Les épreuves du baccalauréat

Objectif BAC

À la fin de l'année, vous allez passer le baccalauréat.
L'épreuve de langue vivante (LV1 ou LV2) comprend deux parties : une partie écrite et une partie orale. Le niveau attendu est B2 (LV1) et B1 (LV2) en référence à l'échelle de niveau du Cadre Européen Commun de Référence pour les Langues (CECRL).

Coefficient de l'épreuve d'anglais

Dans la série STMG, le coefficient est de 3 (LV1) ou 2 (LV2). La note finale est obtenue en additionnant les notes des différentes épreuves passées au cours et à la fin de l'année.
L'oral a autant de poids que l'écrit.

L'ÉPREUVE ORALE

► Compréhension orale

- **Période :** au cours du deuxième trimestre, dans votre lycée
- **Durée :** 10 minutes pour rédiger le compte rendu
- **Note** sur 20 points
- **Déroulement**

Vous entendrez trois fois un enregistrement d'une durée d'une minute trente. Il pourra s'agir d'un monologue, d'un dialogue, d'un discours, d'une discussion, d'un extrait d'émission de radio, d'un documentaire, d'un film, ou d'un journal télévisé. Les trois écoutes seront entrecoupées d'une minute de pause.

Vous prendrez des notes puis rendrez compte par écrit et en français de ce que vous aurez compris (10 minutes).

► Expression orale

- **Période :** au cours du troisième trimestre, dans votre lycée
- **Durée :** 10 minutes
- **Temps de préparation :** 10 minutes
- **Note** sur 20 points
- **Déroulement**

Vous tirerez au sort une des quatre notions étudiées au cours de l'année :
– **Mythes et héros**
– **Idée de progrès**
– **Espaces et échanges**
– **Lieux et formes du pouvoir**

Vous devrez présenter cette notion en anglais (10 minutes).
= 5 minutes en prise de parole en continu
+ 5 minutes en prise de parole en interaction : échange avec l'examinateur

L'ÉPREUVE ÉCRITE

- **Période :** fin du troisième trimestre, avec les autres épreuves du baccalauréat.
- **Durée :** 2 h
- **Note** sur 20 points (10 points par épreuve)
- **Déroulement**

► Compréhension de texte

L'épreuve porte sur **plusieurs documents** : extraits d'œuvres littéraires ou d'articles de presse notamment ; ils peuvent être informatifs, descriptifs, narratifs ou argumentatifs. Ils renvoient aux notions du programme sans exiger de connaissances trop spécifiques. Certains sujets peuvent comporter des éléments iconographiques.
Chacun de ces documents est associé à un **questionnaire**. Une ou plusieurs **questions comparatives** sont posées ensuite. Il s'agit de trouver les points communs et les différences entre les différents supports.

► Expression écrite

Ensuite vous devrez rédiger en anglais un texte lié aux documents proposés en compréhension (écrire une lettre, un article de journal, continuer une histoire…). Il faudra donner votre point de vue, exprimer un jugement dans une langue aussi correcte et précise que possible.

Présenter les notions

Objectif BAC

En vue du baccalauréat en classe de Terminale, il faut vous entraîner à parler des **quatre notions** inscrites au programme : ***Myths and Heroes* • *The Idea of Progress* • *Spaces and Exchanges* • *Locations and Forms of Power***.
Nous vous conseillons de vous familiariser avec les notions et de vous entraîner à les relier aux documents étudiés en classe.

Structurez votre présentation :

1. Expliquez la notion.
2. Introduisez la problématique *(key question)*.
3. Faites le lien avec les documents étudiés en cours.
4. Organisez vos idées.
5. Donnez des exemples précis.
6. N'oubliez pas une conclusion personnelle. Vous pouvez mentionner un film, un reportage que vous avez vus, un livre ou un article que vous avez lus. Vous pouvez donner votre opinion si le thème s'y prête.

A few definitions

MYTHS AND HEROES

MYTH

1. an ancient story about gods, heroes and magic
2. **a.** popular belief or tradition embodying the ideals and institutions of a society
   b. an unfounded or false notion
3. a theme or character type embodying an idea

HERO

1. **a.** a mythological or legendary figure often endowed with great strength or ability
   b. a person admired for his/her achievements, noble qualities and great courage
2. the main character in a literary or dramatic work, an event, period, or movement
3. an object of extreme admiration and devotion: icon/role model

LOCATIONS AND FORMS OF POWER

POWER

1. the ability or official capacity to exercise control • authority (the State, the government, political organization)
2. strength or force exerted or capable of being exerted • might *(puissance)*
3. a person, group, or nation having great influence or control over others

SPACES AND EXCHANGES

EXCHANGE

movement or circulation
all types of exchanges: people, trade, media, communication, etc.

THE IDEA OF PROGRESS

PROGRESS

1. forward movement • advance • development
2. gradual betterment; especially: the progressive development of humankind

Comment parler d'une notion

Objectif BAC

1 Explain the notion

● Give a definition of the key words (→ p. 4)

- The notion I'm going to deal with is…
- First, let me define the notion.
- To start with, I'd like to define the notion.

Note down key words only, don't write complete sentences!

● Think of other possible meanings

- On the one hand a myth/a hero/progress means… but on the other hand it can also be understood as…
- It is also important to bear in mind another aspect of…

2 Introduce your key question

- We may wonder to what extent… *(On peut se demander dans quelle mesure...)*
- We must weigh the pros and cons… *(peser le pour et le contre)*

3 Make the link with what you have studied in class

- This notion can be illustrated with the example of…
- I have chosen to illustrate this notion with the theme/article/video we studied in class.
- After introducing the notion, I will deal with the example of…
- In class, we studied a passage/a report/a film that is connected to the notion and it will help me answer the key question.

Make the link with what you have studied in class:
• Define the terms of the notion.
• Choose the themes studied which best illustrate the notion.
• Pick out precise examples.

4 Organise your ideas

- First of all/First, let's speak about…/Let's examine why…
- Let's begin with…
- Besides, *(de plus)*
- Similarly, *(de la même façon)*
- This brings me to another aspect of the question.
- Let's move on to another point, namely *(à savoir)*…

Look and sound convinced!

5 Insist on a particular point

- We should bear in mind that… *(Il faut garder à l'esprit que…)*
- It is worth mentioning that… *(Cela vaut la peine de mentionner que…)*

6 Conclude your presentation React personally, give your opinion

- I think/feel/believe that...
- To sum up…/To conclude…

Comprendre les consignes

Repérer

- *In this* ***excerpt*** (ou ***extract***):
  Dans cet extrait
- ***List the characters*** *present* ***in the scene****:*
  Faites la liste des personnages présents dans la scène.
- ***Locate****.../Find* ***the location****:*
  Situez/Trouvez le lieu.
- *Who are the* ***main characters****?*
  Qui sont les personnages principaux ?
- *Who* ***is mentioned*** *in this scene?*
  Qui est mentionné/cité dans cette scène ?
- *When/Where does the scene* ***take place****?*
  Quand/Où se passe l'action ?
- ***Find*** *the* ***key word****/the name of.../*
  one adjective/one verb/a ***clue****.*
  Trouvez le mot clé/le nom de.../
  un adjectif/un verbe/un indice.
- *Find the* ***equivalent****/the* ***opposite*** *of/*
  the word ***corresponding to the following definition****:*
  Trouvez l'équivalent/le contraire de/le mot correspondant à la définition suivante.
- ***Choose/Pick out/Select*** *the words...:*
  Choisissez/Sélectionnez/Relevez/Repérez les mots...
- ***List*** *the words which* ***are connected with/ are related to****:*
  Relevez les mots qui se rapportent à/qui font référence à...

Résumer

- ***Fill in*** *the* ***blanks*** *in the* ***summary****:*
  Écrivez les mots qui manquent pour compléter le résumé du texte.
- ***Sum up the story****:*
  Résumez l'histoire.
- ***Sum up*** *this text* ***in your own words****:*
  Résumez ce texte en utilisant vos propres mots.

Justifier vos réponses

- ***Give a quote/quotation:***
  Donnez une citation.
- ***Justify*** *using* ***key words*** *from...:*
  Justifiez vos réponses à l'aide de mots clés tirés de...
- ***Quote*** *one* ***sentence****:*
  Citez une phrase.
- ***Quote*** *one* ***phrase****:*
  Citez un groupe de mots/une expression.

Remettre dans l'ordre

- ***Put*** *the following words* ***in the corresponding column****:* Classez les mots suivants dans la colonne correspondante.
- ***Reorder*** *the* ***events*** *in* ***chronological order****:*
  Classez les événements par ordre chronologique.

Associer

- ***Match*** *the following words* ***with their definitions****:* Associez les mots suivants à leur définition.
- ***Which*** *of the following words* ***apply to****...?*
  Lesquels de ces mots s'appliquent à... ?
- *What do these* ***figures*** *refer to?*
  À quoi ces chiffres font-ils référence ?
- *Who or what do the* ***underlined*** *pronouns* ***refer to****?*
  À qui ou à quoi les pronoms soulignés font-ils référence ?

Agir

- ***Act out*** *the dialogue/scene:*
  Jouez le dialogue/la scène.
- ***Compare*** *your results with your neighbour:*
  Confrontez/Comparez vos résultats avec ceux de votre voisin.
- ***Write down*** *on a* ***blank sheet*** *of paper:*
  Écrivez sur papier libre.
- ***Fill in*** *the* ***grid/table/columns below****:*
  Remplissez la grille/le tableau/les colonnes ci-dessous.

Relire son devoir

RELIRE

Formes verbales

Auxiliaire modal (*may/ must/ will*, etc.)
- suivi d'une base verbale (infinitif sans *to*)
- il est invariable
- pas de -s à la 3e personne du singulier

He must remember that.

Want/would like sb to do sth
Do you want me to help you?
His parents would like him to work harder.

Formes interrogatives : penser à l'auxiliaire
Do you need anything else?
Did you tell them the truth?

Ordre des mots
Attention ! Ne pas « calquer »

Adjectif devant le nom qualifié
This is a scary story.

COD directement après le verbe
She speaks Chinese very well.

▯ *He ~~learns English for six years~~*
*He **has been learning** English for six years.*

▯ *~~They are married since 2010.~~*
*They **have been** married since 2010.*

▯ **Attention à *as soon as* et *when* :** pas de *will* dans une subordonnée de temps.
*He will take a year off when/as soon as **he graduates**.*

Ne pas confondre *They are* et *There are*

They are exhausted. Ils sont épuisés.
There are drawbacks. Il y a des inconvénients.

Attention aux verbes irréguliers

p. 214

Accords

***People* + pluriel**
*People **are** worried about the crisis.*

***Every/ Each* + singulier**
Is everybody ready?

-*s* à la 3e personne du singulier au présent
*He play**s** a lot of video games.*

Adjectifs invariables :
*These books are **new**.*

Emploi de *the*

I love cookies. (en général)
*I love **the** cookies you have bought.* (nom défini)

Équivalents anglais de «pour»:

***For* + nom/pronom**
*This present is **for you**.*

***(in order) to* + BV**
*He stopped **to look** at the map.*

Les sons de l'anglais

1 Voyelles (anglais britannique)

/iː/	/ɪ/	/i/	/e/	/æ/	/ɑː/	

/ɒ/	/ɔː/	/ʊ/	/uː/	/ɜː/	/ʌ/	/ə/

2 Diphtongues

/eɪ/	/aɪ/	/ɔɪ/	/aʊ/	/əʊ/	/ɪə/	/eə/	/ʊə/
			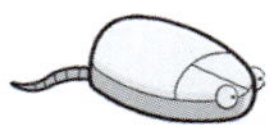				

3 Consonnes

/j/	/ð/	/θ/	/ʒ/	/ʃ/	/ŋ/
yes	**th**is	**th**anks	plea**s**ure	**s**ure	so**ng**

MP3 N°1 CD1 PISTE 1

4 Observez les signes phonétiques (transcription des sons)

a. Trouvez les mots repères qui y sont associés puis prononcez-les.
b. Écoutez l'enregistrement et vérifiez à l'écoute. Exemple : /iː/ = *key*.

5 Prononciation de *-(e)s*

La terminaison *-s* peut être soit la **marque du pluriel** d'un nom *(three car**s**)* soit la **marque de la 3ᵉ personne du présent** d'un verbe *(Sue play**s** the guitar)*.

*pass**es*** • *box**es*** • *judg**es***	La terminaison ***-es*** est utilisée quand le nom ou le verbe se termine par *-s*, *-x*, *-z*, *-ce*, *-ge*, *-ch* ou *-sh*. Elle se prononce /ɪz/.
*play**s*** • *know**s*** • *go**es*** • *lie**s*** • *look**s*** • *sit**s***	Dans tous les autres cas, la terminaison écrite ***-s*** ou ***-es*** se prononce soit /s/ soit /z/.

Attention : ***does*** *se prononce* /dʌz/, *et* ***says*** *se prononce* /sez/.

6 Terminaison *-ed* du prétérit ou du participe passé

*want**ed*** • *need**ed***	On prononce /ɪd/ **SEULEMENT** après ***t*** ou ***d***.
*play**ed*** • *remember**ed*** • *work**ed*** • *miss**ed***	Dans **TOUS** les autres cas, on prononce soit /d/ soit /t/.

MP3 N°1 CD1 PISTE 2

7 Maintenant entraînez-vous.

Classroom English

➜ Pour vous excuser :

Sorry, I'm late.
I apologise for being late.
I'm sorry, I've forgotten my notes, my copybook, my worksheet.
I'm afraid I've forgotten to do my homework.

➜ Quand vous ne pouvez pas voir le tableau :

Could you step aside, please? I can't see the board.

➜ Quand vous ne connaissez pas la réponse :

I'm afraid I don't know.
I don't have a clue /kluː/.
I'm afraid I haven't got the slightest/faintest idea /aɪˈdɪə/.
I'm sorry, but I haven't understood the question.
Sorry, I don't know what you mean.
I am not sure I can answer.
I'm sorry, but I don't know what to say.
Sorry, I can't remember what's next.
May I have a few minutes to think about it?

➜ Quand vous hésitez :

I may be wrong but I think...
I'm not so sure of the answer.

➜ Pour corriger ce qui vient d'être dit :

You should have said...
I think there's a mistake/I think you made a mistake.
Instead of... you should have said...

➜ Pour saluer votre professeur :

Good morning/afternoon Mr X, Mrs Y.
See you on Thursday/on...
Have a nice day.
Have a nice weekend.

➜ Pour demander de l'aide :

How do you spell this word?
Could you write it on the board, please?
I didn't understand this word, could you spell it, please?
What's the English for... ?
What does the word ... mean?
What's the meaning of... ?

➜ Pour vérifier que l'on vous a bien compris.e :

Do you know what I mean?
... if you see what I mean.
I hope that's clear.
Do I make myself clear?

➜ Pour vérifier une prononciation :

How do you pronounce this word?
Is that the right way to say it?
Is that correct?

LOCATIONS AND FORMS OF POWER

Unit 1 YES, WE CARE!
► What power do young people have to promote change today?

YOUR TASK p. 27

Write a cover letter.
OR
Act out an interview.

Unit 2 BLACK VOICES OF PROTEST
► To what extent does music have the power to change society?

YOUR TASK p. 41

Post a video to explain what impact music has on people.
OR
Write one verse of a rap song and perform it!

Unit 3 GUNS UNDER FIRE
► To what extent does the gun issue divide the USA?

YOUR TASK p. 53

Write a comment to a post on Facebook.
OR
React on a radio station phone-in.

SPACES AND EXCHANGES

Sommaire

Unit 4 SCREEN TOURISM
► What is the impact of screen tourism today?

Unit 5 BUILDING A GLOBAL WORLD
► What impact do new forms of communication have on the world today?

Unit 6 THE NEW FACE OF AMERICA
► Is it true to say: "Immigrants come and change America and are changed by America"?

THE IDEA OF PROGRESS

Unit 7 WORK IN PROGRESS
► What is the impact of technology on the workplace?

Unit 8 MORE THAN MEETS THE EYE
► Why is fighting prejudices a step towards progress?

Unit 9 WIND OF CHANGE FOR WOMEN?
► Is gender inequality a thing of the past in developed countries?

Sommaire

MYTHS AND HEROES

Unit 10 — DREAMERS

► The American Dream, a myth or reality for immigrants to the USA?

Unit 11 — SPORTS HEROES

► Are sports champions true heroes?

Unit 12 — AMBASSADORS OF CONSCIENCE

► Are whistleblowers the heroes of modern times?

Annexes

Pictos utilisés dans ce manuel

Écrire

Parler en continu

Parler en interaction

Comprendre un document oral

Comprendre un texte écrit

video **Renvoi au DVD-Rom**

WORKSHEET 41 **Fiche d'aide à la compréhension écrite ou orale téléchargeable sur : www.editions-hatier.fr/langues**

WORKSHEET BAC N° 12 **Fiche d'exploitation des documents du *Get ready for the exam***

CD 2 PISTE 1 **Renvoi aux CD classe**

MP 3 N° 1 **Fichier MP3 téléchargeable sur : www.editions-hatier.fr/langues-eleves**

Les *flashcodes* (ou QR codes) présents tout au long des pages du manuel et sur les fiches « Apprendre à apprendre » vous permettent d'accéder directement aux enregistrements MP3 via votre *smartphone* ou votre tablette.

Quelques conseils pour bien flasher :

1. Téléchargez une application (gratuite) de lecture des *flashcodes* dans votre *store*.

2. Lancez l'application et visez le *flashcode* avec l'appareil photo.

3. Vérifiez que le *flashcode* est bien centré.

4. Vérifiez que la luminosité est suffisante.

5. Flashez et écoutez !

Sommaire

Vidéos présentes sur le DVD

▲ *Hunger Games*, a film by Gary Ross (2012)

Locations and Forms of Power

Unit 1 — Yes, We Care!

WHAT POWER DO YOUNG PEOPLE HAVE TO PROMOTE CHANGE TODAY?

YOUR FINAL TASK
- Write a cover letter. (p. 27)
- **OR**
- Act out an interview. (p. 27)

p. 18-29

Unit 2 — Black Voices of Protest

TO WHAT EXTENT DOES MUSIC HAVE THE POWER TO CHANGE SOCIETY?

YOUR FINAL TASK
- Post a video to explain what impact music has on people. (p. 41)
- **OR**
- Write one verse of a rap song and perform it! (p. 41)

p. 30-43

Unit 3 — Guns Under Fire

TO WHAT EXTENT DOES THE GUN ISSUE DIVIDE THE USA?

YOUR FINAL TASK
- Your friend has posted a recording on Facebook. Write your comment. (p. 53)
- **OR**
- React on a radio station phone-in. (p. 53)

p. 44-55

À la fin de chaque unité, vous trouverez un entraînement type bac complet (compréhension et production écrite, compréhension et expression orale).

Unit 1
LOCATIONS AND FORMS OF POWER
What power do young people have to promote change today?

Yes, We Care!

1 Tune In!

1 Observe and react

a. Who are the people in the photo? What are they doing?
b. What cause do you think the people here are defending? Justify.

2 Back from the demonstration

CD 1 PISTE 3

Listen to two young people who took part in the demonstration.
a. Pick out their names and ages.
b. Focus on the reasons why they took part, their feelings and impressions.

Help!

Actors	Means *(moyens)*	Actions	Causes
activist demonstrator = marcher: *manifestant* protester teenager	banner demonstration protest march slogan peaceful	act: *agir* demonstrate: *manifester* draw attention to get involved in: *s'impliquer dans* make sb aware of: *faire prendre conscience à qqn de* stand up for ≠ against support: *soutenir*	abortion: *avortement* climate change freedom of speech LGBT rights: laws affecting lesbian, gay, bisexual and transgender

2 Zoella

1 Read and understand

a. Read either text A or text B and find out about Zoella.Then share with the rest of the class: real name • age • nationality • job.
b. Pick out elements showing that she is very successful or how she became successful.
c. In text A, find the reasons why Zoella was chosen as an ambassador for the #Don'tPanicButton campaign.

Text A

YouTube star Zoella – aka[1] British vlogger Zoe Sugg – [...] is also taking a role as digital ambassador for mental health charity[2] Mind. The news was announced as Sugg launched[3] her #DontPanicButton campaign to raise awareness of anxiety and panic attacks in young people. It will encourage people to wear red buttons and upload photos to social networks using the hashtag to show their support. Sugg's large online audience – her main YouTube channel has more than 6.1m subscribers, while her MoreZoella channel has 2.3m – should help the campaign reach a large number of young people. [...] Her new role won't come as a surprise to Zoella's fans, as she has spoken publicly about her own experience of panic attacks and anxiety, including a video posted in November 2012 that has been watched nearly 2.6m times.

■ www.theguardian.com, 9 October, 2014

1. also known as 2. *association caritative* 3. *lançait*

Text B

The rise of the internet generation has been reflected in the latest Debrett[1]'s set of the 500 most influential people in Britain.
Zoella, the 24-year-old vlogger, who is also the author of the online book *Girl Online*, is listed along 500 influential people across society including politicians, advertisers, architects, chefs, athletes, educators and journalists.

■ Adapted from www.telegraph.co.uk, 25 January, 2015

1. specialist publisher, founded in 1769

DEFINITION

A vlog is an online blog made via videos. Zoella uploads her 10 to 20 minute videos to her YouTube channel.

2 A new phenomenon

PREPARE YOUR TASK

You are taking part in a British radio show about vloggers. The journalist speaks about Zoella and interviews French students about their favourite vlogs. Act out the show.

3 Become a vlogger!

In groups, make a short film to defend a cause of your choice.

Get ready for the Oral Exam

Do you think demonstrators or vloggers like Zoella have the power to make things change?

3 Sign Up!

1 Before reading

Read the title of the article and observe the bar chart (→ p. 181): How did people answer the question? Use the following prompts: The chart is about... • Most people... • There are four times more... who... than... • twice as many... who... as ...

WORKSHEET 1

2 Now read and understand the different viewpoints

Straight Talk for Teens: Should 16-year-olds have the right to vote?

POSTED: 6:03 PM, May 9, 2015
UPDATED: 8:34 AM, May 11, 2015
TAG: straight talk for teens

SACRAMENTO, California

Dear Straight Talk: I read that the voting age was lowered to 16 in two cities and that San Francisco is considering the same. I don't feel kids this age have the maturity or education to make informed decisions. I think most honest teenagers would agree.
— Parent in Santa Rosa, California

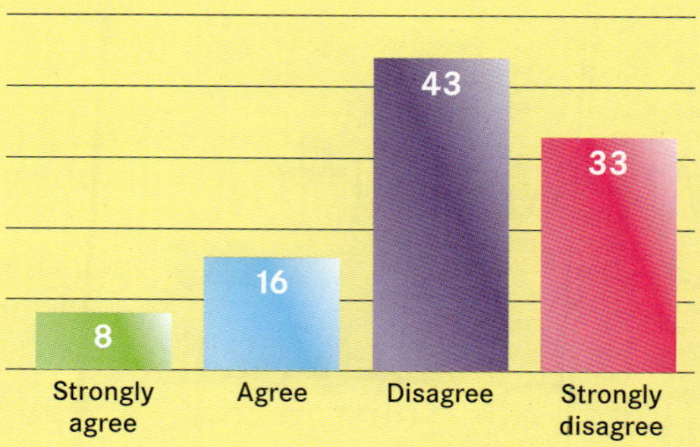

Kat, 20, Eugene, Oregon: Maturity level depends more on the person than age. Many 16-year-olds are more informed and interested than people I know in their 30s who aren't even registered to vote.

Justin, 17, Brentwood, California: I agree that teens lack adequate maturity. Very few high school kids care about politics or have mental capacity to separate what's popular versus[1] what's right.

Karlee, 17, Bentleyville, Pennsylvania: Where I live, kids pay more attention to politics than most adults. [...] We're constantly hit with politics in our history, current events, journalism and English classes. [...] A 17-year-old can't possibly be mature, right? Except when you have divorced parents and help pay bills[2] with two after-school jobs. We've been silenced too long [...]. The voting age should absolutely be lowered.

Lara, 23, Vienna, Austria: I'm a dual citizen and grew up between California and Austria, where the voting age is 16. I was always impressed by how informed and involved[3] my Austrian peers[4] were in global politics and positive change. Lowering the voting age is a great idea.

www.straighttalkadvice.org

1. as opposed to **2.** *factures* **3.** *impliqués* **4.** person who belongs to the same age group or social group

3 Class survey

"Should 16-year-olds have the right to vote?": Does your class strongly agree • agree • disagree • strongly disagree?

a. Ask the question to your classmates and draw a bar chart with your results.
b. Compare your findings with the results in the bar chart above.

PREPARE YOUR TASK

4 Write your own comment on the forum

Help!

What to do	Where to go
go to the polls: *aller voter*	ballot box: *urne*
register to vote: *s'inscrire sur les listes électorales*	polling station: *bureau de vote*
cast a ballot: *mettre son bulletin dans l'urne*	voting booth: *isoloir*

4 Youth Parliament

Culture Tip

The UK Youth Parliament is a youth organisation in the United Kingdom, consisting of democratically elected members aged between 11 and 18. Formed in 2000, the parliament now consists of around 600 elected members. Over 500,000 young people vote in the elections each year.

SICK OF THE SYSTEM?

video

WORKSHEET 2

1 Watch a video

Running for a seat

a. Get ready. Turn to your worksheet for help.

b. Watch the video. What issues do the young people talk about? To help you organise your notes, draw a midmap for each candidate:

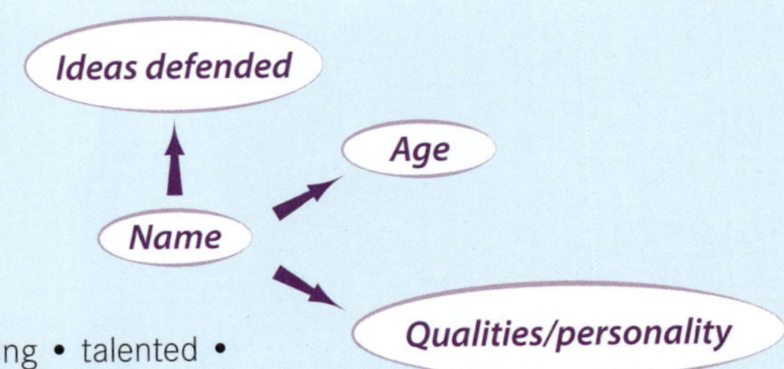

c. Watch Sarah again.
- Do you find her convincing • boring • talented • enthusiastic • hesitant? Justify your choice.
- What speaking techniques does she use?

d. Now watch the video again and compare the three speakers. Who do you find is the most effective *(efficace)*?

2 Become a speech writer

PREPARE YOUR TASK

- You want to be elected to the Youth Parliament. List three things that you would try to do if you were elected.
- List your qualities for the task.
- Write your speech beginning with "Dear fellow classmates, ...".

3 Vote for me!

a. Read your speech and underline the elements you want to insist on.

b. Read it out loud to your neighbour.

c. Once you are sure about the pronunciation, you may use an online prompter to deliver your speech (www.cueprompter.com). You can film yourself too.

d. Vote for the most convincing candidate.

Get ready for the Oral Exam

- **How important is it for young people to be involved in politics?**
- **Do young people have the power to influence politicians?**

5 A Year Off to Volunteer?

WANTED
People to make a difference to others

1 How to make a difference?

In groups, observe the word cloud and select words and phrases to explain what people can do to help people in developing countries.

Travel · Donate money · Participate · Discover · Cultivate · Learn · Work · Paint · Adventure · Share experience · Repair · Exchange · Teach · Go abroad · Support · Build · Raise funds · Grow · Clean · Help · Volunteer

CD 1 PISTE 5
WORKSHEET 3

2 Taking a gap year

a. Listen to a news report and learn more about gap years. Turn to your worksheet for help.
b. With the help of the recording and the word cloud, give your own definition of a gap year.

3 Letty's experience

Diary of my gap year

It's January 3rd […], I take a deep breath… my mum is waiting downstairs for me, to take me to the airport, […] it is time for the journey[1] to begin. […]

From the many appealing options, I was particularly drawn to two projects. An "Ocean Safari" project in South Africa, monitoring dolphins and marine life, and an "Elephant Experience" in Sri Lanka's famous Pinawala Elephant Orphanage[2]. […] I eventually[3] opted for the Sri Lankan placement. It was the appeal of deserted beaches, washing elephants in a river at sunset, ripe fruit, big smiles and a destination so different to England in every way that seduced me. This was the experience I yearned for! […]

My next destination was Thailand. […] I was ready to take on anything now. I was no longer scared of the unknown, but quite addicted to it! My confidence had grown as had my self-reliance, patience and empathy. […]

The achievements of a gap year away cannot be measured. It looks good on your CV, certainly, but the real accomplishment is internal. The first-hand[4] experience of seeing the world offers the opportunity to break boundaries and test your limits. You come back stronger for it and with a bank of special memories and life-long friends.

Time out from that routine existence they call reality is something everyone should experience. It will change your perceptions, and you never know… it might even change your life. It certainly changed mine.

LETTY HARDY

www.travellersworldwide.in

1. *voyage* **2.** *orphelinat* **3.** finally **4.** direct

a. Use the context to find the synonym for each word in the list below.

- **appealing**: attractive • horrible
- **yearned for**: wanted very much • was afraid of
- **monitoring**: teaching • observing
- **self-reliance**: autonomy • helplessness

b. Answer the following questions:
– Who does "I" (l. 1) refer to?
– Read paragraphs 1 and 2. Name the countries that he/she will visit during their "journey".
– What will he/she do while abroad: Work with dolphins? • Work with elephants? • Study marine life?
– Read paragraphs 3 and 4. What are the effects of a gap-year on "gappers"? Organise your ideas: Relationships with other people • Professional life • Personal life
– Conclude: Who seems to have benefited most from this gap year? Locals or the "gapper"?
– Rephrase the gapper's advice in the last paragraph: "Taking a gap-year is..."

4 A testimony

Twenty-two year old Liz McKay, from Glasgow, followed in her mother's footsteps by volunteering overseas when she took up an ICS placement in early 2014. Liz travelled to Ghana where she supported the Football for Hope programme helping to support livelihoods[1] projects for unemployed young people as well as a range[2] of other local needs. [...]

"Our work ranged from developing resource to help improve the school curriculums,[3] writing lesson plans and teaching children ranging from five to sixteen years old as well as young adults. [...]

"I feel we had a great impact on the community. All the volunteers felt that their ten weeks in Cape Coast had been worthwhile[4] for both them and the community."

www.yearoutgroup.org

1. *moyens d'existence* **2.** *gamme* **3.** *programme (scolaire)* **4.** beneficial

a. – Where does Liz McKay live? What country did she visit in 2014?
– Observe the word "overseas". How is it built? Use your answers to question **a.** to translate it.

b. True or False? Justify with a quote from the text.
The main character was not the first family member to volunteer.

c. – Pick out the different activities that volunteers took part in when Liz was there.
– Who seems to have benefited from these activities? The community? • The gappers? • Both?

5 Compare and contrast

What vision of a gap year is given by the two testimonies and the poster?
You can use the following prompts: on the one hand... on the other hand... • both in... and in... • both testimonies... • whereas... • as opposed to... • unlike... • similar/different from...

PREPARE YOUR TASK

6 Join me!

You explain to a friend on Facebook why you have decided to take a gap year and you try to persuade him/her to do the same.

Help!

Experience

gapper: a person taking a gap year
(work) placement (GB) = internship (US): *stage*

apply for a job: *postuler à un emploi*
take a gap year: *prendre une année de césure*

Results

self-confidence: *confiance en soi*
memories: *souvenirs*

achieve sth: *accomplir qqch*
benefit from
broaden (one's horizons): *élargir*
improve = make better

Get ready for the Oral Exam

Do gappers have the power to make a real difference?

6 Video Corner

Helping the Homeless

1 Before watching

a. Look at the two stills from the report carefully. Where does the scene take place? Who and what can you see?
b. In pairs, decide which of the following words you expect to hear. Check the meaning in a dictionary if necessary.

company • factory/plant • sewing machine • worker • failure • succeed • graduate • addict • assignment • sleeping bag • prototype • issue • hire: *embaucher* • pride • opportunity • put on (a coat) • jobs

2 Watch the beginning of the video (to 1:08) with the sound off

Explain what you understand about the story.

3 Watch the video with the sound on

a. Which words from the list above did you hear? Copy them out.
b. Take notes.

4 Watch the video again

Take as many notes as you can. Then, classify them.
a. Veronika Scott: age • job • where she is from • education • family.
b. A turning point in her life.
c. Her first idea. Why?
d. Reaction(s) to this idea.
e. What she finally did and the impact it had.
f. What is Veronika Scott's conclusion?
Use "even if" or "although" to rephrase what she says.

Help!

CEO: *P.-D.G.*
scholarship: *bourse d'études*
self-worth = self-esteem
plant (US) = factory (GB): *usine*
shelter: *abri*
empowerment plant: *(ici) usine de réinsertion sociale*
tackle: *s'attaquer à*
sew /səʊ/: *coudre*

5 Watch the video one last time

a. Complete your notes.
b. Write a short article about Veronika Scott's story: what she did, her qualities.

Get ready for the Oral Exam

Why can Veronika be given as an example to show that young people can make things change?

Play with words

MP3 N° 3 — CD 1 PISTE 6

Getting involved

take a gap year: *faire une année de césure*

- do voluntary work
- do charity work = volunteer: *faire du bénévolat*
- go abroad: *aller à l'étranger*
- travel: *voyager*

- gapper: *étudiant qui fait une année de césure*
- inhabitant
- local community
- have an impact on

awareness campaign: *campagne de sensibilisation*

- make people react
- make people aware of: *faire prendre conscience aux gens de*
- get people involved: *impliquer les gens*
- focus on = concentrate on
- empower sb: *donner à qqn les moyens de*

- advertisement: *publicité*
- flyer: *prospectus*
- leaflet: *brochure*
- poster

voting

- candidate
- election
- manifesto: *programme*
- polling station: *bureau de vote*
- register to vote: *s'inscrire (sur les listes électorales)*

protest (verb)

- speech: *discours*
- protest (noun)
- march = demonstrate: *manifester*
- chant: *scander*
- deliver a speech: *faire un discours*

- citizen: *citoyen*
- crowd: *foule*
- demonstrator: *manifestant*
- protester

- peaceful = non-violent

- banner: *banderole*
- sign: *pancarte*

A Choose words from the list to fill in the blanks.

charity · homesick · volunteering · committed · interns · open-minded

a. Students often work as ... to get some work experience before their first job.
b. Giving some of your time to work to help without a salary is called ... .
c. Living in a developing country for a year makes you more ... .
d. When you are away from home and your family you can be... .
e. When you are willing to give your time and energy to something that you believe in, you are ... .
f. An organisation that gives help and raises money for those in need is a ... .

B Match words with similar meanings. Choose one from list A and one from list B.

List A: abroad • college • internship • focus on • peaceful • march • brochure

List B: leaflet • concentrate on • foreign country • non-violent • demonstration • university • work placement

C Draw a similar grid and classify the words below in the right column.

Nouns	Verbs	Adjectives	Adverbs

persuade • persuasion • persuasive • persuasively
demonstration • demonstrator • demonstrate
convince • convincing • convincingly
believer • believe • belief
volunteer • volunteering • volunteer
peace • peacefully • peaceful

D Dictation time

Listen to three sentences and write down what you heard.

LANGUAGE AT WORK

«Apprendre à Apprendre»
Téléchargez la fiche n°1
www.editions-hatier.fr/langues-eleves

Corrigés p. 216-221

A Apprenez à mieux utiliser les mots de liaison

1. Associez chaque mot de liaison de la liste A à son équivalent français dans la liste B.

List A: even if • although • however • nevertheless • in spite of • despite

List B: *bien que* • *malgré* • *néanmoins* • *cependant* • *même si*

2. Choisissez le mot de liaison qui convient dans chaque énoncé.

a. *(Although / Despite / However)* the bad weather, lots of people demonstrated in London and marched for hours in the rain.

b. *(Even if / Despite / However)* you are young, you should fight for what you believe in.

c. I think the government is totally wrong, *(even if / despite / however)* I don't believe that demonstrating is the best way to be heard.

d. *(Although / Despite / However)* we had planned all the details very carefully, some people forgot their banners and signs.

B V-ING ou *to* + BV ?

(Précis grammatical 45 p. 213)

3. Complétez ces énoncés en utilisant un des verbes suivants à la forme qui convient (*to* + BV, ou V-ING) : *speak* • *travel* • *remember* • *help* • *be* • *register* • *become* • *post*.

a. ... other people can be a worthwhile experience.

b. I need ... before I can vote next month.

c. I'm really looking forward to ... able to vote in the next election.

d. I'd love ... a Youth Parliament member.

e. You should avoid ... in English all the time, try to speak the local language.

f. He's very enthusiastic about ... some more videos on his blog.

g. We spent a lot of time ... with some Australian friends.

h. I can't help ... all the fun times we had.

C Comparatif / superlatif

(Précis grammatical 9 p. 196)

4. Mettez l'adjectif entre parenthèses au comparatif ou au superlatif. Faites les changements nécessaires.

a. Taking a gap year was the (+ good) ... decision I have ever made.

b. After a gap year in China, Tom thinks Chinese is (+ difficult) ... language in the world.

c. When I was in Australia, the weather was even (+ hot) ... in Africa.

d. I have felt much (+ happy) ... since my gap year. Now I know what I really want to do.

e. The (+ amazing) ... thing happened to me when I was in Africa.

f. The schools in Columbia were (+ bad) ... in India.

D *Suggesting*

5. Complétez ces phrases en utilisant *how / what about* + V-ING, *shall we…, let's…* .

a. ... get to the Amnesty meeting early.

b. ... volunteering at the homeless centre?

c. ... go there by bus or by train?

d. ... register to vote instead of complaining!

e. ... showing that we feel concerned after all?

f. ... starting to act?

YOUR TASK

SCENARIO 1

You are Ben/Lucy Miles and you have just read the following ad in a youth magazine. Write a cover letter *(lettre de motivation)* to apply.

We are currently offering **FULLY FUNDED** overseas volunteer opportunities, for those with a passion to make a difference and desire to experience another culture. Apply today and you could be in South Africa by January.

Projects last for an incredible **10 WEEKS**. You will work on projects that focus on:
- Children and young people, including those living on the streets
- People living with disabilities
- People living with and affected by HIV/AIDS

Send your cover letter and CV to: A Better World, 154 The Leas, Folkestone, CT20 2DY, UK

► **Read the ad carefully.**
Pick out the qualities required to be the best candidate for the job.

► **List all the elements that you want to mention:**
- Why you are interested in the offer.
- What qualities can you offer? (skills, experience, motivation)
- When you are available.

► **Revise how to present a cover letter p. 189.**
- Don't forget the appropriate greetings at the start and at the end of the letter.
- Organise your ideas.
- Sign your letter.

► **Avoid basic mistakes (→ *Relire son devoir* p. 7).**

SCENARIO 2

You are in charge of recruiting volunteers for a charity abroad. You interview a candidate to explain the job profile (necessary qualities, experience, practical abilities) and ask them questions to find out more about them. In pairs, act out the interview.

► **Each student** will prepare both roles, but will only act out one.

► **Get ready** to ask and answer questions about age, skills, experience, motivation, availability, etc.

► **Revise** how to ask questions p. 202.

► **Revise** useful expressions p. 178-179.

Compréhension écrite et expression écrite

Answer the questions on the worksheet the teacher will give you.

WORKSHEET BAC N° 1

DOCUMENT A

Home | Young Global Citizen Club | Project Work | Global Citizen Certificate | Support us | About Us

16-right-2-vote — Home / Young Global Citizen Club / Annual Global Meeting / 16-right-2-vote

Global Citizen Academy

Campaign 16-right-2-vote

We believe that young people are perfectly capable of understanding the challenges that our societies are facing today when they become 16. There is no reason that a 16-year-old high school student is less capable in this respect than a 60-year-old uneducated person. In other words: For people after the age of 16 not the age but the general education level is the crucial factor of determining good judgment in elections.
On the other hand, it is quite clear that older people have interests that are quite different to those of the younger generation. [...]

How does the campaign work?

We cannot and we do not want to substitute the many campaigns that are already on the way on national levels. In particular in the United States and in Canada the movement for a voting age of 16 already has a strong momentum with many organizations promoting it.
But we can raise funds for these organizations and seek a cooperation to form an international alliance of 16-right-2-vote organizations.
Please contact us to tell us what you think about this and to provide other ideas for a global campaign.

www.global-citizen-academy.org

DOCUMENT B

The INDEPENDENT

General Election 2015: E4 to shut down on polling[1] voting day to encourage young people to vote

Thousands of young people across the country will miss out on watching repeats of *Made in Chelsea* and *The Big Bang Theory* on election day when E4 will shut down for the day to encourage 16-34-year-olds to vote.
Channel 4 has announced it will be switching off E4's regular schedule on 7 May in a bid to stop young people watching TV and to get them out to vote in the general election.
The channel will shut down when polling stations open at 7am, and will resume its usual schedule at 7pm. [...]
Dan Brooke, Channel 4's chief marketing and communications Officer, said: "Less than half of under-25s voted at the last election so we've engaged the most powerful weapon that we have at our disposal to try and boost that number – switching off their favourite TV channel for the day!" [...]
E4 is the number one digital channel for 16-34 year old viewers, attracting a 5.2 per cent share of the youth demographic to date this year – beating BBC2 and Channel 5.
The E4 shut down is one of many initiatives Channel 4 has in store to engage young people with the general election. [...]
In an online exclusive, seven youth party leaders will go up against each other as they tackle the key issues for young voters.

www.independent.co.uk, Wednesday 22 April, 2015

1. voting

DOCUMENT C

Compréhension de l'oral

CD 1 PISTE 7

Daniela Papi's experience

→ Écoutez l'enregistrement trois fois.

→ Prenez des notes puis faites en dix minutes le compte rendu de ce que vous avez compris en français.

→ Utilisez les expressions données p. 183.

USEFUL WORDS

- Pepy: Daniela Papi's organisation
- Sri Lanka • voluntourism = form of tourism in which travellers participate in voluntary work

Expression orale

LOCATIONS AND FORMS OF POWER — What power do young people have to promote change today?

Comment parler de la notion ?

1. Which documents did you study in the unit? In each document, select appropriate elements to illustrate the notion.
2. Use the mind map below to organise your ideas.

What power do young people have to promote change today?

first of all/besides: *de plus*
for example = for instance

Why is it important for young people to get involved (in politics or other)? What means do they have to do so?

because of + noun
at stake: *en jeu*

Do gappers have the power to make a real difference?

Do you think demonstrators or vloggers like Zoella have the power to make things change?

To what extent is Veronika Scott a good example to show that young people can make things change?

Limits to their power: voting age, age, lack of experience, etc.

although...
even if...
On the one hand... on the other (hand)...

3. Present your ideas and be ready to answer questions about what you have just said. Defend your arguments.
4. If you prefer, find your own key question around the notion and prepare an outline.

Black Voices of Protest

1 Tune In!

1 Websearch

a. What do you think were the key words in the search bar to find these videos?
b. Do you recognize these artists? Get ready to give the class some details about them:
name • type of music • famous songs...
c. Do you listen to them?

2 Online survey

CD 1 PISTE 8
WORKSHEET 4

a. Listen to an interview with a teenager about his music tastes. Turn to your worksheet for help.
b. Pick out the questions and report to the class what you have understood.
c. Now use these questions to create your own survey. You may add a few others.
d. Poll your classmates and discuss the results with the class.

Tip
You can use websites to create your survey online. Try Google Forms or SurveyMonkey.

2 From Slave Songs to Hip-Hop

CD 1 PISTE 9

WORKSHEET 5

1 Did you know?

a. Listen to a recording on African-American music. Turn to your worksheet for help.
b. With your notes fill in the timeline of musical genres you were given.
c. Rap or hip-hop: what is the difference?

→ Recap

What characteristics of slave songs can be found in today's music?

2 Blind test

a. Choose one of the genres from your timeline and find an example on the Internet.

spirituals • blues • work songs • freedom songs • rap

b. Bring it to class.Your classmates will guess which genre it belongs to. Be ready to give them some details about it (→ *Enrichir sa prise de parole*, p. 178-179).

Help!
roots: *racines*
strength: *force*
(a) means of: *(un) moyen de*
ghetto/inner city
struggle = fight

3 What is hip-hop?

Read this definition given by a hip-hop singer. Pick out the words in the lyrics that best describe the photo.

Hip means to know
It's a form of intelligence
To be hip is to be up-to-date and relevant[1]
Hop[2] is a form of movement
You can't just observe a hop
You got to hop up and do it
Hip and Hop is more than music
Hip is the knowledge
Hop is the movement
Hip and Hop is intelligent movement
Or relevant movement
We selling the music.

KRS-One, *Hip-Hop Lives*, 2007

1. *(ici) à la mode et dans le coup* 2. *sauter*

4 On air

PREPARE YOUR TASK

You work for your high school radio station. Prepare a short progamme on the roots of hip-hop. Make sure you include extracts of music to illustrate your ideas.

Get ready for the Oral Exam

- **What are the roots of today's music?**
- **What have Black Americans used music for?**

3 Across the Lines

1 Observe and react

a. What is the girl trying to do? In your opinion, what does the red balloon symbolise?
b. In groups, read the following key words from the song and imagine what the song is about. Then compare your stories with the other groups.

guns · blacks · whites · girl · riots · streets · hurt · blacks · kill · bridge · angry · assault

2 Read the lyrics and understand

WORKSHEET 6

Turn to your worksheet for help.

Across the lines
Who would dare[1] to go
Under the bridge
Over the tracks[2]
That separates whites from blacks

Choose sides
Or run for your life
Tonight the riots[3] begin
On the back streets of America
They kill the dream of America

Little black girl gets assaulted
Ain't no[4] reason why
Newspaper prints the story
And racist tempers fly
Next day it starts a riot
Knives and guns are drawn
Two black boys get killed
One white boy goes blind

Little black girl gets assaulted
Don't no one know[5] her name
Lots of people hurt and angry
She's the one to blame

Tracy Chapman, 1988

1. *oserait* **2.** *rails de chemin de fer. Les rails séparaient les villes en deux parties : d'un côté la ville blanche, de l'autre la ville noire.* **3.** *émeutes* **4.** = there is no **5.** = no one knows

3 Express yourself

PREPARE YOUR TASK

A fan writes on his/her blog why he/she considers *Across the Lines* one of the most powerful songs Tracy Chapman wrote and sang.

Help!

Incident	Songwriter	Goals
witness: *témoin*	frustration	racial divide /dɪˈvaɪd/
unbearable: *insupportable*	despair	make sb angry/react
deep-rooted: *profondément ancré*	concerned: *inquiet*	protest against
pretend to: *faire semblant de*	committed: *engagé*	denounce = expose
	emotional	condemn /kənˈdem/
	shocked/outraged	threaten: *menacer*

Get ready for the Oral Exam

- **What are protest songs written for?**
- **What impact should protest songs have on listeners?**

4 A Colorblind Society

1 Get ready

a. Look at the cartoon. What does the little boy dream of?
better schools • job opportunities • the end of violence • equal rights • the end of gang warfare • the end of discrimination • better health care • a higher standard of living

b. Is Santa Claus optimistic? Justify your answer.

2 A racial divide in the US

When President Barack Obama was elected the nation's first black president in 2008, it suggested a move toward a post-racial America, the kind of society that Martin Luther King Jr. envisioned in his "I Have a Dream" speech nearly a half-century before. But six years into the Age of Obama, relations between blacks and whites are arguably worse in communities across the nation.

Obama has pushed for many policies to boost[1] blacks, with some success: increasing access to health care, making college more affordable, and he launched My Brother's Keeper, a program designed to empower[2] young minority men.

Yet vast disparities between blacks and whites remain. Blacks earn less money, graduate from college at lower rates[3] and are imprisoned at disproportionately higher rates than whites. The unemployment rate for blacks is more than double the national average,[4] 11.1 percent, while it's 4.9 percent for whites.

Improving African-Americans' quality of life may help empower them and narrow[5] the gap between black and white. But ultimately race relations come down to what's in a person's head. And even the first black president can't change how people feel about each other.

■ Adapted from www.mcclatchydc.com, December 11, 2014

1. *(ici) améliorer la situation de* **2.** give power to **3.** *pourcentage (de reçus)* **4.** /ˈævərɪdʒ/ *moyenne* **5.** *réduire*

a. Read the text and pick out the names of two people. What are they famous for?
b. What do the following numbers, dates and expressions refer to?
2008 • half-century before • 6 • 11.1% • 4.9%
c. Focus on the words highlighted in pink. How are they built? What prefix and/or suffix is used? Find the root *(racine)*. Check their meanings with a dictionary. Translate them into French.
d. Use the context to guess the meaning of the word in blue.
e. How are the words in green built? Translate them into French.
f. In what ways has the situation improved for African-Americans thanks to Obama?
g. List four spheres where racial inequality still exists.
h. Which sentence best sums up the text? Justify your choice.

➜ Recap
- Sum up what you have learnt about racial inequality in the US today.
- Is the article optimistic or pessimistic? Why?

Get ready for the Oral Exam

Has the situation evolved for African-Americans over the last fifty years?

5 The Power of Music

1 Get ready

Read this quote:

> *We are the voice for those without a voice.*
> T.I., an American rapper

a. Who is "We"?

b. In the following list, imagine who "those without a voice" could be:
ordinary citizens *(citoyens)* • people who are excluded • political leaders • minorities

2 Read and understand

The New York Times

Friday, June 19, 2015 | Today's Paper | Video | 77°F |

In the wake[1] of recent killings of unarmed African-American men, [R&B singer] D'Angelo has grown increasingly frustrated with racial injustice and has been looking at the political movements of the past for ideas for change. [...] After the killing of [black teenager] Michael Brown [by a white police officer] in Ferguson, Mo.,[2] last year, he felt compelled[3] to speak out. In December, he surprised fans by suddenly releasing the album "Black Messiah". [...] On "The Charade", D'Angelo sings, "All we wanted was a chance to talk / 'Stead[4] we only got outlined in chalk." [...]

Does music play a role in helping ignite[5] social change?

D'ANGELO: Now more than ever is the need to sing about it and to write songs about it. And no one's doing it. There's only a chosen couple of people. I think **it just takes one little snowflake to start a snowball to go down the hill**. My contribution and say, Kendrick Lamar's and some chosen others' start the snowball.

That's all I can hope for. I don't know if I'm comfortable being quote-unquote[6] a leader. But I do realize and understand that [...] as a musician, and in the medium that I am, that people are listening to me. Kids are listening to me. We have power to influence minds and influence lives. So I respect that power. I really do.

1. *À la suite* **2.** Missouri /mɪˈzʊəri/ **3.** obliged **4.** = instead, *au lieu de cela* **5.** *provoquer* **6.** *entre guillemets*

a. Pick out three names. Who are the people mentioned?

b. Find the name of a state and a town. What happened there?

c. Focus on the first paragraph. Pick out the words related to:
problems the country is confronted with • feelings • what the singer wants.

d. With the help of the picture in the article, explain the words in green.
Which part of the underlined sentence refers to non-violence? Which part refers to violence?

e. – Observe the sentence in blue.
– Focus on the words "snowflake" and "snowball". How are they built? Translate them.
– What does this sentence mean? One single person can start a movement and make a difference. • If only one person acts, nothing is going to change.

f. Focus on the end of the article. Classify the information given:

Who? (names + job)	→	Power and influence	→	Over whom?

→ **Recap** what you have understood with the help of the vocabulary p. 35.

3 Baltimore

a. Go on the Internet and watch the video clip for the song "Baltimore" by Prince.
b. After watching it, which words do you remember?
c. What do you think the song is about?
d. Now turn to the worksheet your teacher will give you.

WORKSHEET 7

Nobody got in nobody's way
So I guess you could say it was a good day
At least a little better than the day in Baltimore
Does anybody hear us pray
For Michael Brown or Freddie Gray?
Peace is more than the absence of war
Absence of war

Chorus
Are we gonna[1] see another bloody day?
We're tired of the crying and people dying
Let's take all the guns away

Absence of war, you and me
Maybe we can finally say
Enough is enough, it's time for love
It's time to hear
It's time to hear the guitar play, guitar play
Baltimore, ever more

If there ain't[2] no justice then there ain't no peace

Chorus
If there ain't no justice then there ain't no peace

We have to interrupt the regular scheduled programming
To bring you up to date on a developing situation in Los Angeles

■ Prince, *HITnRUN phase two*, 2015

1. going to **2.** isn't

4 Testimony

PREPARE YOUR TASK

Act out the interview of a protester in Ferguson by a journalist.
Don't forget to include:
– why people are protesting
– the protester's reactions to Prince's song.

Help!

songwriter
messenger
social change
peace = non-violence
(large) audience: *public*

powerful
committed: *engagé*
determined
influential

demand: *exiger*
promote
speak out against: *s'élever contre*
make sb realize
protest = march = demonstrate

Get ready for the Oral Exam

- **Do you believe music can help fight injustice?**
- **To what extent is music a powerful force for change?**

6 Video Corner High Hopes

I can.

1 Get ready

a. React to the still from the video clip (person, place, activity).
b. Why is this photo surprising? Use the words in the Help! box.
c. Read the song title. Imagine how the girl would finish the sentence: "I can..."

Help!

vacant lot: *terrain vague*
(poor) neighborhood: *quartier*
ghetto / inner city
low cost housing: *HLM*
mattress: *matelas*
power line: *câble électrique*
sunrise: *lever de soleil*

deprived: *démuni*
incongruous = out of place
underprivileged
hopeful ≠ hopeless

expect sb to + BV: *s'attendre à ce que qqn...*

2 The chorus

I know I can
Be what I wanna be
If I work hard at it
I'll be where I wanna be

a. Read the lyrics opposite. Give the equivalent in standard English of "wanna".
b. Pick out key words and phrases:
– referring to determination
– showing what is necessary for the singer to succeed.

3 Watch the video

Watch from the beginning to 0:36. Where does it take place?

First stanza (from 0:37 to 0:47)

a. Who is the singer talking to?
b. Find three professions. Why does he mention them?
c. Pick out one expression referring to success.
d. Fill in the blanks: "But nothing comes ... , it takes much ..." What is necessary to succeed?

Last two stanzas (from 1:07 to 1:17 and from 3:18 to 3:28)

Pick out key words. Organize your notes with the help of the words below.

education power pride

WORKSHEET 8

4 The whole first verse *(couplet)* (from 0:37 to 1:17)

Read the lyrics on the worksheet your teacher will give you.

a. Match the following titles with the corresponding stanzas. One title will be used twice.

... and Fall — School empowers kids — Rise... — Believe in yourself — Choose your friends wisely

b. Is the message of the song positive or negative? Explain why.

5 Focus on the musical elements

a. The chorus uses "call and answer". Explain. Which music genre is this characteristic of?

b. What other music genres can you hear? Why does Nas superimpose different music styles?

PREPARE YOUR TASK

➜ Recap

These words appear in the video. Write your opinion of the video to post in the comment section of YouTube using all of the following words:

ACHIEVE — CAREFUL — BEAUTIFUL — TRUTH — READ — LEARN — LISTEN — PRACTICE — EMPOWER

WORKSHEET 8

6 Work on pronunciation

Listen again to the chorus, stanzas 1, 5 and 6. Read the lyrics on your worksheet.

a. Highlight the words that are particularly stressed.

b. Where will you breathe *(respirer)*? Mark pauses with a vertical bar (|).

c. Read this passage aloud, paying attention to the rhythm.

d. Choose the stanza you prefer. Learn it by heart and recite or sing it in front of the class.

7 Hold on to your dreams

PREPARE YOUR TASK

You were one of the kids in the video. Ten years after this song was released you go back to your high school to talk to the students about how this song inspired you.

Help!

courage
determination = will-power
self-discipline

ambitious
determined /dɪ'tɜːmɪnd/
self-confident
optimistic
energetic
hopeful

fulfill one's dreams = achieve one's dreams = make one's dreams come true
The singer urges everyone to...: *le chanteur incite tout le monde à...*
overcome obstacles: *surmonter des obstacles*
express one's personality

Get ready for the Oral Exam

How does a singer use music to empower young people (=make them more confident)?

7 Slam Poetry

Why I Think this World Should End

The people are depressed and angry
We can't live with each other and we can't live with ourselves
So everyone's medicated[1]
We pass each other on the streets
And if we do speak it's meaningless[2] robotic communication
More people want fifteen seconds of fame
Than a lifetime of meaning and purpose[3]
Because what's popular is more important than what's right
Ratings[4] are more important than the truth
Our government builds twice as many prisons than schools
It's easier to find a Big Mac than an apple
And when you find the apple
It's been genetically processed[5] and modified
Presidents lie, politicians trick[6] us
Race is still an issue[7] and so is religion [...]
Instead of trying to change others we can change ourselves
We can change our hearts [...]
So yes, the world is coming to an end
And the path[8] towards a new beginning starts within you

■ Prince Ea, *The World Is Coming to an End*, 2014

1. *sous médicaments* **2.** without any sense **3.** *(ici) projets d'avenir* **4.** *(ici) cotes de popularité* **5.** *transformée génétiquement* **6.** *trompent* **7.** problem **8.** *chemin*

Slam poetry is a spoken form of poetry influenced by the music and rhythm of hip-hop.

Slam poems often have a political message, calling for social change.

Slam Poetry: The only thing known to man that makes anyone under the age of 30 like poetry.
Urban Dictionary

CD 1 PISTE 10

1 Read the lyrics, then listen to the song

a. What does Prince Ea protest against? Which topics are mentioned? Choose from the following list:

pessimism – the economic situation – unemployment – lack *(manque)* of communication – a superficial world – pollution – drugs – lies – repression – junk food – racism

b. Which three topics are the most important to you? Compare your list with your neighbor's and justify your choices.

WORKSHEET 9

2 Slam it!

Focus on lines 1 to 9 and use the worksheet your teacher will give you.

PREPARE YOUR TASK

3 Creative workshop

Write your own short slam poem using the steps given opposite. Record it or perform it in class and vote for the best in the class.

Tips

4 Steps to Slam Poetry

- **STEP 1:** Write it all down. Think of one event or a protest topic. Write down anything that you can think of.
- **STEP 2:** Read it out loud. Say the words. Hear how they sound. Feel them in your mouth.
- **STEP 3:** Add flavor! Add powerful words, movement, emotion.
- **STEP 4:** Read it out loud again. Listen to yourself. Feel it! Share it!

Play with words

MP3 N° 4 · CD 1 PISTE 11

A Lisez les mots suivants. Puis écoutez-les.

Who for?
public
audience
spectators

Songs
songwriter
lyrics
release an album
perform: *jouer, donner un spectacle*
give a performance

What for?
tool: *outil*
(a) means of + noun/V-ING: *(un) moyen de*
express
reach: *atteindre*

Protest
riot /ˈraɪət/: *émeute*
social unrest: *agitation sociale*
injustice
be politically engaged
denounce

Goals
promote
overcome (differences...): *surmonter*
break down barriers
convey a message: *transmettre un message*
fight prejudices: *combattre les préjugés*
raise awareness: *sensibiliser*

B Entraînez-vous à prononcer les mots suivants. Sont-ils accentués sur la première ou la deuxième syllabe ? Recopiez le tableau ci-dessous sur papier libre et complétez-le. Puis vérifiez à l'écoute.

album • audience • barriers • lyrics • message • prejudice • injustice • express • committed

Première syllabe	Deuxième syllabe

C Utilisez les mots dans les bulles ci-dessus pour compléter les phrases suivantes. Mettez les verbes à la forme qui convient.

Tracy Chapman is a ... . She writes her own ... . She has already ... several albums. Her concerts usually attract a large ... . Writing a song is a means of ... her feelings and reactions. She has often reacted to ... in certain neighborhoods. She denounces social ... and ... . She wants to ... ... barriers and ... better race relationships. She would like to ... . She is a ... singer who dreams of a better world.

D Go further

a. Go on the Internet. Find the Apple music commercial 2015 "History of Sound".

b. Put these listening devices in chronological order.

CD player • radio • iPod • phonograph • cassette player • walkman • record player • mobile phone

LANGUAGE AT WORK

«Apprendre à Apprendre»
Téléchargez la fiche n°2
www.editions-hatier.fr/langues-eleves

Corrigés p. 216-221

A L'infinitif

(Précis grammatical 45 p. 213)

1. Réécrivez les énoncés suivants au discours indirect à l'aide des amorces proposées.

a. "Don't fight anymore." Prince asks them ...
b. "The government should fight against discrimination." He expects *(attend du gouvernement qu'il)* ...
c. "Let's take the guns away." He advises *(conseille)* ...
d. "Don't give up hope." He advises ...
e. "Stop violence." He encourages people ...
f. "When will people live in peace?" He would like/ prefer people ...

2. Traduisez.

a. Le chanteur veut défendre la paix dans son pays.
b. Il a écrit cette chanson pour protester contre la violence.
c. Il veut que les émeutes s'arrêtent.
d. Il s'attend à ce que des mesures soient prises.
e. Il encourage le gouvernement à prendre des mesures.
f. Dans les années soixante les chanteurs voulaient aider les gens à combattre pour leurs droits.
g. Ils ont utilisé la musique pour surmonter les obstacles et faire tomber les barrières.

B Les subordonnées relatives

(Précis grammatical 40 p. 210)

3. Complétez les énoncés suivants avec *who*, *that* ou ∅ (plusieurs choix possibles).

a. Have you paid attention to the lyrics of the songs in the album ... Pharrell Williams has just released?
b. Tracy Chapman has a voice ... I like very much.
c. What are the songs ... you know by heart?
d. Is this the singer ... denounced racial injustice in his last album?
e. Is rap the only musical genre ... you listen to?

4. Complétez les énoncés suivants avec *that*, ∅ ou *what* (plusieurs choix possibles).

The song ... I prefer is *Strange Fruit* by Billie Holiday. It is a song ... she wrote to express her disgust because the Ku Klux Klan used to lynch Blacks in the South of the USA in the thirties. Billie Holiday wanted to denounce ... was going on in the South. ... she describes is horrible. She never forgot ... some people suffered. Writing a song was the best solution ... she found to make people realize the situation. The song ... you can listen to today is very moving, it's one of the most beautiful songs ... I know. ... Billie Holiday wrote is a masterpiece.

5. Traduisez.

a. La chanson que tu écoutes est émouvante *(moving)*.
b. Ce qu'il écrit est très beau.
c. Prince parle des émeutes qui ont eu lieu à Baltimore en 2015.
d. Il rend hommage à *(pay tribute to)* une chanteuse qu'il aime beaucoup, Nina Simone.

▲ Billie Holiday

YOUR TASK

STEP BY STEP

Go over your notes from the unit.

- Listen again to the songs you have studied.
- Learn the vocabulary and practice the grammar points studied.

SCENARIO 1

Imagine you are Prince, Tracy Chapman or Nas. Prepare a short speech talking about why you write songs and what impact music has on people. Make a video of your speech to post on your official website.

► **Take notes.**
– Choose the singer you want to be and the song you will talk about.
– Write down key ideas only. Include:

A SHORT DESCRIPTION OF THE SONG

WHAT THIS SONG DENOUNCES

HOW YOU WANT PEOPLE TO REACT

► **Practice speaking.**
Remember to say the stressed syllables louder.

► **Make a video selfie or have a friend film you.**

SCENARIO 2

Write one verse of a rap song or slam poem. You can add a verse to a song from the unit or think of a cause you want to support or a problem you want to denounce. Perform it live in class or make a video.

► **Prepare your lyrics.**
– Brainstorm for vocabulary.
– Put your ideas into short sentences.

► **Give it a strong rhythm or beat.**

► **Practice your pronunciation.**

► **Perform it!**
Perform it in class or make a video.

Tip
Clap your hands or tap your desk to give yourself the rhythm.

► **The jury (formed by the rest of the class) will vote for the best performance based on the following criteria:**

a. The song had a clear rhythm or beat: yes • most of the time • not really
b. The pronunciation was authentic and the message was clearly delivered:
yes • most of the time • not really
c. The vocabulary was rich and the grammar points studied were used correctly:
yes • most of the time • not at all
d. The ideas were original: yes • not really • not at all
e. The performance: It was very entertaining. • It wasn't entirely convincing.
The singer didn't look at the audience and didn't look convinced.

Compréhension écrite et expression écrite

WORKSHEET BAC N° 2

Answer the questions on the worksheet the teacher will give you.

DOCUMENT A

I was born by the river in a little tent
Oh and just like the river I've been running ev'r since
It's been a long time, a long time coming
But I know a change gonna come, oh yes it will

It's been too hard living, but I'm afraid to die
'Cause I don't know what's up there, beyond the sky
It's been a long, a long time coming
But I know a change gonna come, oh yes it will

I go to the movie and I go downtown
Somebody keep tellin' me don't hang around[1]
It's been a long, a long time coming
But I know a change gonna come, oh yes it will

Then I go to my brother
And I say brother help me please
But he winds up[2] knockin' me
Back down on my knees, oh

There have been times that I thought I couldn't last for long
But now I think I'm able to carry on
It's been a long, a long time coming
But I know a change is gonna come, oh yes it will

■ Sam Cooke, *A Change Is Gonna Come*, 1964

1. *(ici) traîner* 2. gets angry

DOCUMENT B

“I have a dream that my four little children will one day live in a nation where they will not be judged by the color of their skin but by the content of their character. I have a dream today! I have a dream that one day, […] right there in Alabama little black boys and black girls will be able to join hands with little white boys and white girls as sisters and brothers.
I have a dream today!”

■ Martin Luther King Jr., speech in Washington, D.C., 1963

DOCUMENT C

Singing helped the Freedom Riders[1] in the face of great danger. Following one impromptu songwriter on the bus, the Freedom Riders sang as they entered Jackson, Mississippi. […]
In Jackson, the Freedom Riders were arrested and jailed. Rider James Farmer: “The prison officials wanted us to stop singing, because they were afraid our spirit would become contagious and the other prisoners would become Freedom Riders as a result of our singing.” The guards threatened to take away the mattresses[2] – their only luxury in a steel cell – if they continued to sing.
As Farmer recalled, one Freedom Rider called for the guards. “He said, ‘Come get my mattress. I'll keep my soul.’ And everybody started singing, *Ain't gonna let nobody turn me round, turn me round, turn me round…*”
“They came in and took the mattresses away and people sang as they had never sung before. We thought we were winning the battle; they were on the run.”

■ Bernice Johnson Reagon, www.pbs.org

1. In the 1960s, black and white activists took buses in the south of the US to protest against segregation on public transport.
2. *matelas*

Compréhension de l'oral

CD 1 PISTE 12

Music for a cause

→ Écoutez l'enregistrement trois fois.
→ Prenez des notes puis faites en dix minutes le compte rendu de ce que vous avez compris en français.
→ Utilisez les expressions données p. 183.

Expression orale

LOCATIONS AND FORMS OF POWER { To what extent does music have the power to change society?

Comment parler de la notion ?

1 Définissez le mot « pouvoir ». Reportez-vous à la page 4.
2 Pour répondre à la problématique, recopiez le schéma ci-dessous sur papier libre et complétez-le avec les documents étudiés en classe.

To what extent does music have the power to change society?

What are the roots of today's music?
slavery
rhythm
drums

Has the situation evolved for African-Americans over the last 60 years?
racial divide
inequality
gap
take measures
improve

What have Black Americans used music for?
What are protest songs written for?

To what extent is music a powerful force for change?
self-confident
advise sb to do sth
encourage sb to do sth
overcome
take up a challenge

How does a singer use music to empower young people?
committed
rebel against
denounce
criticize sb for
stand for = defend

What impact should protest songs have on listeners?
shock
provoke
amaze
make sb react
inspire
raise awareness
protest against = speak up against

3 Utilisez le vocabulaire donné (p. 5, rubriques *Help* et p. 39) pour enrichir votre expression.
4 Préparez-vous à prendre la parole à partir de notes : ne rédigez pas votre présentation ; notez les idées clés et les mots importants.
5 N'oubliez pas une conclusion personnelle.

Unit 3

LOCATIONS AND FORMS OF POWER
To what extent does the gun issue divide the USA?

Guns Under Fire

1 Tune In!

React to the photograph

a. What catches your eye first?
b. Where does the scene take place?
c. Which adjectives best describe the woman?

protective | dangerous | loving | relaxed | carefree *(insouciante)* | careless *(négligente)* | scared | enthusiastic | self-confident

d. Why do you think the woman is carrying a gun? Make a sentence with the help of these words:

everyday objects | family | want | protect | defend

Tip

How to give your opinion:
I think...
I believe...
In my opinion/To my mind...
It seems to me that...

Help!

shoulder: *épaule*
machine gun
pop-gun: *pistolet en plastique*
toy: *jouet*
24 hours /aʊəz/ a day

astonishing: *très surprenant*
disturbing: *troublant*
gruesome/horrid
usual = commonplace
unusual = out of place

YOUR FINAL TASK

OR

Your friend has posted an audio recording on Facebook. Write a comment. (p. 53)

React to a testimony on a radio station phone-in. (p. 53)

2 The Right to Bear Arms

1 The Second Amendment

CD 1 PISTE 13

a. Listen to this recording of the Second Amendment and reorder the balloons.

A well-regulated Militia • to keep and bear Arms • shall not be infringed. • to the security of a free State, • being necessary • the right of the people

b. What does this amendment mean? (Several possible answers)
American citizens are forbidden to buy guns. • They are allowed to defend their communities. • They can have weapons in their homes as well as on them. • The government can take away what citizens own privately. • Only members of the army can be armed.

2 Points of view

a. Look at the poster.
– Who is speaking?
– What is the message?
approve of • want sb to • criticize sb for V-ING • refuse • support • compare sb to

b. Read the two quotations below.

c. What do these people have in common with the women on this double page?

CLINT EASTWOOD: "I have a very strict gun control policy: if there's a gun around, I want to be in control of it."
He is a strong supporter of the Second Amendment and a member of the NRA (National Rifle Association).

BRUCE WILLIS: "Everyone has a right to bear arms. If you take guns away from legal gun owners, then the only people who have guns are the bad guys."

3 How many guns out there?

CD 1 PISTE 14

PREPARE YOUR TASK

a. Listen to the recording and take notes.
– Focus on numbers and percentages.
– Note down the American states you have recognized.
– Classify the states in two groups: easy access to guns • strict laws.
– How long does it take to buy a gun? (several possible answers)
30 minutes • 30 days • 2 weeks • 2 years

WORKSHEET 10

b. Complete the map of the USA the teacher will give you. Note down the number of guns per inhabitant for each state mentioned and if laws are restrictive or not.

4 Writing workshop

Use the information collected to write a short article entitled "The USA, a gun nation". (120 words)

3 Who's Next?

▲ *Crayons*, graffiti mural by Gamma Acosta, Longmont, Colorado

1 Read and understand

Two teenage girls are in the high school restrooms at break time.

Part 1

Dot. Dot—

So loud this time—close and mechanically bright—that both girls scream. Their screams are followed by a silence that sounds foolish, cold and hard as the tile[1] on the girls' room walls. One says in a whisper,[2] "It's Michael Patrick. Yesterday, in trig,[3] he told me he was going to bring a gun to school, that he was going to kill…"

"Who? Kill who?"

"Everybody."

"What?"

"'All you fuckheads,' he said. I thought he was joking, you know what a freak[4]—"

"Why didn't you tell anybody?"

On the other side of the door to the girls' room, there's another scream. It sounds desperate and pointless as music, and it's followed by a man asking for help.

"Help," is all he says.

Part 2

[…] Then he opens the door slowly, and steps in. He's holding a big blue-black gun with both hands, pointing it in front of him, aiming at nothing.

When he sees them, Michael Patrick laughs. "Hey," he says.

One of the girls, trying not to sob,[5] swallows,[6] then says, "Michael."

He's wearing a shiny shirt—a clean and pale white shirt, but there are large ugly sweat stains[7] under his arms. There's an angry rash[8] under his chin, where he must have shaved too fast that morning.

Michael Patrick smiles. He's breathing hard. He takes one of his hands off the grip of the gun and puts the hand in the pocket of his jeans. He's wearing white shoes with blue lightning bolts on the sides, laces untied.

"So," he says too loudly in the quiet softness of the girls' room, and both girls flinch.[9]

"So," he says more softly, as if sorry to have startled them.

"Which one of you girls should I kill?"

■ Laura Kasischke, *The Life Before her Eyes*, 2002

1. *carrelage* **2.** *murmure* **3.** trigonometry **4.** *dingue/taré* **5.** *sangloter* **6.** *avale sa salive* **7.** *taches*
8. *plaque rouge* **9.** *tressaillent*

Part 1

a. Name the characters present in this part.
b. Who else is mentioned?
c. What plan was revealed the day before?
d. Pick out sounds. What is going on?

Part 2

e. Who are the characters present in the room now?
f. Pick out movements and sounds showing the characters are scared.
g. Describe the boy in your own words.
h. What is going to happen in the end?

2 Radio interview

One of the girls tells a journalist about that terrible day in her school. Imagine the radio interview.
She explains: what happened • her reaction • Michael Patrick's motivations.

Help!

Shock and fear	Violence
helpless: *impuissant*	slaughter /slɔːtəʳ/: *massacre*
desperate /despərɪt/: *désespéré*	in cold blood: *de sang froid*
scared stiff/to death: *mort de peur*	aim at sb/target sb: *viser qqn*
fear for one's life: *craindre pour sa vie*	threaten sb with sth
realize/become aware of	shoot sb down: *abattre qqn*

CD 1 PISTE 15

PREPARE YOUR TASK

3 Columbine High School, Colorado, 1999

a. Get ready. Listen to a few words from the recording and write them down.
b. First listening
– Note down as many words as possible.
– Who is speaking: a journalist • a student • a teacher • a police officer?
c. Second listening

Part 1
Listen for key information about the killers and organise it into two groups: their enemies • their friends.

USEFUL WORDS
- a couple of = two
- get even with sb = to get one's revenge

Part 2
– Pick out key words. Note down all the places mentioned.
– How did the students get guns into the school?
  • The guns were hidden in a schoolbag.
  • They were in their lockers.
  • They were under their long coats.

USEFUL WORDS
- shoot at point-blank range: *tirer à bout portant*
- trap: *piéger*

The end of the tragedy Are the following statements true or false? Justify with key words you have heard.
Many students in the library were executed. • The killers were arrested by the police. • Some victims called their family for help.
d. Third listening. Complete your notes.
e. Compare the story in the text p. 46 and the recording.

4 Teen Talk

Write the inside of this leaflet (80 words). Use the information collected to speak about gun violence in schools. Here are some possible headings:

Friends at risks

Do you need a gun?

Your friend brings a gun at school

Get ready for the Oral Exam

What impact do testimonies and stories on gun violence have on people?

4 Video Corner

Guns With History

1 Get ready

a. Read the title of the video and look at the photo on the right. What do you think the video is about?

b. Who are the potential customers *(clients)*?

c. Read the words below, then close your book and say which ones you remember.
protection • safety • revolver • semi-automatic • shooter • bedroom • injured: *blessé* • target practice

2 Go on the Internet, type the title. Then watch the video without the sound.

a. Read the information on the screen.
– What do most people buy a gun for?
– What are the risks of having a gun at home?
– What are the campaigners' goals?

b. Focus on the experiment.
– What did the campaigners do? Where?
– What is special about the objects sold there?
– What technical device is used? Why?

c. Watch the video again from 1:20 to 2:53. How do the customers react?
They look: appalled (horrified) surprised scared furious enthusiastic.

d. Why? Because of the price • Because of the stories the man tells them • Because of what they can read on the labels *(étiquettes)*.

USEFUL WORDS
- **Walmart superstore**
- **Sandy Hook Elementary School**
- **blindsided:** ***désagréablement surpris***

3 Watch and listen

a. Pick out one word repeated twice. What are the customers' motive?

b. Focus on numbers.
– Which ones did you hear? 2 • 5 • 9 • 12 • 19 • 20 • 21 • 26 • 90
– What do they correspond to? age (months, years) • number of victims (adults, children, killed, injured: *blessé*) • caliber (type of weapon) • date (day, year)

c. Where did the tragedies happen? at home • in a school • in a hospital • in a supermarket • in a prison • in a fast food restaurant • in a cinema • in the street

d. True or false? justify your answers.
– Guns have been used in school shootings.
– A young child took one gun out to play.
– Guns caused death by accident.
– People committed suicide with these guns.
– The guns usec are mostly police guns.
– A gun was used to kill in a supermarket.

e. Which adjectives are used to qualify guns?
cheap: *peu cher* handy: *facile à manier* deadly: *mortel* easy to use popular automatic

f. What do the customers decide when they leave? Why?

g. Explain the slogan in your own words.

> **"Every gun has a history. Let's not repeat it."**

4 I've changed my mind

PREPARE YOUR TASK

One of the customers in the video returns home and explains to his/her partner why he/she didn't buy a gun.

5 Music Corner — No Guns Allowed

1 Read this stanza *(strophe)* from the song

a. Rephrase the stanza in standard English *(anglais considéré comme correct)*.
"Let the music play, ... don't want ... more gun-play, ..."
b. Pick out words referring to a dangerous game • its consequences.
c. Who does "me" stand for?
d. What is Snoop Lion's message?

> Let the music play, me don't want no more gun-play
> When the bodies hit the ground, there's nothing left to say ay ay
> Me don't want to see no more innocent bloodshed
> Me don't want to see no more youth dead
> Come hear me now
>
> ■ Snoop Lion, 2013

PREPARE YOUR TASK

2 Go on the Internet and watch the clip of the song

a. Concentrate on the voice-overs *(voix off)*. Who is speaking? the president • witnesses *(témoins)* • the police • a journalist • shooters • parents • teachers • politicians
b. Focus on the visual elements. Note down people, places, objects, actions and dates. Then organize your notes.

People
- **Children:** games, school...
- **Adults:** police, demonstrators *(manifestants)*...

Violence
- Objects
- Tragedies
- **Consequences:** people mourning *(en deuil)*...

3 Compare

Which do you like better, the campaign on p. 48 or the song above? Explain your choice.

Help!

Campaigns
- informative/educational
- shocking
- effective: *efficace*
- striking
- unusual: *peu ordinaire, original*
- eye-catching: *qui attire l'attention*

Goals
- alert sb to/warn sb about
- condemn
- criticize sb for V-ING
- denounce
- make sb realize
- support ≠ oppose
- prevent sb from V-ING

4 Role play

Act out an interview between a talk show host *(animateur)* and Snoop Lion who explains why he wrote this song. Imagine the dialogue.

Get ready for the Oral Exam

Can the tactics used in anti-gun campaigns change the public's opinion?

6 Hollywood and Gun Violence

1 React to the film poster

a. How does the man look?
powerful • scared • calm • violent • fearless

b. Can you name films with gun violence?

c. Do you enjoy watching them? Why? Why not?

2 Gun violence in movies

a. Read the article.

GUNS BLAZING ON THE SILVER SCREEN

What a new study on movie violence tells us about gun control.

A new study coming out in next month's issue of "Pediatrics" shows that the level of gun violence in the top PG-13 films[1] is rising. Violence with a gun shows up, on average, twice an hour! [...] Living 20 minutes from Hollywood here in Los Angeles, I know how much both guns and movies mean to our society, and I also know that Hollywood's all about the supply and demand[2] when distributing its products. Hollywood gives us violent movies, specifically shoot 'em up[3] violent films, and we eat them up. The problem, though, is that our children are acting on that behavior. Violence sells, but what if the audience can't handle[4] what Hollywood's selling? [...] Our children simply can't handle the violence that they're taking in. And we have no way of truly knowing what transpires once that amount[5] of violence is stored in that wonderful computer called our brain.

US News, November 13, 2013

1. films children under thirteen can't see **2.** *l'offre et la demande* **3.** *(ici) où tout le monde se fait flinguer* **4.** *(ici) gérer* **5.** *(ici) dose*

b. According to the article, what impact do violent films have on the audience *(public)*?

3 Speak up

PREPARE YOUR TASK

Go on the Internet (type: gun control • celebrities • demand a plan) and watch the video.

a. Which of these tragedies are mentioned by the celebrities?
Fort Worth, 1999 (Wedgwood Baptist Church) • Columbine High School, 1999 • Virginia Tech, 2007 (University) • Omaha shopping mall, 2007 • Fort Hood, 2009 (army base) • Tucson supermarket, 2011 • Charleston church, 2015 • Aurora movie theater, 2012 • Newtown, 2012 (Sandy Hook School) • Oak Creek, 2012 (Wisconsin Sikh temple)

b. Note down the repeated words and sentences. Which one is the slogan?

c. Do you find this campaign effective? Why? Why not?

d. Why can these celebrities be called a lobby?

ABC **DEFINITION**

A lobby is a group of people seeking to influence politicians or public officials on a particular issue.

4 A radio phone-in

An anxious mother calls because her child is addicted to violent movies. You are the radio host, what would you advise her to do?

Get ready for the Oral Exam

To what extent do film makers and celebrities influence the public?

Play with words

MP3 n° 5 — CD 1 piste 16

A **Savoir utiliser des données chiffrées.**

a. Écrivez ces nombres et ces pourcentages en toutes lettres.

– Each year, there are 9,484 victims of guns in the USA. Yet, only 200 die because of firearms in Canada and 35 in Australia. The total cost of gun violence is $229,000,000.

– In America, 80% of suicide attempts with a gun are successful. 4,257 teenagers died in 2014.

– Among 15-24 year-olds, gun deaths surpass car accidents. 64.3% of teenagers have held a gun at least once.

– The police found 749 rifles, revolvers and automatic weapons in a house in Compton, a Los Angeles district. They also arrested 48 members of a gang of young offenders.

b. Sur la fiche que votre professeur vous donnera, écrivez en toutes lettres les nombres et les pourcentages que vous allez entendre.

WORKSHEET 11

Tips

- **Les nombres sont invariables** *(ten million)*, sauf dans l'expression : *millions/thousands of...*
- Observez : 2,853 = *two thousand, eight hundred and fifty-three.*
- Point ou virgule ? 1,5 se dit en anglais *one point five (1.5)* (→ p. 181).

B **Classez les mots ci-dessous en trois groupes :** Weapons | People | Motives

Certains mots sont proches du français ; utilisez un dictionnaire si nécessaire pour les autres.

rifle • attacker • shotgun • robbery • firearm • revenge • ammunition • shooter • protection • robber • bullet • shooting-practice • intruder • victim • hatred • cartridge • hunting • revolver • pistol • assault

C **Associez les mots de la liste A avec un mot de sens voisin de la liste B. Utilisez un dictionnaire si besoin.**

List A	List B
aim at sb • carry a weapon • prohibited • slaughter • horrid • frightening • dangerous • determined • denounce • disapprove of	massacre • disagree with • condemn • target sb • gruesome • unsafe • banned • scary • resolute • bear arms

D **Observez le document ci-contre. Sur papier libre, associez chaque chiffre en jaune à l'un des mots suivants. Vérifiez à l'écoute.**

awareness • limit • denounce • support • approve • prevent • saved • access • warn

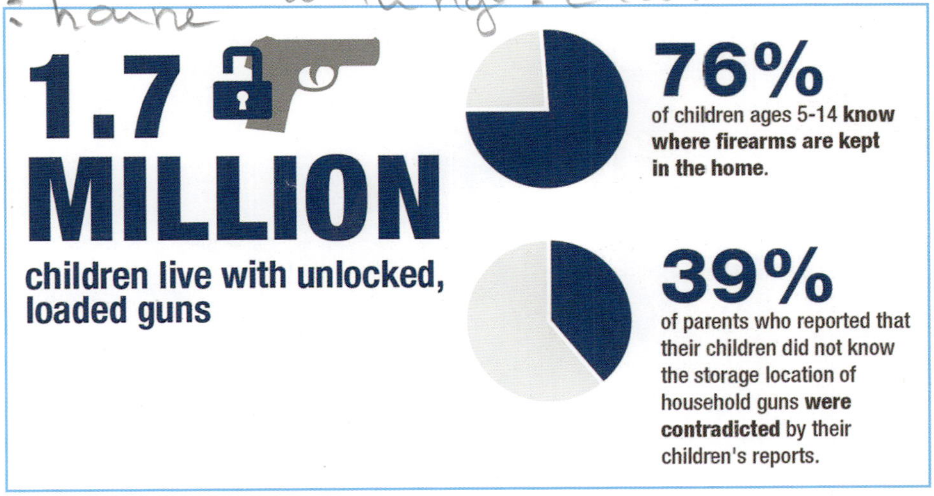

This is an **1** campaign to **2** parents about the danger of having guns at home. Many children are killed by a parent's gun. The campaigners **3** the free **4** to guns and would like to **5** the number of firearms in the home. They want to **6** parents from keeping a gun at home. They want to make homes, schools and communities safer. Many lives would be **7** . They hope more and more parents will **8** of their action and **9** them.

LANGUAGE AT WORK

« Apprendre à Apprendre »
Téléchargez la fiche n°3
www.editions-hatier.fr/langues-eleves

Corrigés p. 216-221

A Le passif

(Précis grammatical 28 p. 204)

Sujet + *be* + participe passé du verbe { **verbe irrégulier = 3e colonne de la liste p. 214-215** / **verbe régulier = V + *-ed***

1. Complétez ce paragraphe en utilisant des formes passives. Attention au marqueur de temps souligné à chaque fois.

a. In the US today, moviegoers' bags and pockets (check) by some movie theaters before entering.
b. A young boy (shoot) in the street yesterday.
c. In 2015, people (shoot) in a church in Charleston, South Carolina.
d. A criminal just (arrest).
e. Stricter gun control (demand) for years.

2. a. Complétez ce paragraphe en utilisant des formes passives.
In 1989 Troy Davis, an American man, (accuse) of the murder of a police officer. He (send) to jail and (take) to court. He (try) and (execute) because seven witnesses said Davis had shot the police officer. He (convict) of murder, (put) on death row and (condemn) to death.

b. Lisez le paragraphe à voix haute et vérifiez à l'écoute. MP3 N° 6 — CD 1 PISTE 17

3. Mettez le verbe entre parenthèses à l'actif ou au passif.

a. New restrictive gun ownership laws ... in Pennsylvania last year. (vote)
b. The gun industry ... by many politicians in western states. (support)
c. Young offenders ... easy access to guns at home or on the black market. (have)
d. The Second Amendment ... by pro-gun supporters. (often/quote: *citer*)
e. Many Americans ... a weapon to protect their family. (buy)
f. The NRA ... in 1871 and is the most important gun organization in the USA. (create)

B *Can, can't, mustn't, be forbidden to, be allowed to, don't have to*

(Précis grammatical 24 p. 203)

4. Complétez avec une des formes modales proposées.

a. In Colorado, you ... buy a gun when you are 18 years old but only if you have no criminal record, and you ... carry arms.
b. You ... register for any type of weapon, handgun or rifle but citizens ... buy automatic weapons.
c. Anti-gun people think too many US citizens ... have free access to arms. But because of the lobbies, gun violence ... be stopped.

ON YOUR OWN!

An anti-gun activist reacts to the cartoon and writes a short comment on the newspaper website. Don't forget to use the passive voice and modal auxiliaries.

USEFUL WORDS

• vending-machine: *distributeur* • free sale • free access to • denounce • danger • law • alert sb about • be in favor of • limit • take measures

YOUR TASK

1. Get ready

a. Go over your notes again on gun ownership, gun control, and the dangers of guns.

b. Look at the cartoon.
- List as many words and expressions as possible.
- What sort of family is portrayed? What is their opinion about guns?

CD 1 PISTE 18

2. Listen to a recording entitled *Gun Education*

a. First listening
- Focus on numbers (date, quantity, age, percentage).
- Which words are repeated?

b. Second listening
List as many key words *(mots accentués, porteurs de sens)* as possible.

c. Third listening
Complete and check your notes.

d. Write an account of what you have understood (10 minutes). Use the expressions given p. 183.

USEFUL WORDS
- **firing range:** *stand de tir*
- **pop-gun:** *pistolet en plastique (jouet)*

SCENARIO 1

Your friend has posted this recording on Facebook. Many people liked it. You don't understand why. Write your comment. (100 words)

SCENARIO 2

You have just heard the testimony on the radio. React on the radio station phone-in.

- What I've heard is incredible/unbelievable.
- I'm shocked/outraged by this report.
- Does this man/woman realize...?
- He/She should/shouldn't...
- Let sb do sth: *laisser qqn faire qqch*
- I would never...

Write your draft *(brouillon)*.

Include these points:

- Introduce yourself briefly.
- Give your opinion (→ *Enrichir sa prise de parole*, p. 178-179).
- Sum up the narrator's opinion and the anecdote she relates.

Compréhension écrite et expression écrite

Answer the questions on the worksheet the teacher will give you.

WORKSHEET BAC N° 3

DOCUMENT A

Jennifer Longdon was one of at least 750,000 Americans injured by gunshots over the last decade, and she was lucky not to be one of the more than 320,000 killed. Each year more than 11,000 people are murdered with a firearm, and more than 20,000 others commit suicide using one. Hundreds of children die annually in gun homicides, and each week seems to bring news of another toddler[1] accidentally shooting himself or a sibling[2] with an unsecured gun. And perhaps most disturbingly, even as violent crime overall has declined steadily in recent years, rates of gun injury and death are climbing (up 11 and 4 percent since 2011) and mass shootings have been on the rise.

■ www.motherjones.com, Mark Follman, Julia Lurie, Jaeah Lee and James West

1. *tout-petit* **2.** *frère/sœur*

DOCUMENT B

In an artist's statement on her website, Calton writes that "growing up in Houston was synonymous with an induction into Texas gun culture." The 55-year-old photographer wanted to explore the significance of the concealed weapons for women in Texas and found that the owners had diverse backgrounds and also owned the weapons for different reasons, not just because they are Texans and were born with them.

"Often these women are unassuming and unexpected," she writes, "a young mother with her baby at the grocery store checkout counter, a grandmother walking her dog, or perhaps a woman in the parking space next to you at the shopping mall. My photographs showcase the diversity of this population. However, I found a commonality in their response to the question "are you prepared to pull the trigger to protect yourself or your loved ones?" The answer from the women in this collection of portraits is a resounding "yes."

■ www.complex.com

DOCUMENT C

Gun violence costs more than $700 per American a year. We spend more on it than on obesity, and almost as much as we spend on Medicaid.

www.motherjones.com

Compréhension de l'oral

CD 1 PISTE 19

More firearms in American schools?

→ Écoutez l'enregistrement trois fois.
→ Prenez des notes puis faites en dix minutes le compte rendu de ce que vous avez compris en français.
→ Utilisez les expressions données p. 183.

USEFUL WORDS

- Sandy Hook Elementary School
- Kathy Steinhoff
- Columbia, Missouri /mɪˈzʊərɪ/

Expression orale

LOCATIONS AND FORMS OF POWER { **To what extent does the gun issue divide the USA?**

Comment parler de la notion ?

1. Définissez la notion *Locations and Forms of Power*. Revoyez la définition de *lobby* p. 50.
2. Sélectionnez les documents qui vous permettent de répondre aux questions suivantes.

To what extent does the gun issue divide the USA?

What are the laws in the different states?
free sale/access to
right to carry/bear arms
contrast between and…
contrary to
whereas

Media Power: What impact can Hollywood films have on the public?
(dis)agree with
oppose
side with: *prendre le parti de*
take a stand: *prendre position*
voice one's opinion

Anti-Gun Lobby: What tactics/devices are used to make the public aware of gun violence?
make people aware of
warn sb about
underline: *souligner*
prevent sb from V-ING
ban: *interdire*

Pro-Gun Lobby: What arguments do pro-gun people put forward?
threaten: *menacer*
feel insecure ≠ safe
protect sb
fear sb might + BV: *craindre que*

3. Utilisez le vocabulaire donné dans la carte mentale ci-dessus et p. 5 pour enrichir votre expression.
4. Préparez-vous à prendre la parole à partir de notes : ne rédigez pas votre présentation, contentez-vous de noter les idées clés, les mots importants.
5. N'oubliez pas une conclusion personnelle.

▲ *Mad Men*, season 1, a series by Matthew Weiner (2007)

Spaces and Exchanges

À la fin de chaque unité, vous trouverez un entraînement type bac complet (compréhension et production écrite, compréhension et expression orale).

Unit 4

SPACES AND EXCHANGES
What is the impact of screen tourism today?

Screen Tourism

1 Tune In!

React to the ad

a. In groups, get ready to talk about the document. Is this an advert for:
a TV series /ˈsɪəriːz/ • a videogame • visiting a place • an app • a theme park?

b. What strikes you about this ad? (people, clothes, objects, landscape, atmosphere)

c. What is the aim of the advertiser? Who is targeted?

d. What do you know about the series mentioned and Northern Ireland?

Help!

Setting
sword /sɔːd/: *épée*
cape
ruins

fantastic
desolate
surreal = strange

dress up as: *déguiser en*

Advertisement
logo
layout: *disposition*
aim = goal

appeal to: *attirer, plaire à*
target: *cibler*

Goals
tourist/holidaymaker

attract
cash in on (the success of): *tirer profit de*
make sb feel like V-ING: *donner envie à qqn de*
get sb to do sth: *convaincre qqn de*

YOUR FINAL TASK
In groups, prepare a report on the impact of film tourism. (p. 67)
OR
Leave a comment on a forum. (p. 67)

2 Tourists Welcome!

1 Marketing campaigns

a. In groups, study one of the marketing strategies on this page: country • film • medium used • aim/goal

b. Present the ad to the other groups.

c. Go on the Internet and watch an Air New Zealand safety video based on *The Hobbit*. Type: http://tinyurl.com/mmzrohg

d. Which campaign do you find the most clever? The most effective? Why?

2 Design your ad

PREPARE YOUR TASK

a. Choose a series or a film you like and design a magazine ad to attract tourists to the country/city where it was filmed.

b. Present your ad to the class and vote for the best one.

Tips

- Choose a memorable place.
- Find a logo, a slogan and a punchy catchphrase.

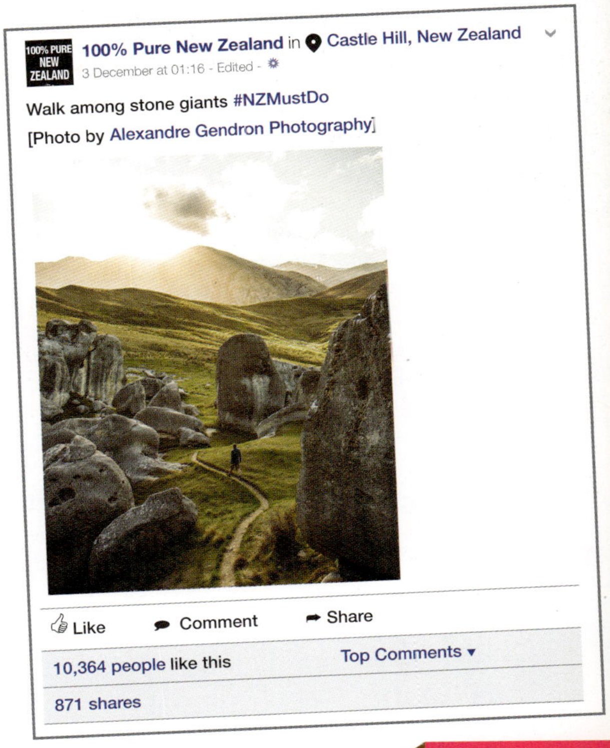

3 An Economic Boost

1 Get ready

a. React to the picture opposite.
What kind of document is it? What does it advertise?
b. Locate Belfast on the map of the UK (see the front flap of your book).
c. Read the article's headline. What does it suggest?
- Thanks to *Game of Thrones*, people can now locate Northern Ireland on a map.
- *Game of Thrones* is a Northern Irish series.
- *Game of Thrones* attracts tourists to Northern Ireland.

"Game of Thrones" puts Northern Ireland on the map

BELFAST, Northern Ireland (AP) – Giants, dragons and vengeful queens have for generations populated Northern Ireland's folk tales.[1] Now, such creatures are visiting the land in a different version – on the sets[2] for the hit TV show "Game of Thrones". But rather than spells[3] and destruction, they're bringing an economic boost to this British province still healing from[4] its past of political violence.[5]
Fans of the HBO fantasy drama would recognize here the landscapes from the fictional land of Westeros – the castle of Winterfell, the seaside cliffs of the Iron Isles and the King's Road leading to the north. About 75 percent of the show is filmed in Northern Ireland, both in natural settings and in the Titanic Studios in Belfast. […]
Cara and Tom Collins from Springdale, Arkansas, were in Ballintoy Harbour recently to see the rocky coastal setting used in the show for the "Iron Isles", a kingdom of rugged sailors.[6] "You can just close your eyes and picture everybody there," said Tom.
The season four finale of "Game of Thrones" last week was watched by 7.09 million viewers in the United States. […] For Northern Ireland's tourism industry, that represents a huge pool of potential visitors. The province hopes to use the show's popularity to increase the number of tourists to over 2 million annually by 2016, from 1.8 million in 2013 – more than the region's population of just 1.8 million.
Coach operators[7] have created "Game of Thrones" tours, for which demand hit a record as the show reached its season finale this month.

■ *The Daily Mail*, 22 June 2014

1. /teɪlz/ *contes et légendes* **2.** *plateaux de tournage* **3.** *formules magiques* **4.** *qui se remet de* **5.** see Culture Tip below **6.** *marins bourrus* **7.** *compagnies de cars*

2 Find out more about tourism in Northern Ireland

WORKSHEET 12

Read the text, then turn to your worksheet for help.

Culture Tip

In Northern Ireland, from 1969 to 1997, a violent political conflict opposed Irish nationalists (who wanted Ulster to be unified with the Republic of Ireland) and Unionists (in favour of staying part of the UK). This conflict is known as **The Troubles**.

CD 1
PISTE 20
WORKSHEET 13

3 Back from the tour

First listening

With the help of the map your teacher will give you, retrace the itinerary.

Second listening

– Pick out as many stressed words as you can (reasons for travelling • activities • feelings • opinion of the tour).
– Organise the pictures in chronological order. Justify with key words you have heard.

Third listening

– Complete your notes.
– Pick out the numbers given. Associate each of them with one of the balloons below.

- Companies using *Game of Thrones* to promote their services
- Part-time jobs created
- Full-time jobs created
- *Game of Thrones'* contribution to the country's economy

➜ **Recap**

– Cara and Tom's reasons for travelling?
– Places visited? Activities? Reactions?

4 Create a flyer

You work for a company offering *Game of Thrones* excursions in Northern Ireland. Design a flyer to encourage tourists to go on a tour. Include:
– information about the tour (number of days, places to visit, various activities offered)
– details about and stills from the TV show, which will convince fans to go on the tour
– your contact details, price of the tour and illustrations.

Help!

Economic impact

film-induced tourism /tʊərɪzəm/ = screen tourism

increase: *augmenter*
boost (the economy): *donner de l'élan à*
benefit from

Activities

archery /ɑːtʃəri/: *tir à l'arc*
sword /sɔːd/-fighting

go on/take a (guided) tour

Tourists

holiday destination

consume
buy = purchase
spend money on

Get ready for the Oral Exam

What means are used to attract tourists to film locations?

4 Another Movie Set

TOURISM IRELAND LAUNCHES SKELLIG MICHAEL VIDEO TO ENTICE STAR WARS FANS

Tourism Ireland have already predicted that the appearance of beautiful Skellig Michael in the latest "Star Wars" film will attract a whole new set of travellers to the monastic site and now they've launched a video to prove the real-life island is just as fantastic as it appears in the film.

The mystic Skellig Michael, an uninhabited pinnacle of rock with the ruins of an ancient monastery, rises 230 meters above the sea 11 miles from the small Kerry fishing town of Portmagee. It was named as a UNESCO World Heritage Site in 1996. [...]

"We needed to find somewhere from another time and place," said Martin Joy, the film's Supervising Location Manager.

"Rick Carter [Production Designer] stumbled across[1] a picture of Skellig Michael which is an island off the Irish coast.

"We were just blown away by it.[2] It's an extraordinary place. It certainly fed into[3] our 'Star Wars' universe." [...]

The increase in visitors is expected to bring a further $4.7 billion to the Irish economy. [...]

Tourism Ireland will share the promotional video across 14 markets: Britain, the United States, Canada, Germany, France, Italy, Spain, the Netherlands, the Nordic region, Australia, New Zealand, India, the Gulf Cooperation Council and South Africa.

■ www.irishcentral.com, January 6, 2016

1. est tombé sur/a trouvé par hasard 2. époustouflés 3. (ici) contribuait à créer

1 Main facts

Read the article and make notes about the following points:
- Where is Skellig Michael located? How was the film location found? What were its advantages?
- What impact will the film have on the economy of the country? What will travellers discover?

2 Watch a video

a. Type http://tinyurl.com/jjjobn2 and watch the video. Complete your notes.

b. Give an account of what you have understood (in the article and the video).

3 Role play

PREPARE YOUR TASK

You are a *Star Wars* fan. You want to convince a friend to go to Ireland on holiday. Act out the dialogue.

Get ready for the Oral Exam

How important are film locations for a film and the economy of a country?

5 London in the Spotlight

1 "My name is Bond, James Bond"

a. React to the poster. How many London sights can you identify below?
b. Have you ever seen any James Bond films? Which one(s)? Who is James Bond? What are the main characteristics of a Bond movie?

2 Find out why Bond is Britain

Introducing Great Britain's $1M Tourism Ambassador: James Bond

By Mark Johanson @MarkJohansonIBT
on October 2, 2012

Though he may roam[1] the globe, James Bond will always be a British gentleman. But is his intrinsic tie to the Union Jack[2] marketing gold? Great Britain's tourism board is betting roughly $1 million that it is. [...]
Just as Scotland did with "Braveheart" and New Zealand is doing with the [...] "Hobbit" trilogy, Britain hopes to transform filmgoers into travelers.
"It's what we like to call vacation[3] on location, and it's something Britain excels at," Clarkson said. [...]
VisitBritain claims that, on average,[4] 120 million people worldwide will see a blockbuster film in the first three weeks of its opening and that research shows that film locations can be a major draw[5] for overseas tourists. Moreover, it claims[6] that almost half of potential visitors to Britain say they want to visit places they've seen featured in films or TV.
"[Bond] represents the quintessential[7] British gentleman," Clarkson asserted. "A lot of men aspire to be him and a lot of women aspire to be on his arm."
There's a certain timelessness to Bond, she added. He's got one foot in the past and one foot planted firmly in the future.

International Business Times

1. *sillonner* **2.** *lien essentiel avec le drapeau britannique* **3.** holiday **4.** *en moyenne* **5.** *attraction* **6.** *affirme* **7.** typical

WORKSHEET 14

a. Turn to your worksheet for help.
b. Sum up the article briefly: Why is Bond associated with Britain? What does the British tourist board plan to do? Why?

3 Organise a poll

PREPARE YOUR TASK

a. Choose a film or a series set in an English-speaking country. Explain why it can make people feel like visiting the place where it was shot.
b. Gather the different places chosen by the class. Then go to padlet.com to organise all your ideas on a virtual collaborative wall.
c. Which country or city is the favourite in the class?

Help!

Nouns	Verbs
plot: *intrigue*	give an assignment: *donner une mission*
spy/secret agent	explode/blow up
villain	have gadgets at one's disposal
chase scene: *scène de course-poursuite*	embody: *incarner*
stunt: *cascade*	attract
showdown/confrontation	cash in on: *tirer profit de*

6 Video Corner — A Fan's Dream

1 Get ready

CD 1 PISTE 21

a. Listen to a short recording to understand the meaning of the following words:
Middle Earth • Hobbiton • fantasy.

b. Use your notes to describe the photo opposite.
Where does the scene take place?

2 Watch and understand

First viewing

a. Type http://tinyurl.com/z4qj8jn and scroll down to the second video: *"See die-hard Hobbit fans CRY as they see middle earth set."* Watch the report once and write down as many words as possible:

groups of people involved | **numbers** | **other elements**

USEFUL WORDS
• weep = cry • (a) highlight = special moment during an event

b. Which places are mentioned: Waikato (a place in New Zealand) • Auckland • Perth • Australia • Barbados • Japan • Bulgaria • England • North Island • Queenstown?

Fans

Who?
How many?
Where?
Where from?

How did they get there?
How were they selected?
How many competitors?

Emotions

Second viewing

c. Watch again, organise your notes and give an account of what you have understood.

d. Locate where the visitors were at the beginning of the trip and after. See map opposite.

Third viewing

e. Listen for more details. Sum up the main points of the video with the help of the following words:
thrilled/excited • moved • enthusiastic • film location • can't believe one's eyes • fulfil: *réaliser* • come true

3 Tweet your reactions

PREPARE YOUR TASK

You are one of the visitors in the video. You were disappointed with your tour. Give your impressions. (140 characters)

Get ready for the Oral Exam

What makes film fans travel to distant places?

Play with words

MP3 N° 7 — CD 1 PISTE 22

Movie industry

blockbuster film
media hype: *battage médiatique*
a TV series /ˈsɪəriːz/
viewer
audience
film set: *plateau de tournage*
enthusiastic fan
influence → influential

fascinated by
be released (film): *sortir*
feature in: *apparaître dans*
increase: *augmenter*
shoot (a film): *tourner*

Tourism

site/place
travel agency
landscape: *paysage*
tourist destination
holidaymaker: *vacancier*
traveller
trip: *voyage/séjour*
sight = tourist attraction

sightsee/go sightseeing: *faire du tourisme*

Economic impact

phenomenon
trend: *tendance*
economic benefits
tourism revenues

benefit from
attract
boost tourism

A **Complétez ces questions à l'aide d'un mot de la liste ci-dessus.**

a. When was *Spectre* ... ? In 2015.
b. Who ... ... this film? Daniel Craig.
c. Where was the film ... ? Mexico City, Rome and London.
d. Was there a lot of ... ... around this film? There were ads absolutely everywhere.

B **On a separate sheet of paper, fill in the blanks with words taken from the lists above.**

1 films are seen by a large **2** when they are **3** . **4** fans of *The Hobbit* dream of going to New Zealand. Viewers are **5** the locations where the films were shot. TV series like *Sherlock* have already **6** many tourists to London. Screen tourism is a new **7** which **8** tourism. The places that **9** in films attract many holidaymakers. Northern Ireland, Malta and Croatia have become popular tourist **10** since the release of *Game of Thrones*. The **11** benefits are huge. Tourism **12** are increasing. Indeed, tourists need to go to **13** to organise their **14** . They need **15** in camping grounds or hotels; they spend money on food and in restaurants. They go **16** , go to **17** , want to see famous buildings, watch plays in theatres. They also go to the country to admire beautiful **18** . Screen tourism creates many jobs.

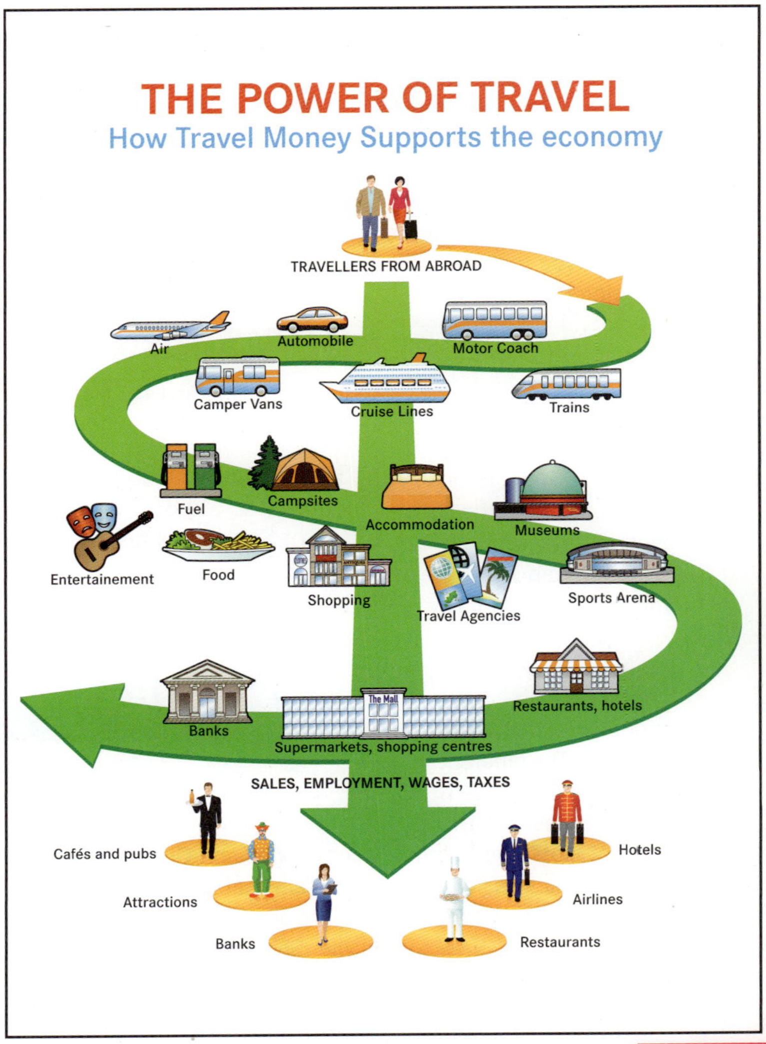

LANGUAGE AT WORK

« Apprendre à Apprendre »
Téléchargez la fiche n°4
www.editions-hatier.fr/langues-eleves

Corrigés p. 216-221

A Les déterminants

(Précis grammatical 3 p. 194 et 23 p. 202)

1. Complétez les phrases suivantes avec *a/an*, *the* ou *Ø*.

a. Many people want to go to ... Northern Ireland because they are ... great fans of *Game of Thrones* and they want to see with their own eyes ... places where ... scenes they loved in ... series were shot.

b. ... New Zealand became ... popular tourist destination after *Lord of the Rings* was shot there. Many tourists also want to see ... famous locations in ... USA. For example, ... *Sex and the City* tours are organised in ... New York City and take ... fans to ... spots that people enjoyed in ... series.

c. A few years ago, ... Wales tried to attract ... travellers thanks to *Doctor Who*.

d. ... Australia hoped to attract ... foreign tourists thanks to ... film *Australia*, in particular tourists from ... Japan, ... China and ... United States.

e. ... film tourism is really becoming ... means *(moyen)* for ... tourist boards to boost ... tourism industry in their countries.

B Infinitif ou gérondif (V-*ING*) ?

(Précis grammatical 45 p. 213)

2. Recopiez ce paragraphe et mettez les verbes entre parenthèses à la forme qui convient.

After (watch) films or series, many viewers suddenly discover that a place is worth (visit) and decide (go) there. What they see makes them feel like (travel) and they want (discover) what the film locations really look like. In fact, many people consider (go) to a place just because they saw it in a film. Fans enjoy (take) selfies in front of famous landmarks. For them, (go) to a place where a film was shot is an unforgettable experience. Thanks to *Game of Thrones*, many fans now look forward to (spend) their holidays in Northern Ireland.

3. Recopiez ce paragraphe et mettez les verbes entre parenthèses à l'une de ces deux formes : infinitif avec *to* ou base verbale (infinitif sans *to*).

The detective series *Sherlock* has helped (boost) tourism in London, because it is largely set there and has been watched by nearly seven million people in the UK. The authors make us (discover) Sir Arthur Conan Doyle's universe, but manage (transpose) it in the contemporary world. Everything is done (modernise) the main character. The different characters use modern technologies in the different plots: the Internet, smartphones and GPS are used to make Sherlock Holmes (look) modern. The film director invites us (follow) the two main characters in many typical locations of London or the British countryside. Sherlock's fans are targeted here. The aim of the travel agency is (make) visitors (want) (go) to London and get them (visit) the places where scenes with Sherlock or Doctor Watson take place. Sherlock is popular all over the world with people of all ages, so the aim is (get) visitors (come) in greater numbers and (spend) more money across Britain. Would you like (go) on such a tour? Would you be ready (visit) Sherlock's house on Baker Street?

BBC Sherlock Locations Tour

Guided mini coach tour of locations featured in the BBC drama including the site of Sherlock's fake death, 221B Baker St, Magnusson's office and much more.

MORE INFO | BOOK TOUR

YOUR TASK

SCENARIO 1

You are the host of a travel show. You prepare a presentation on the impact of film tourism in English-speaking countries. Work in groups and present your results to your audience.

STEP BY STEP

1. Go over your notes from the unit.

a. Choose a country or a city.

b. With the help of the word cloud opposite, recap the impact screen tourism can have on a country:

- **tourism**: number of tourists/visitors, holiday destinations...
- **economy and tourism industry**: travel agencies, tours, film locations, local businesses...
- **culture**: people learn more about...

c. Pick out statistics in the documents you have studied.
Complete them with the help of the worksheet your teacher will give you.

WORKSHEET 15

2. Work on your slideshow presentation.

a. Include statistics, graphs, images and text (just type some key words to help your audience follow what you are saying).

b. Get ready to speak from notes. Don't write full sentences.

c. Look at your audience. If you sound convinced, you will be convincing!

d. Don't forget to share the speaking time equally between all the speakers.

e. Think of what questions the audience may ask you.

Tip

Use gap fillers if you hesitate or need time to think (→ *Enrichir sa prise de parole* p. 178-179).

SCENARIO 2

You are browsing an Internet forum when you see the following question:
Has your holiday destination ever been influenced by a film or series?

- **React and leave a comment.** (80-100 words)

→ *Relire son devoir* p. 7

Compréhension écrite et expression écrite

WORKSHEET BAC N° 4

Answer the questions on the worksheet the teacher will give you.

DOCUMENT A

How does movie tourism change a city's environment?
As the old Hollywood cliché goes: the location is a character in itself – and doesn't stop being so after the director has called cut.

Film has long had a means of making even the most ordinary of places something extraordinary, meaningful and, of course, cinematic. It's why, in 2012, Tourism Competitive Intelligence found that 40 million international tourists chose their destination because they'd seen a film in that particular location – a way, surely, to bask in[1] the reality of fiction.

Yet such a statistic is not only being enjoyed by fans, but also of the towns, cities and countries that are being visited too; proving that TV and film can be one of the biggest boosts to a local tourism industry. […]

With the movie industry pulling in $1 billion a year into the local economy, Canada has struck gold, becoming one of the major players for movie-sets. Dubbed "North Hollywood", huge franchises such as *X-Men* and *Twilight* hail from the windy city.[2]

Due to becoming an attractive and diverse location for directors, Vancouver specifically has had to step up its game – adapting the city into a movie-friendly society, and building its own film services department. […]

The technology is also beginning to shape around[3] movie-goers' fascinations. Take for example, app-culture. Michel Reilhac developed an app to further encourage starry-eyed fans to re-enact their own Parisian movie experience. Chatting to *Variety,* Reilhac explained that the Smartphone app "Cinema City" would further embolden France's tourism. "It's geo-activated, meaning that when you are in a spot where a scene from a film was shot, you will be able to see that scene in the smartphone," Reilhac says. "You'll then get a link to a DVD platform where you can watch the whole film."

A fascinating study by Dr. Walaiporn Rewtrakunphaiboon […] called "Film-induced Tourism: Inventing a Vacation to a Location" revealed how major movies benefited their country of origin. For example, after Mel Gibson's war classic *Braveheart,* Scotland saw a 500% rise of visitors. The Crowne Hotel, featured in Richard Curtis' comedy *Notting Hill*, is usually booked up three years in advance […]. From the stats alone, it really is true that the magic of a film can become true.

■ www.virgin.com

1. *baigner dans* 2. *sont originaires de la ville battue par le vent* 3. *(ici) s'adapter à*

DOCUMENT B

When I hear talk about the power of a single movie to increase tourism (especially international tourism), I am concerned, particularly when the sites are in relatively remote areas that are traditionally difficult for international visitors to access. This is the case with the site of Baz Luhrmann's *Australia* in the Kimberley region, some 100km west of Kununurra. International visitors, especially the desirable Japanese and Americans, have extremely limited time for their visit, and even getting to Darwin will be problematic and require them to forego[1] visiting other places in Australia. […]

■ Professor S. Beeton, www.abc.net.au

1. *renoncer à*

Movie Map London

DOCUMENT C

Follow your favourite films throughout London. This handy app pinpoints famous sites used in London-based films over the years, so you can visit Will's blue door from *Notting Hill*, follow James Bond throughout the city, and more.

Compréhension de l'oral

CD 1 PISTE 23

The benefits of *Game of Thrones*

→ Écoutez l'enregistrement trois fois.
→ Prenez des notes puis faites en dix minutes le compte rendu de ce que vous avez compris en français.
→ Utilisez les expressions données p. 183.

USEFUL WORDS
• plotline: *intrigue* • props: *décors, accessoires*
• cast: *distribution* • scenery: *paysage*

Expression orale

SPACES AND EXCHANGES { What is the impact of screen tourism today?

Comment parler de la notion ?

1 Définissez le mot « échanges ». Reportez-vous à la page 4.
2 Pour répondre à la problématique, recopiez le schéma ci-dessous sur papier libre et complétez-le avec les documents étudiés en classe.

Reasons
What makes film fans travel to distant places?

film-induced tourism
holidaymaker/tourist
icon/tourism ambassador
boost the economy
spend money on
embody: *incarner*

What is the impact of screen tourism today?

The economic boost
How can countries benefit from the success of famous films or series?

enthusiastic
thrilled
fulfil one's dreams

Advertising
How do advertisers use films and series to promote tourism in some countries?

strategy
effective
appeal to
target sb

3 Utilisez le vocabulaire donné p. 5 et dans l'unité pour enrichir votre expression.
4 N'oubliez pas une **conclusion personnelle**.

Building a Global World

1 Tune In!

Snapchat More Popular Than Twitter Among Millennials[1]

Most popular social media apps among Americans aged 18-34 (% of smartphone users)

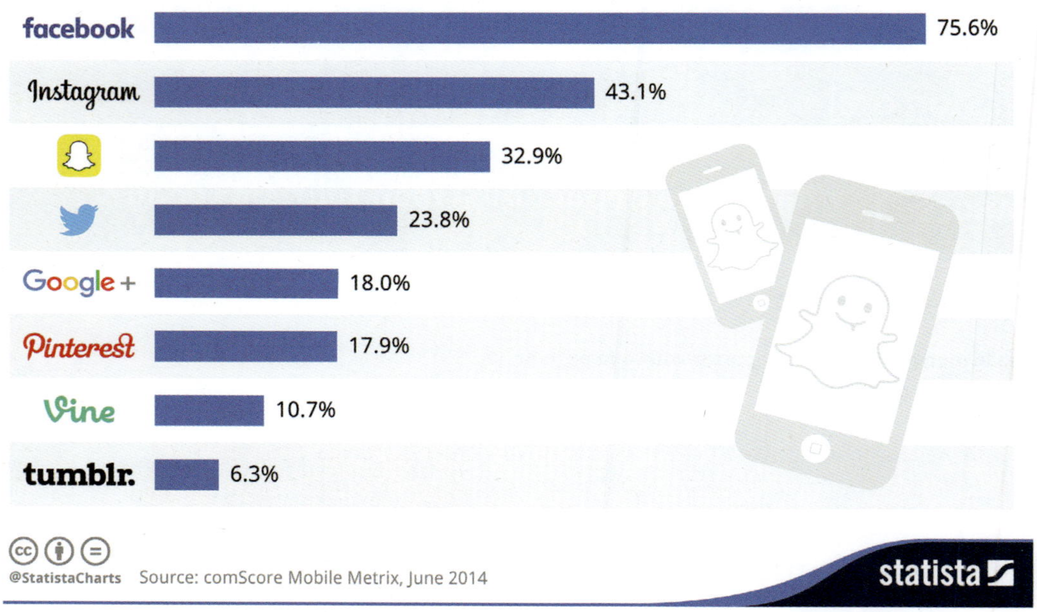

1. millennial: individual born between the early 1980s and the early 2000s

1 Popular apps

a. React to the chart above: Which apps do you know? What are they used for?

b. Compare the percentage of users: twice as many people use ... as • three times more ... than • almost *(presque)* • over *(plus de)* → *Nombres et graphiques*, p. 181

c. Class survey

– Think of the three apps you use the most.

– List the five favourite apps of the class and find out the percentage of users of each app.

– Compare your results with the results above.

PREPARE YOUR TASK

d. You are taking part in a study about teenagers and apps. Present one of your favourite apps. Explain what you use it for, how often you use it, how it works, and list its advantages and drawbacks.

Help!

device: *appareil*
instant messaging

user-friendly = easy to use
entertaining = fun
convenient = handy: *pratique*
useful ≠ useless = pointless
popular

communicate
enable sb to: *permettre à qqn de*
find one's way: *trouver son chemin*
share: *partager*
facilitate exchanges

OR

Post a video message to your friends. (p. 79)

Organise a crowdfunding campaign. (p. 79)

2 Builders of new empires

a. In groups, work on the photomontage below. List the similarities and the differences between the two parts of the picture: colours • people/gender • period of time • objects • dress code.

DEFINITION

Swag
(adj.) cool, stylish
(n.) money or free merchandise distributed as part of the promotion of a product, company, etc.

b. Learn about some of the people in the picture.
Go to www.biography.com/people and search for:
Jeff Bezos • Andrew Carnegie • Bill and Melinda Gates • Henry Ford • Larry Page • John D. Rockefeller • William H. Vanderbilt • Mark Zuckerberg.

c. Organise what you have learnt about them with the help of the mind map below and present them to the class.

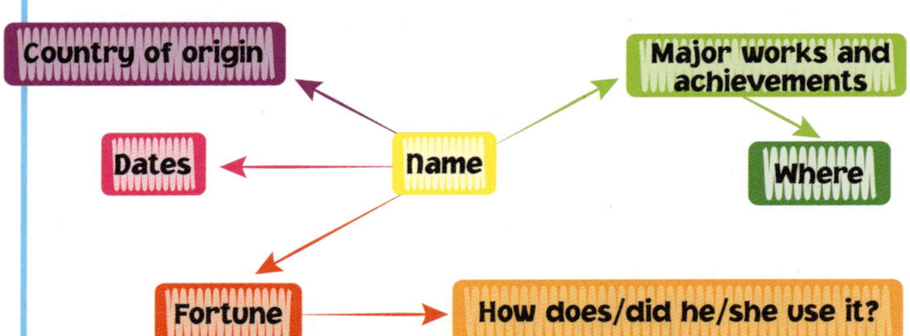

d. What are the people in each group standing on? What does each object symbolise?

➜ **Recap:** What do all these people have in common? What does the right-hand side of the picture show about the place of new technologies today?

Help!

Past
moustache
steel beam: *poutre en acier*
top hat
(three-piece) suit /suːt/: *costume*

Present
casual clothes /kləʊðz/
laptop computer
colourful/bright
relaxed

Comparison
(bank)note: *billet*
modern ≠ old-fashioned
successful
similar to ≠ different from

Get ready for the Oral Exam

To what extent have new technologies revolutionised our world?

2 Can the Internet Save the World?

Mark Zuckerberg and Priscilla Chan Welcome Baby Girl, Plan to Donate $45 billion to Charity
By Kunle Mark December 1, 2015

Like 1 G+1 0 Tweet

Mark Zuckerberg and wife **Priscilla Chan** have welcomed a baby daughter named Max. The billionaire couple married in 2012 said they intend to donate "99 per cent" of their Facebook shares – worth approximately $45 billion – to **"advancing human potential and promoting equality".**

1 Get ready

a. Look at the headline and subheading of the article on the left and find the equivalents of the following words: *faire don de* • *œuvre de bienfaisance* • *actions (en bourse)* • *d'une valeur de*

b. Mark and Priscilla plan to donate money to *"advancing human potential and promoting equality".*

– **In groups**, explain why the following initiatives could fit their plan.

- building schools in poor countries
- building libraries and funding them
- giving Internet access to everyone in the world
- building hospitals in poor countries
- financing education for girls
- developing infrastructures

– Which one would you consider the most urgent? Why?

2 A letter to our daughter

WORKSHEET 16

a. Read this passage from Mark Zuckerberg and Priscilla Chan's letter to their daughter. Which of the initiatives above are they explaining?

b. Turn to your worksheet for help.

ONE
@ONECampaign

YES: We're joining forces with Mark Zuckerberg to #ConnectTheWorld & achieve the #GlobalGoals: one.org/connecttheworld

I BELIEVE
INTERNET ACCESS
IS ESSENTIAL FOR ACHIEVING HUMANITY'S #GLOBALGOALS

December 1, 2015

Dear Max,

Many of the greatest opportunities for your generation will come from giving everyone access to the internet.

People often think of the internet as just for entertainment or communication. But for the majority of people in the world, the internet can be a lifeline.[1]

It provides[2] education if you don't live near a good school. It provides health information on how to avoid[3] diseases or raise healthy children if you don't live near a doctor. It provides financial services if you don't live near a bank. It provides access to jobs and opportunities if you don't live in a good economy.

The internet is so important that for every 10 people who gain internet access, about one person is lifted out of poverty and about one new job is created.

Yet still more than half of the world's population - more than 4 billion people - don't have access to the internet.

If our generation connects them, we can lift hundreds of millions of people out of poverty. We can also help hundreds of millions of children get an education and save millions of lives by helping people avoid disease.

This is another long term effort that can be advanced by technology and partnership. It will take inventing new technology to make the internet more affordable and bring access to unconnected areas. [...]

As you begin the next generation of the Chan Zuckerberg family, we also begin the Chan Zuckerberg Initiative to join people across the world to advance human potential and promote equality for all children in the next generation. Our initial areas of focus will be personalized learning, curing disease, connecting people and building strong communities.

1. (here) vital **2.** *fournit* **3.** *éviter*

3 The digital divide

a. Read these Internet facts from *The Atlantic*. What strikes you most?

How Much of the World Has Regular Internet Access?

A new United Nations study shows who can and cannot connect to the web.

→ Only five percent of the world's 7,100 languages are represented on the Internet.

→ In the developing world, 25 percent fewer women have Internet access than men—that number goes to 50 percent in parts of sub-Saharan Africa.

→ Roughly 300 million people gained Internet access in the past year.

→ Ninety percent of the population of the world's poorest 48 countries remain offline.

■ www.theatlantic.com, September 22, 2015

b. Go to www.globalgoals.org. On a separate piece of paper complete the following mind map.

c. Use the article from *The Atlantic* and the Internet page to explain why #GlobalGoals supports Mark Zuckerberg's initiative.

4 Become a Global Citizen

a. Go to www.tinyurl.com/hsun4lq. Watch Bill Gates trying to convince us to become Global Citizens. Pick out key information and fill in the blanks:

"We want to ignite *(susciter)* people's desire for **1**. The power of digital technology can bring people **2** and **3** barriers. That's where *Global Citizen* comes in. The way to **4** millions of people and take action **5** to help create a better world. This year represents an incredible opportunity for people to show their support for these issues, to use their voice, to use their time, and to go beyond their own communities to **6** with something larger."

b. What are the common points and differences between Bill Gates's and Mark Zuckerberg's initiatives?

5 A radio interview

You are a journalist interviewing Mark Zuckerberg or Priscilla Chan on their commitment to provide Internet access to the whole world. Act out the interview.

Help!

Philanthropy	Goals	The Internet
financial aid charity work: *bénévolat* finance /faɪnæns/ commit oneself to	medicine vaccine cure diseases prevent from V-ING reduce inequalities	knowledge: *connaissance* a means of V-ING: *un moyen de* bridge the digital divide: *réduire la fracture numérique* enable sb to do sth: *permettre à qqn de*

Get ready for the Oral Exam

To what extent can the Internet help to solve global problems?

3 New Opportunities

1 Work on words

On a separate piece of paper, fill in the blanks with one word from the following list:
app • brand *(marque)* • earn a living • hire *(embaucher)* • on vacation • snapped.

a. Snapchat is an ... that enables users to send pictures with captions *(légendes)* to their friends.
b. Sharon was so pleased with her new camera that she ... many photos when we were ... ... in New York.
c. We need to get a job to ... ... decent ... .
d. They will ... a new employee for the summer.
e. Nike is a famous ... all over the world.

video

2 Watch a video

Living with Instagram

USEFUL WORDS
- stroll: *flâner*
- stunned = very surprised
- millennial: individual born between the early 1980s and the early 2000s

a. Get ready: Judging from the title of the report, what do you think the video is about?
b. Watch the report once, then write down the elements you remember on a sheet of paper.
c. Watch again, organise your notes and give an account of what you have understood.

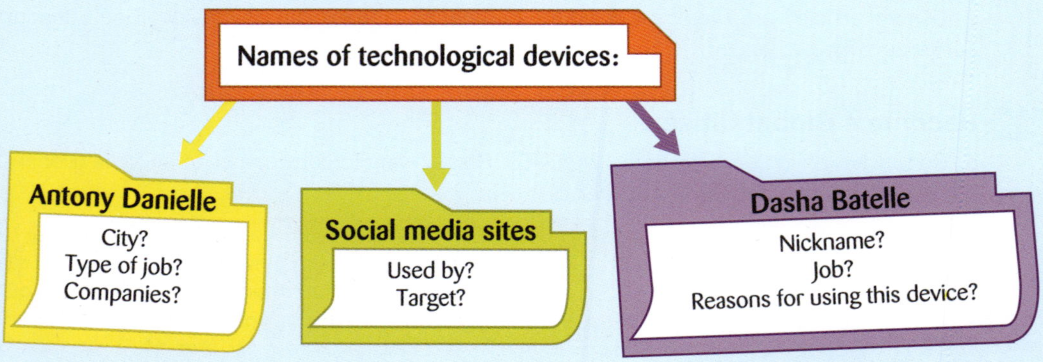

d. Listen for more details and sum up the video with the help of the following words:
opportunities • exist • technology • use • promote • companies.

PREPARE YOUR TASK

e. Write a short newspaper article using the headline below:

New Careers for Millennials

- Recap what you have understood in the report.
- Find a photo to illustrate your article and write a caption.
- What is the impact of technology on jobs?

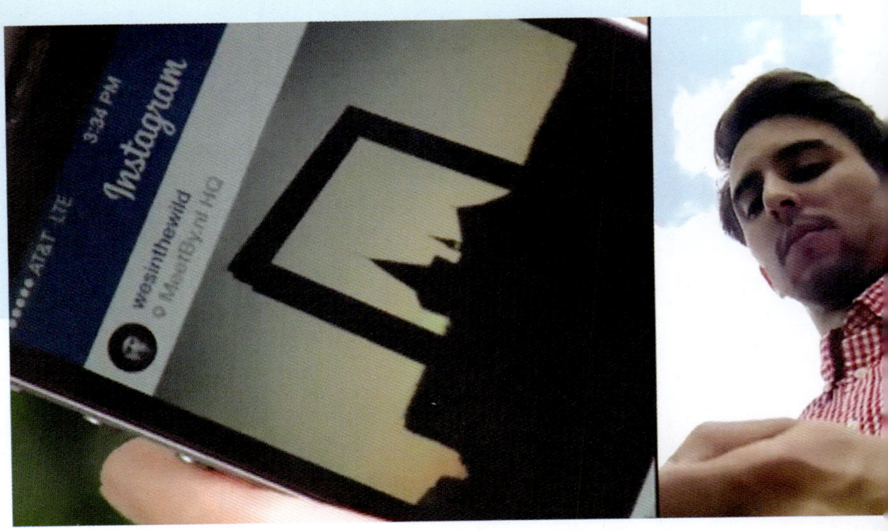

3 Elite athletes find help

a. Read the definition of crowdfunding opposite. Associate each underlined word with its translation:

entreprise commerciale (risquée) • *sommes* • *en récoltant* • *financer*

b. Now read the headline of the article and the caption under the photo. What do you think it will be about?

c. Read the article and check your answers.

DEFINITION

Crowdfunding (noun): the practice of <u>funding</u> a project or <u>business venture</u> by <u>raising</u> many small <u>amounts</u> of money from a large number of people, typically via the Internet.

Crowdfunding a huge help to schools

Candace Hill, a rising junior at Rockdale County (Conyers, Ga.[1]) High School and a 2016 Olympic hopeful, ran the 100-meter dash[2] in 10.98 seconds at an invitational meet June 20 in Seattle, becoming the first 16-year-old in the world to run the distance in less than 11 seconds and the first American girl under 19 to accomplish the feat.[3]

It was one of the numerous races across the country that she attended with her parents and younger sister this summer, and after budgeting conservatively and soliciting donations, the family set up a fundraising page on YouCaring.com.

"She can't go to those places by herself," said Rockdale track coach Venson Elder, who raises money for the school's football team using OurFund.us. "Someone has to go with her. She's only 16 years old. The cost was astronomical this summer." [...]

"We put our heads together and said, 'How can we generate some money, have people come on board and be supportive?' And I did a little research to see which websites were legitimate and basically 100% of the money would go to the fund."

The campaign sought to raise $5,000 to help Candace Hill reach the IAAF World Youth Championships on July 15-19 in Columbia where she'd set records in the 100- and 200-meter dash.

"It was heaven sent," Lorri Hill [Candace's mother] said. "We were recharged knowing that a lot of Americans were behind Candace. That was a good feeling. It made us proud. It made her proud when she was going over there to represent the USA."

USA Today Sports, July 30, 2015

With crowdfunding help, Candace Hill was able to compete in a qualifying event and eventually the IAAF World Youth Championships.

1. Georgia **2.** *(ici) course* **3.** *exploit*

WORKSHEET 17

PREPARE YOUR TASK

d. Turn to your worksheet for help.

e. You are a journalist and work for a sports channel. You make a report on Candace Hill after her victory race. Include the following points:

Sports background and past successes • What did crowdfunding help her achieve?

Get ready for the **Oral Exam**

- **Which new forms of exchanges are illustrated on this double page?**
- **What impact can they have on people's careers?**

4 Video Corner

Connections

1 Get ready

a. React to the picture:
– People (age, relationship, clothes)
– Place (room, usual activities there)

b. What are they doing? Which object has been removed from the picture?

c. Conclude: What message(s) does the photographer, Eric Pickersgill, want to convey?

The members of this family are all in the same room so they don't need to speak or interact.

They are so addicted to technology that they don't communicate anymore.

Technology helps people to communicate.

Technology isolates people.

People are more connected to their phones than to each other.

2 Watch a video clip

***Can we auto-correct humanity?* by Prince Ea**

Part 1 (beginning – 1:10)

a. Complete the lyrics at the beginning: *"Did you know the average* (moyen) *... spends four years of his ... looking down at his ... ?"*

b. What is the singer's opinion? Pick out one key word.

c. List all the words related to technology.

d. What is the impact of technological devices on people? In the following list, which words does the singer use?

lose touch • together • selfish • separate • socialise • anti-social • friendless • alone • popular

e. Rephrase what you have understood in your own words.

Part 2 (1:11 – end)

WORKSHEET 18

f. Turn to your worksheet for help.

Help!

lack of: *manque de*
screen: *écran*

addicted to = hooked on

be engrossed = absorbed in
ignore /ɪgˈnɔː/ ≠ pay attention to
stare at: *regarder fixement*
blame sb/sth for V-ING
do without: *se passer de*
prevent sb from V-ING: *empêcher qqn de*
stand for = represent

3 React!

PREPARE YOUR TASK

a. Post a comment on the photographer's website: do you agree with his opinion on technology?

b. The end of Prince Ea's video clip has no lyrics. Suggest a short stanza (5-7 lines) to add to the song.

Get ready for the Oral Exam

- **What is the two artists' opinion on technology?**
- **Why can technology disconnect us?**

Play with words

MP 3 N° 8 — CD 1 PISTE 24

A **Choisissez parmi les mots ci-contre et complétez les phrases suivantes sur papier libre.**

a. Do you think the Internet will help … … … between the rich and the poor?
b. Mark Zuckerberg wants to use his money to … poverty all over the world.
c. Bill Gates encourages people to … … … the fight against hunger and to protect the environment.
d. They both want to make people aware of global … .
e. Their goal is to … water and sanitation, as well as ensure human rights and education for all.
f. Because of …, people will have to work collaboratively across … .
g. Preventing the emergence of a … … between developed and developing countries must be a priority.

B **Entraînez-vous à prononcer les mots suivants. Sont-ils accentués sur la première, la deuxième ou la troisième syllabe ? Recopiez le tableau ci-dessous sur papier libre et complétez-le. Puis vérifiez à l'écoute.**

abroad • connect • transformation • obstacle • transform • eliminate • innovate • participate • innovation

Première syllabe	
Deuxième syllabe	
Troisième syllabe	

WORD LIST

Nouns
globalisation: *mondialisation*
border: *frontière*
digital divide: *fracture numérique*
(social) network: *réseau (social)*
knowledge: *savoir, connaissance*
the haves and the have-nots = the rich and the poor
issue = problem

Adjectives and adverbs
isolated /aɪsəleɪtɪd/
global: *mondial*
worldwide: *dans le monde entier*
abroad = overseas: *à l'étranger*

Verbs
improve = make better
foresee: *prévoir*
bridge the gap: *combler le fossé*
provide sb with: *fournir qqch à qqn*
share: *partager*
connect
transform
innovate
participate in = take part in
be involved in: *être impliqué dans*
struggle = fight: *combattre*
overcome obstacles: *surmonter les obstacles*
eliminate = eradicate

C **Dictée. Observez l'image ci-dessous puis, sur papier libre, notez les phrases que vous allez entendre.**

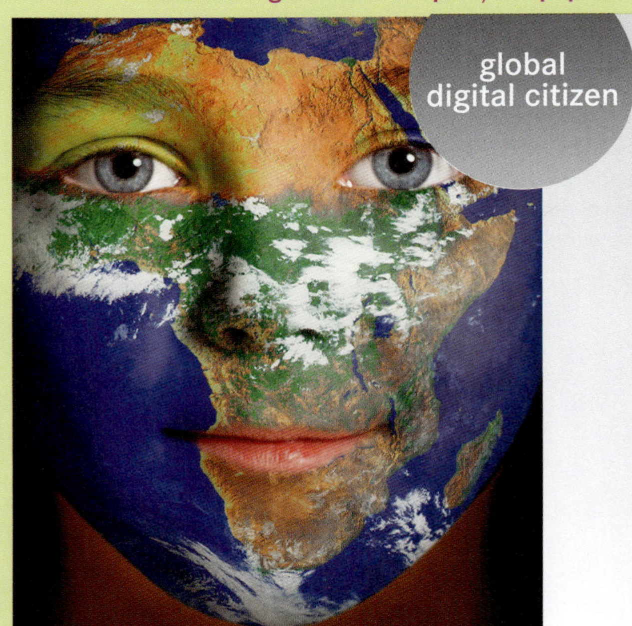

personal responsibility
global citizenship
digital citizenship
altruistic service[1]
environmental stewardship[2]

1. *aide à autrui* 2. *gestion de l'environnement*

LANGUAGE AT WORK

« Apprendre à Apprendre »
Téléchargez la fiche n°5
www.editions-hatier.fr/langues-eleves

Corrigés p. 216-221

A Les quantifieurs

(Précis grammatical 5 p. 194)

1. Complétez avec a *lot of*, *much*, *many*, *little* ou *few.*

a. Facebook has changed the world in ... ways. ... users give ... information about themselves. ... people list their interests on Facebook, and as a result ... brands can target them easily. Advertisers pay ... money for that.

b. Unfortunately, ... social network users give too ... information about themselves, and forget that ... employers will check their future employees' profiles.

c. Thanks to the Internet, we now have ... tools to communicate and build ... social connections. Mobile devices offer ... ways to stay in touch.

d. Having ... friends on social networks does not mean we are unpopular.

e. At ... parties or lunches some guests stare into their digital devices and text messages to others. They pay ... attention to all the people around. ... people can do without their mobile phones.

B Les déterminants

(Précis grammatical 3 p. 194 et 23 p. 202)

2. *The*, *a/an* ou *Ø* ?

a. Mark Zuckerberg announced he would invest ... money to combat ... global problems. He said he would give away 99% of his fortune for ... good causes.

b. Zuckerberg and Chan's decision received ... praise of Sheryl Sandberg. "From ... moment I met Mark and Priscilla I knew they would change ... world. Their decision to invest now in ... future is smart and important – it will fund ... kind of work that no-one else will," Sandberg wrote in ... post on her personal Facebook page. Those funds will help "advance ... human potential and promote ... equality in ... areas such as ... health, ... education, ... scientific research, and ... energy."

c. Will Mark Zuckerberg's billions help solve ... world's problems?

C Les modaux

(Précis grammatical 24 p. 203)

3. Complétez à l'aide de *may*, *will*, *would* ou *could*. Plusieurs réponses sont parfois possibles.

Mark Zuckerberg's decision to fund good causes ... encourage other billionaires to do the same and it ... lead to progress against poverty in the world. Zuckerberg has said that any money earned by the foundation ... be put back into charitable efforts. However, the money that he and his wife have decided to give away ... not be enough to solve all the global problems. In their letter, Zuckerberg and his wife said they wanted to fund education in the US. This ... be a good idea but this money ... be of greater use in countries where education ... also mean greater life expectancy. It is true that we now often wonder how we ... cope without the Internet. If there was no Internet, life ... indeed be very different.

ON YOUR OWN!

Décrivez et commentez cette image. N'oubliez pas d'utiliser des auxiliaires modaux pour formuler des hypothèses.

YOUR TASK

SCENARIO 1

You want to promote one of the global goals above. Post a video message to your friends.

► **Explain why the cause you chose is important.** Give the number of the goal and some details about the cause you have selected. Why have you decided to promote this one in particular?

► **Convince them that their selfies could help.**
– How can the Internet and social networks be useful to share ideas and make things change?
– Why should everyone be involved in global issues?

► **In class, vote for the five most convincing videos.**

SCENARIO 2

You want to help build a school in a deprived area *(région défavorisée)* in South Africa. In groups, create a crowdfunding campaign to help your class finance the project.

► **Use the Internet to raise awareness *(sensibiliser le public)* and get money for your campaign. Think about the following points:**
#1: Which social networks can you use to promote your campaign?
#2: Create a campaign hashtag.
#3: Write a paragraph:
- Explain what your goal is.
- Say why people should give money for your cause.
- How will this money be used?

► **Post your campaigns on the class blog or on a collaborative wall (Padlet, for example). Vote for the best one.**

Get ready for the Exam BAC

Compréhension écrite et expression écrite

WORKSHEET BAC N° 5

Answer the questions on the worksheet the teacher will give you.

DOCUMENT A

The narrator is sitting in an Internet café in Indonesia.

I sat and wrote – in one effortless draft – a fund-raising e-mail to all my friends and family across the world.

I told everyone that my birthday was coming up in July and that soon I would be turning thirty-five. I told them that there was nothing in the world that I needed or wanted, and that I had never been happier in my life. I told them that, if I were home in New York, I would be planning a big stupid birthday party and I would make them all come to this party, and they would have to buy me gifts and bottles of wine and the whole celebration would get ridiculously expensive. Therefore, I explained, a cheaper and more lovely way to help celebrate this birthday would be if my friends and family would care to make a donation to help a woman named Wayan Nuriyasih buy a house in Indonesia for herself and her children.

Then I told the whole story of Wayan and Tutti and the orphans and their situation. I promised that whatever money was donated, I would match the donation from my own savings.[1] Of course I was aware, I explained, that this is a world full of untold suffering and war and that everyone is in need right now, but what are we to do? [...]

By the next morning, when I checked my emails, $700 had already been pledged.[2] The next day, donations passed what I could afford to match. [...]

Let's just wrap up this episode by saying that – a mere seven days after the original plea went out over the wires – my friends and my family and a bunch of strangers all over the world helped me come up with almost $18,000 to buy Wayan Nuriyasih a home of her own.

■ Elizabeth Gilbert, *Eat, Pray, Love*, 2006

1. *économies* 2. promised

DOCUMENT B

SECTIONS HOME SEARCH **The New York Times** SUBSCRIBE NOW LOG IN

To Unite the Earth, Connect It

By **BONO and MARK ZUCKERBERG** SEPT. 26, 2015

Today over half the people on this planet don't have access [to the Internet]. That is not good for anyone — not for the disempowered and disconnected, and not for the other half, whose commerce and security depend on having stable societies.

In this century, global development and global connectivity are closely linked. If you want to help people feed, heal, educate and employ themselves around the world, we need to connect the world as well. The Internet should not belong to only three billion people, as it does today. It should be seen as a necessity for development, and a tool that makes larger things possible.

In Ethiopia and Tanzania, for example, farmers connect to get better prices, track inventory and make mobile insurance payments in case of bad weather. In Nigeria, citizens use BudgIT, a mobile app, to assess whether governments keep their spending promises. The opportunity is especially great for women. Men have significantly more access to the web, but when women get connected, they use technology as a pathway to better education, health, economic status and security. In Guatemala, cellphones inform mothers how to have healthy pregnancies. In Kenya, women receive financial services via their cellphones thanks to the brilliant M-Pesa microfinance scheme.

Compréhension de l'oral

CD 1 PISTE 25

Multilingualism and global citizenship

→ Écoutez l'enregistrement trois fois.
→ Prenez des notes puis faites en dix minutes le compte rendu de ce que vous avez compris en français.
→ Utilisez les expressions données p. 183.

USEFUL WORD

OU = Oklahoma University

Expression orale

SPACES AND EXCHANGES { **What impact do new forms of communication have on the world today?**

Comment parler de la notion ?

❶ Définissez le mot *exchanges*. Reportez-vous à la page 4.
❷ Pour répondre à la problématique, recopiez le schéma ci-dessous sur papier libre et complétez-le avec les documents étudiés en classe.

What impact do new forms of communication have on the world today?

To what extent have new technologies revolutionised our world?
- instantly
- enable sb to do
- facilitate
- bring closer /ˈkləʊsə/

To what extent can the Internet help solve global problems?
- awareness campaign
- online action
- become aware of
- bridge the gap
- share information

What impact can new forms of exchanges have on people's careers?
- career opportunity
- raise funds
- finance a project

Why can technology also disconnect us?
- isolated /ˈaɪsəleɪtɪd/
- lose contact with

❸ Utilisez le vocabulaire donné p. 5 et dans l'unité pour enrichir votre expression.
❹ Ne rédigez pas votre présentation, notez les idées-clés, les mots importants.
❺ Anticipez les questions qui pourront être posées (points à approfondir, exemples pour illustrer un argument, opinion personnelle...).
❻ N'oubliez pas une **conclusion personnelle.**

The New Face of America

1 Tune In!

By 2060, non-whites will make up 57 percent of the U.S. population.

POPULATION BY RACE AND HISPANIC ORIGIN
Percentage of total population

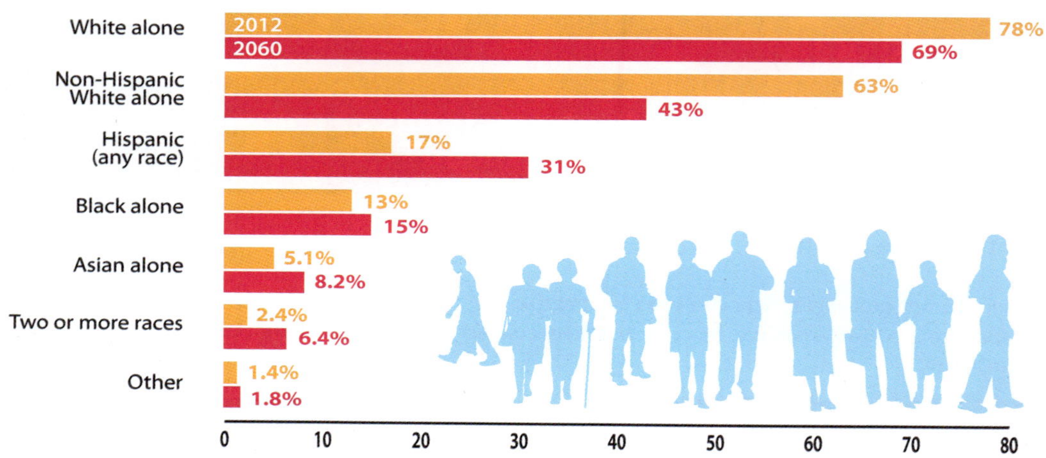

U.S. Census Bureau

1 A demographic shift

a. Look at the graph above and identify the different ethnic groups.
b. Compare the percentages and evolution of these groups (→ p. 181).
c. Recap by completing the following sentences:
- This graph shows the ... racial population in comparison with the 2060 ... .
- The percentages reveal there is going to be a major ... in the number of ... Americans while the ... , ... and ... populations will ... .
- ... people will no longer ... a majority of the American population by 2060.
- A historic ... is taking place and is ... the nation.
- This new demographic ... will have a huge ... on the nation's schools, economy, workforce and electorate.

d. Memorise the sentences and present the graph again on your own.

Help!
decline in
impact on
increase = growth
mosaic
projection: *prévision*
shift = change
current: *actuel*
lower ↓ ≠ higher ↑
grow = rise (rose, risen)
make up: *composer, constituer*
rate: *classer*
reshape: *refaçonner*

CD 2 PISTE 1
WORKSHEET 19

2 A changing identity

a. Listen to an interview to find more information about the changes in the American population. Turn to your worksheet for help.
b. Sum up what you have understood and report to the class.

YOUR FINAL TASK OR

Write an article on the new face of America. (p. 91)

Interview the young woman in the photo. (p. 91)

2 Diversity

1 Get ready

a. Observe the poster and choose the correct statement(s): The fair-haired girl and black-haired girl are looking at each other. • The girls live in different worlds. • They belong to the same ethnic group. • They come from the same country. • They are considered equal.

b. Pick out the adjectives that you believe correspond best to the poster and justify: multi-ethnic • racist • colourful • optimistic ≠ pessimistic • realistic.

➜ **Recap:** what does it show about the USA's population?

PREPARE YOUR TASK

2 Now check your answers

CINCINNATI.com
PART OF THE USA TODAY NETWORK

By Mark Curnutte, 2014/10/21

Lydia Perez is 2 years old, with the curly black hair and dark eyes of her father's Guatemalan heritage. [...] Her white mother, a woman of Appalachian[1] descent grew up in Cincinnati: [...] A place where a quarter of the people speak Spanish; where thousands more Latin Americans, East Africans, Asians and others live and work; and where increasing diversity is having profound influence on our families, schools, workplaces and politics.

The changes are part of dramatic[2] shifts projected across America's heartland[3] in the next 50 years. A new diversity suggests that many of our communities will look less like the Cincinnati we know today and more like multi-ethnic Austin, Texas, or suburban Washington, D.C.

In many of our neighborhoods, chances will be 50/50 that the next person your child or grandchild meets in 2060 will be of a different race or ethnic background.[4] [...] About one-third of us will be non-white, compared to 18 percent in 2010. [...]

Earlier this year, Cincinnati Mayor John Cranley created a task force on immigration, the point of which is to make the city a good place for immigrants to live and start businesses.

Raj Chundur, an immigrant from India and urban planner [...] brings a personal perspective to his role. [...] "My perspective, in terms of economics, is that immigrants bring the power of ideas," Chundur said.

1. from the US Eastern region and of Anglo-Scottish origin 2. major 3. central area 4. origin

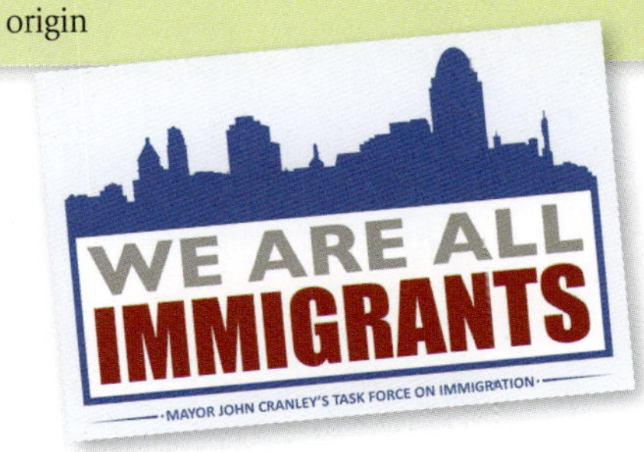

3 Read again for details

a. Pick out the names of the people in the article and find information about them when possible (age, nationality, heritage/origin, job, city...).

b. List the communities living in this American city.

c. Which other cities are mentioned? Why?

d. What do a quarter • thousands • 50 • 50/50 • 2060 • one third • 18 refer to?

4 Action!

Cincinnati's Mayor needs you to work on his project. Create and submit an ad to promote the city and attract new immigrants.

Get ready for the Oral Exam

What is the immigrants' role and impact on America?

3 A New Force

1 America's future

A Observe and react

a. What is represented here?
b. What do the red chili peppers symbolise?
c. What do you expect to read about?

Culture Tip

The Star Spangled Banner is the name of the American flag.

B Read and understand

CNN

By Monica C. Lozano, May 12, 2015

America finds itself on the threshold[1] of a unique demographic opportunity. The explosive growth of the Latino population means Latinos are projected to make up 26% of the U.S. population by 2050. As today's Hispanic population tends to be younger than comparable groups, Latinos literally represent America's future.

With an aging white population reaching retirement, Latino youth[2] are many of our future doctors, lawyers and schoolteachers. America's future economic well-being and competitiveness is increasingly contingent on[3] the success of the Latino population.

Latinos want what all Americans want: quality education, economic opportunity, affordable homes, strong and safe communities, good government and access to health care. Unfortunately, we have lagged behind[4] other groups in most of these areas. If we are serious about bridging these gaps[5] and translating population gains into growing influence on America's institutions, we must work together across communities, with experts and thought leaders, to become part of the fabric[6] of American society.

1. *(ici) à l'aube* **2.** young people **3.** dependent on **4.** *nous sommes à la traîne par rapport à* **5.** *réduire l'écart* **6.** *tissu (social)*

PREPARE YOUR TASK

a. Observe the words in:
– **blue:** find their suffix and/or prefix to get the root *(racine)*. Select the translation from the list below:
malheureusement • compétitivité • croissance • croissante • abordables (= pas trop chères) • retraite • de plus en plus
– **green:** they are transparent. Guess the appropriate translation for each word.

b. Read for details and find the key ideas in each paragraph.
§1: What is said about the Latino population in the US today? in the future?
§2: Which Latino age group is particularly concerned? Pick out the reasons why.
§3: Rephrase l. 8-10, and say what the Latinos are looking for. Have they succeeded yet? Why or why not? What do they have to do?

Get ready for the Oral Exam

Why does the Latino population represent an opportunity for the USA?

2 "Bienvenidos everyone!"

A Get ready

a. Look at the poster and read the slogan. What strikes you?
b. Can everyone understand the message? Why or why not?

CD 2
PISTE 2

B Read this definition and listen to a report about Spanglish.

Culture Tip

Spanish is the USA's second-most spoken language. But with the equal influence of English, a new *lingo* has been created: **Spanglish!** Spanglish speakers, who are members of both communities, mix English and Spanish words.

USEFUL WORDS
- ad lingo = advertising language
- brakes: *freins* • target: *cibler*
- code-switching: *alternance de code linguistique*
- hybrid = mixed

First listening: Answer the following questions.
a. Concentrate on the voices at the beginning of the recording. What immediately strikes you?
b. Which word is repeated several times? Then, find words referring to it.
c. Using the definition above and the beginning of the recording, guess what the main topic is.
d. Write down as many words as possible and classify them: languages nationalities numbers period.
Pick out other stressed words.

Second listening: Organise your notes.

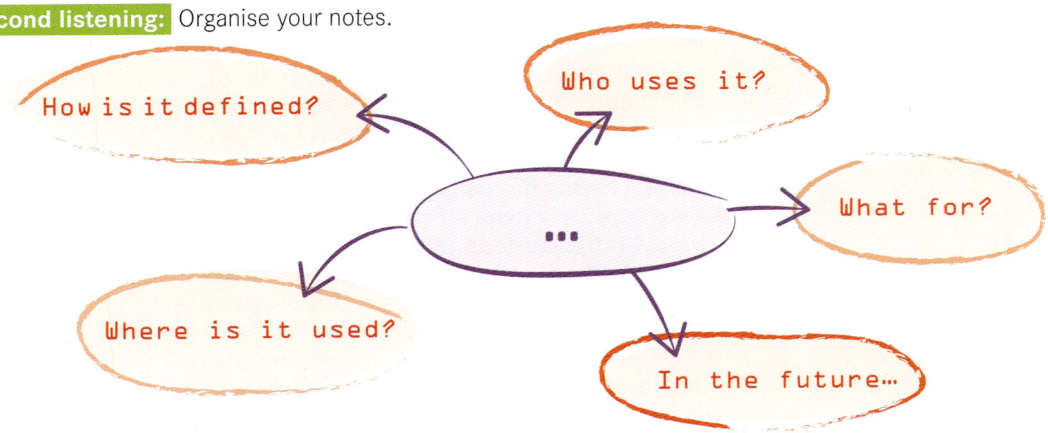

Third listening: Complete your answers, and give an account of what you have understood.

Go further: Try to identify the tone of this speech:
defiant · humorous · threatening · optimistic · pessimistic · critical · serious · light

Get ready for the Oral Exam

What does this recording reveal about the Hispanics' economic force in the USA?

4 The Land of Success

1 The refuge

a. Before you read.
In pairs, use the words below to imagine what happened to the woman in the picture.

hoping • visa • unable • rebuilt • job • earn money • safe • free • survivors • Cambodia • USA • succeed • sent back • terrified • poor • language • family's story • not easy • new life

b. Now read and compare your stories to the real one.

SreyRam Kuy, MD,[1] was born in Cambodia during the "Killing Fields" genocide, after the Khmer Rouge took over the country in 1975. After escaping from Cambodia, she lived in refugee camps in Thailand.

During these years we waited anxiously, hoping to come to America. Our visa application had been denied over and over. Many families were being sent back to Cambodia. We were terrified of returning. One day, we received the incredible news that we had been sponsored to the United States by a Christian Missionary group.

We arrived in the U.S. destitute,[2] haunted by the memories of the Killing Fields, and unable to speak the language. My mom rebuilt a new life, taking any job she could find. She scrubbed[3] toilets at Good Samaritan Hospital during the day, cleaned doctors' houses at night, and on the weekends we worked in the fields alongside Mexican migrant farm workers picking berries[4] and vegetables to earn extra money. It was not easy, but we were safe and we were free. That was all that mattered.

Today, I'm a surgeon myself, taking care of our nation's veterans. My sister works as a podiatrist,[5] caring for underserved[6] patients with diabetic foot problems. We are so grateful[7] to be alive, and that we were given refuge in this land of freedom. This is my family's story as refugees, as genocide survivors and as Americans.

By SreyReath Kuy, DPM and SreyRam Kuy, MD.
Hufftington Post, June 19, 2015

1. Doctor of Medicine **2.** very poor **3.** cleaned **4.** *baies*
5. *podologue = spécialiste du pied* **6.** *défavorisés* **7.** *reconnaissantes*

a. Identify the different places.

b. Who are the people present and mentioned?

c. Who is the narrator?

d. Pick out the time references.

e. According to the different periods of time, the narrator and her family felt: disheartened • worried • hopeful • nervous • scared • thankful?

f. What impact did this event have on their lives?

g. What does the USA represent for the narrator and her family?

WORKSHEET 20

c. Turn to your worksheet to go further.

2 Indians and business

a. Learn more about Indians in the US nowadays.

The Economist

May 23, 2015, Special report

Indians in America are the most promising [group]. They are increasingly prominent[1] in tech companies, on Wall Street and in government, especially in the state department. Around 1% of America's population, over 3.3m people, are "Asian Indians". Perhaps 150,000 more arrive each year, and 90% of them stay permanently. Devesh Kapur, who has studied them, talks of a "flood".[2] He says over half of all Indian-born people in America arrived there after 2000.

On the usual measures of success they outstrip[3] all other minorities, including Jewish-Americans. They are educated and rich.

In 2012 some 42% held first or higher degrees; average family income was over $100,000, roughly double that of white Americans. Over two-thirds of them hold high-status jobs.

1. *visibles* **2.** *afflux* **3.** *dépassent / surpassent*

b. Choose the correct translation of the words in orange.

– *degrés* • *diplômes*

– *revenu* • *arrivée*

– *célèbre* • *à responsabilité*

– *le plus bas* • *moyen*

c. Pick out all the numbers, figures and dates. Then train to read them aloud. Two references to proportions are in letters. Find them out and write their equivalents using numbers. What do they refer to?

d. Say what characterises this community.

Help!

rich = wealthy
enterprising
hard-working

achieve one's goals
make it to the top = succeed in sth/V-ING
set up a business: *monter une entreprise*

video

3 Watch a video

Instacart

CD 2 PISTE 3

a. Get ready

– Listen to a list of words and write them on a separate piece of paper. Find out what their meaning is. Then repeat them.

– What do you expect to hear about?

WORKSHEET 21

b. Watch the report and find out what Instacart is all about. Turn to your worksheet for help.

c. What do all the documents on this page show about Indians in the USA today?

Get ready for the Oral Exam

What do immigrants bring to their new country?

5 Foreign-born Blacks

1 A change of origin?

a. Read and understand.

The New York Times — By Fredrick Kunkle, April 9, 2015

The most recent wave of black immigration began in the 1960s after U.S. immigration laws were changed. In recent years, the pace has increased. The most recent Census Bureau estimates show that immigration accounted for 25 percent of the growth in the U.S. black population between 2010 and July 2013 […].

Half of the black immigrants arrived from the Caribbean. […] The largest source is Jamaica, with 682,000, followed by Haiti, with 586,000. Jamaican immigrants make up 18 percent of the black population in the United States; those from Haiti represent about 15 percent of the U.S. black population.

But a rapidly growing proportion of foreign-born blacks who arrived in the United States in recent years came from Africa, led almost entirely by immigrants from sub-Saharan Africa, the report says. Nigeria and Ethiopia rank first and second, respectively, in the number of African immigrants in the United States. Many sub-Saharan immigrants — 28 percent — were refugees or others seeking asylum. About 8 percent of black immigrants came from South or Central America, the report says.

In terms of socioeconomic profiles, foreign-born blacks have a median age of 42, compared with 29 for U.S.-born blacks. Twenty-six percent have a college education, compared with 19 percent of native-born blacks, and black immigrants are less likely to live in poverty (20 percent vs. 28 percent) and have higher incomes.

b. Complete the graphs below on a separate sheet of paper to test your understanding.

US Black population between ... and ... — **Black immigration**

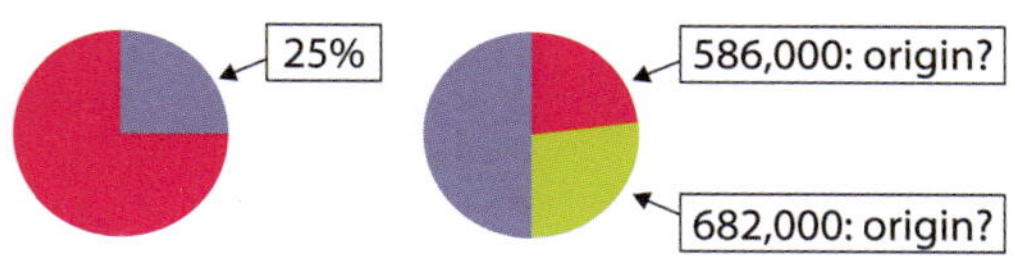

c. Find the caption for each group of bar charts.

d. Locate the two countries where Africans mainly emigrate from.

e. Use the graphs to make a short oral recap to the class or to a classmate.

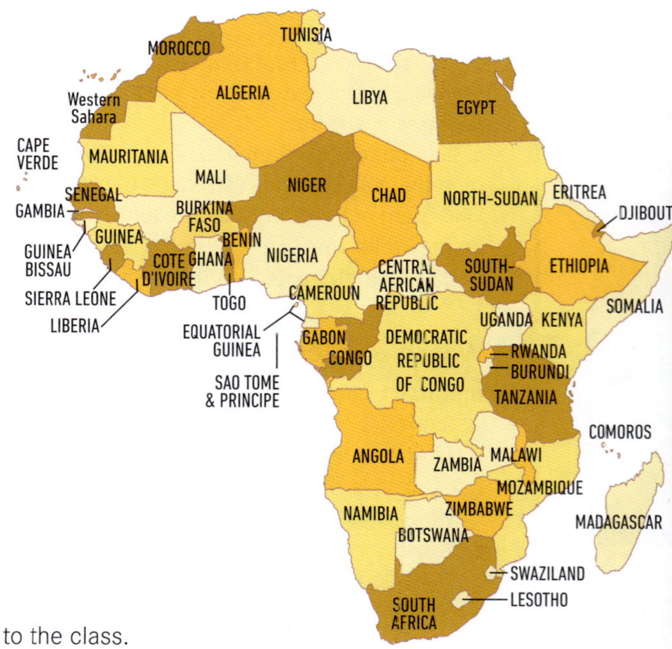

CD 2 PISTE 4

WORKSHEET 22

2 A major difference?

a. Listen to Kara talk about her personal story. Turn to your worksheet for help.

b. Sum up what you have understood and report to the class.

Get ready for the Oral Exam

To what extent is black immigration reshaping the US black population?

Play with words

MP 3 N° 9 — CD 2 PISTE 5

A Lisez les mots suivants. Puis écoutez-les.

Growth: *croissance*
driving force
energy → energetic
economy → economic
politics → political

strong ≠ weak
↓ ↓
strength ≠ weakness

grow/rise
develop → development
increase
shape: *façonner*

Material success
success → successful
wealth → wealthy

succeed
achieve → achievement: *réalisation*

Impact
influence → influential
culture → cultural
incentive

contribute to
benefit from
transform → transformation

B **1. Sur papier libre, à partir des mots donnés dans la colonne de gauche, trouvez les termes de la même famille dans la colonne de droite et entourez la syllabe accentuée.**

Noms	Adjectifs
economy	
politics	
culture	

Noms	Adjectifs
success	
wealth	
influence	

Verbes	Noms
grow	
succeed	
develop	
achieve	

2. Vérifiez à l'écoute puis lisez tous les mots à haute voix en respectant la syllabe accentuée.

C **1. Sur papier libre, complétez ces phrases à l'aide d'un mot choisi dans la liste suivante :**
adapt • customs • diversity • immigrants • maintain • practise • together • traditions • welcomed • language

The USA is a nation of ... because it has ... refugees from all over the world. They had to ... to American ... . Immigrants have always been encouraged to ... their ... and their native ... . They can also ... their religion. This model of racial integration is called a salad bowl model. It means people of different cultures live ... . It refers to the cultural ... of the US.

2. Vérifiez vos réponses à l'écoute.

LANGUAGE AT WORK

« Apprendre à Apprendre »
Téléchargez la fiche n°6
www.editions-hatier.fr/langues-eleves

Corrigés p. 216-221

A Les déterminants

(Précis grammatical 3 p. 194 et 23 p. 202)

1. Complétez les phrases suivantes avec *the* ou Ø.

a. ... Latinos are now more visible in ... press and on ... television.
b. ... impact of immigration on ... country is enormous.
c. Will ... government give ... American citizenship to ... illegal immigrants?
d. ... American Dream means ... equal opportunities and ... happiness for all.

2. Complétez les phrases suivantes avec *a/an* ou Ø.

a. ... immigrants dream of ... peace, ... freedom and ... better life.
b. José arrived in Texas when he was ... child. When he was ... student he worked very hard. He is now ... engineer. His sister is ... doctor.
c. His parents worked in fields fourteen hours ... day to pay for their education. They picked ... fruit and ... vegetables all day long.

3. Complétez les phrases suivantes avec *a/an*, *the* ou Ø.

a. ... USA has always been ... nation of ... immigrants.
b. ... white people will no longer be ... majority in ... US by 2060.
c. ... historic change is taking place and is reshaping ... nation.
d. This new demographic shift will have ... huge impact on ... nation's economy.
e. Will ... Latino become ... president of ... US one day?
f. The governor of New Mexico, Susana Martinez, is ... Latina.
g. ... Latinos come from ... South America, ... Central America and ... Mexico.
h. ... immigration is reshaping one of ... world's biggest nations.

4. Traduisez les phrases suivantes.

a. Aux États-Unis les immigrants changent la vie dans les villes et les quartiers.
b. Les Latinos parlent espagnol.
c. Beaucoup d'Indiens ont monté des entreprises. Ils sont de plus en plus visibles *(prominent)* dans le gouvernement et à la bourse *(Stock Exchange)*.

B Subordonnées de temps et expression du futur

(Précis grammatical 17 p. 200)

On n'emploie **pas *will*** dans les subordonnées de temps :
*Black immigrants hope they will have a better job **when they arrive** in the US.*

5. Quels sont les équivalents français des mots en gras ?

a. **When you go** to the States, you will see many commercials in Spanglish.
b. **As soon as you arrive** in Florida, you will notice the influence of Latinos.
c. I won't move **until I have found** a better job.

6. Traduisez.

a. Ils chercheront un emploi et un appartement dès qu'ils arriveront.
b. Les États-Unis changeront quand les Hispaniques seront le groupe le plus important.
c. Quand les enfants iront à l'école, ils apprendront l'anglais.
d. Ils ne déménageront pas avant de trouver un meilleur emploi.

YOUR TASK

Use the different texts and the other documents studied in the unit and choose one scenario.

SCENARIO 1

You are a journalist. You have to write an article on the new face of America.

▶ **Include the following points:**
- the minorities' current situation in America;
- the economic, social and political changes;
- the reasons why people choose the US as their new home;
- what they have already achieved in the US;
- how they shape the nation's identity.

Where Minorities Are a Majority

In four states plus Washington, D.C., non-whites make up more than 50 percent of the population

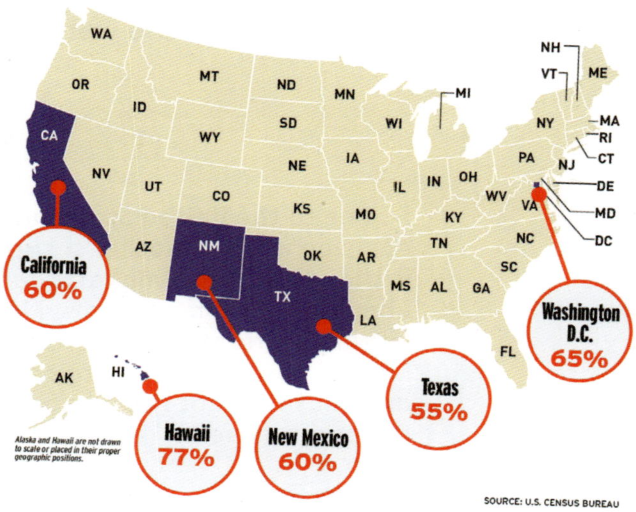

SOURCE: U.S. CENSUS BUREAU

Tips

Proofread your article (→ p. 7):
- check your **tenses**
- **no "s"** at the end of adjectives
- person + **singular**/people + **plural**
- which ≠ who
- want sb to do sth
- **the USA + singular!**

SCENARIO 2

You are a journalist. Imagine you interview the young woman in the photo.

▶ **Include the following points:**
- the person's identity (full name, age, nationality, community...);
- information about her community;
- her education;
- how she feels about being a Latina in America;
- what she and her community have achieved;
- what her hopes are for the future.

Tips

- Use texts p. 83 and 84 too.
- Use the present perfect and future.
- Pay attention to the word order in questions (→ *Précis grammatical* 22 p. 202).

Compréhension écrite et expression écrite

WORKSHEET BAC N° 6

Answer the questions on the worksheet the teacher will give you.

DOCUMENT A

I came to the United States at the age of 14 from Uzbekistan. The decision was my mother's; she felt like we needed a better life after my father died from lymphatic cancer. It was tough at first, but all I cared about is that I'm here now. I knew I had no future in Uzbekistan due to extreme corruption and broken education for which you can pay through. I am 17 now, on my way to college. Although current circumstances aren't as I'd want them to be, I will change that. After all, this is the land of opportunities.

Umar

Los Angeles

www.myimmigrationstory.com

DOCUMENT B

DON'T KILL TEXAS' IMMIGRANT SPIRIT

By Sam Wyly, May 22, 2015

Texas is home to six of the 13 fastest-growing cities in America.

The Dallas-Fort Worth area, where I live, created more jobs last year than any other metro area in the country. I wasn't surprised that the region beat New York, Los Angeles or San Francisco, but I was surprised that we topped Houston — which has now surpassed New York as the favorite city for newcomers to America.

Immigrants enrich us all, and unless we're Cherokee, Choctaw or Comanche, we're all children of those who came to America and to Texas by sailboat, steamboat, covered wagon, horse, railroad, car or a trek through the Cumberland Gap[1] or across the Rio Grande.

Immigrants don't take jobs away from those of us who got here sooner; they create jobs for us, our children and themselves. They're twice as likely to start new businesses, and they do jobs many of us wouldn't do. [...]

Texas has a thriving[2] economy because it celebrates ethnic and intellectual diversity and empowers newcomers to become prosperous citizens who help generate wealth for everyone.

Here's my message to state lawmakers: Please don't pass laws — like a repeal of in-state tuition rates for undocumented immigrants — that will change this. We're all immigrants or children of those who arrived on the shores of this country hoping for a better life for themselves and their families. We all descend from brave immigrants seeking[3] freedom and prosperity.

This is what has made us a great country, and we must keep this American Dream alive. And Texas — the most American of states — should continue to lead.

1. *col dans la chaîne des Appalaches et lieu de passage de nombreux colons vers l'Ouest américain* 2. *prospère*
3. looking for

www.tribtalk.org

Compréhension de l'oral

CD 2 PISTE 6

Wendy Cervantes Celebrates Immigrant Heritage Month

→ Écoutez l'enregistrement trois fois.

→ Prenez des notes puis faites en dix minutes le compte rendu de ce que vous avez compris en français.

→ Utilisez les expressions données p. 183.

Expression orale

SPACES AND EXCHANGES { **Is it true to say: "Immigrants come and change America and are changed by America?"**

Comment parler de la notion ?

❶ Définissez l'expression « Espaces et échanges » (→ p. 4).

❷ Pour répondre à la problématique, recopiez les mots en gras ci-dessous sur papier libre et complétez avec les documents étudiés en classe.

The immigrants' demographic impact on America
Explain the demographic shift today and in the future.

mosaic /məʊ'zeɪɪk/
diversity
ethnic group
reshape
make up

The Latinos: a new force?
Why do Latinos represent an opportunity for the USA?

growth
youth
growing market
influence

African-born Blacks
To what extent is black immigration reshaping the US black population?

income
college education
different from
make their dreams come true

Asians
What do immigrants bring to their new country?
- Personal stories of refugees
- Success stories

escape
start from scratch
struggle
make it to the top

❸ Utilisez le vocabulaire donné p. 5 et 89 pour enrichir votre expression.

❹ Ne rédigez pas votre présentation, notez les idées clés, les mots importants.

❺ Anticipez les questions qui pourront être posées par l'examinateur (points à approfondir, exemples pour illustrer un argument, opinion personnelle...).

Tip

N'oubliez pas une **conclusion personnelle** (film, reportage vus, livre, article lus).

▲ *The Martian*, a film by Ridley Scott (2015)

The Idea of Progress

Unit 7

Work in Progress

WHAT IS THE IMPACT OF TECHNOLOGY ON THE WORKPLACE?

YOUR FINAL TASK

- Write a newspaper article. (p. 105)

OR

- Debate about introducing robots in your company. (p. 105)

p. 96-107

Unit 8

More than Meets the Eye

WHY IS FIGHTING PREJUDICES A STEP TOWARDS PROGRESS?

YOUR FINAL TASK

- Create a short video to fight prejudices. (p. 117)

OR

- Write a short text to introduce the video you have posted. (p. 117)

p. 108-119

Unit 9

Wind of Change for Women?

IS GENDER INEQUALITY A THING OF THE PAST IN DEVELOPED COUNTRIES?

YOUR FINAL TASK

- Write an article about gender equality. (p. 129)

OR

- Design a poster and prepare an oral presentation to promote gender equality. (p. 129)

p. 120-131

À la fin de chaque unité, vous trouverez un entraînement type bac complet (compréhension et production écrite, compréhension et expression orale).

Unit 7

THE IDEA OF PROGRESS
What is the impact of technology on the workplace?

Work in Progress

1 Tune In!

1 Which office for you?

a. In groups, work on one of the pictures above: What strikes you (place • people • atmosphere...)?

WORKSHEET 23

b. MATCHING GAME
Read the card your teacher will give you and associate it with one of the photos above. Justify your answer.

c. Explain where you would prefer to work if you had the choice.

I'd rather work in... because...

I prefer working in... to being...

Working in an office/from home is...

For my part, I would prefer to... rather than...

... would be my first choice because...

Help!

People

co-worker = colleague /kɒliːg/
remote worker: *travailleur à distance*
staff = personnel

busy /bɪzɪ/
professional

collaborate
concentrate = focus
multitask: *faire plusieurs choses à la fois*

Places and objects

cubicle /kjuːbɪkəl/ = cubby /kʌbi/: *bureau sans cloison*
open-plan office
laptop: *ordinateur portable*
desktop computer: *ordinateur de bureau*

distracting
partitioned = separated
stressful

telework = telecommute = work remotely = work away from the office

YOUR FINAL TASK

Write an article for *The Economist*. (p. 105)

OR

Debate about introducing robots in your company. (p. 105)

2 The future of your workplace

A Get ready

Read the title above and the words in pink. Imagine what the text is about.

THE HINDU

Search GO

Home Today's Paper All Sections News National International Opinion Business Sport Features Sci-Tech Entertainment

July 22, 2015

Technology and digital platforms *have transformed* the way we do business, work, interact and collaborate. The *next phase* of *change* and *transformation will be witnessed*[1] at our workplaces. [...] With the connected world, our work is *no longer* limited to the eight-hour window and our "office" *is no longer* what *it used to be*. [...] The workplace of the future *is expected to be* less centralised, more mobile, and more flexible than anything most of us have witnessed before. The *future workplace will not merely be* a physical space shared by employees but an experience that *allows* them to explore newer heights[2] of success and productivity.

[...] Optional work-from-home is *an age-old idea*. With more than 100 billion app downloads in 2014, almost 50 million people from all over the world were enabled to accomplish their tasks on the move.

This implies[3] that the power of smartphones and tabs, cloud computing, wearable devices,[4] and enterprise apps *may soon* make brick-and-mortar[5] offices obsolete.[6]

We may still be reading emails out of our mailbox but the *next* challenge could be – what after the email? Real time messaging *may soon replace* the static mailboxes.

1. *(ici)* observed **2.** *de nouveaux sommets* **3.** *cela implique* **4.** *appareils* **5.** *(ici) classiques* **6.** not used anymore

B Now read the whole text and check your answers.

a. Focus on the highlighted words. Choose the correct translation (in the order of the text):

digital / numérique *en dehors du bureau / en mouvement* *à la mode / portable*

b. Classify the phrases in italics in the text in three groups:

c. Complete your notes. What do the following elements from the article refer to: the past, the present or the future?

digital platforms • eight-hour window • centralised • more mobile • more flexible • work from home • optional work-from-home • brick-and-mortar offices • static mailboxes • real time messaging

d. Why is the word "office" l. 7 between inverted commas *(guillemets)*? Several possible answers:
traditional offices do not exist anymore • we work from different places and not just one place • it is difficult to call them "offices" because they are very different from what existed before.

e. List all the technological devices at the origin of the revolution on the workplace.

f. Share what you have understood with the class. Use the following words:
in the past • used to • disappear • traditional • thanks to *(grâce à)* • technological progress • change • evolve • enable to • technological devices • different places

2 Work on the Move

1 A better workplace?

a. Observe the picture. What strikes you? (Who? What? Where?)

b. Listen to a report and turn to your worksheet for help.

CD 2 PISTE 7
WORKSHEET 24

➜ Recap

- What is the report about?
- Present the average *(moyen)* remote worker/telecommuter.
- What is the interviewee's viewpoint?

Culture Tip

Millenials = individuals born between the early 1980s and the early 2000s.

2 The pros and cons

a. Read the words below. According to you, what top three qualities must all telecommuters have?

motivated · organised · autonomous · independent · productive · flexible · hard-working · focused · committed · reliable *(fiable)* · trustworthy *(digne de confiance)*

b. Read the following article:

Secret to successful telecommuting? Moderation, research shows

New research is adding scientific credence[1] to the popular belief that working remotely can be a good thing for both employees and employers — as long as certain guidelines are followed.
[...] While there have been many documented advantages to working from home — including saving employers thousands of dollars — there could be potential drawbacks for employees when it comes to work-life balance.[2] Even though telecommuting may give you more control over your time, Allen said, it can also blur[3] the lines between work and family. Not only do some telecommuters often put in longer hours, but they may get saddled[4] with more family responsibilities because they're at home. That distraction can sometimes make things more stressful. [...] The arrangement may not suit everyone, Allen points out. A telecommuter should have good discipline and self-regulation.

Patricia Kozick, *Global News*, September 28, 2015

1. *crédibilité* **2.** *équilibre* **3.** *brouiller* **4.** *supporter la charge de*

c. Classify the ideas in two columns:

Advantages	Drawbacks = disadvantages

d. What are the advantages and disadvantages for the employer and the employee? Discuss with your neighbour and complete your notes.

3 Working from home

PREPARE YOUR TASK

You have a meeting with your manager to convince him/her that you could telecommute one day a week. Imagine your arguments and the manager's counter-arguments and act out the conversation.

Help!

win-win situation

convenient: *pratique*
beneficial
efficient

meet deadlines: *respecter des délais*
suit /suːt//fit sb: *convenir à qqn*
miss out on (opportunities): *laisser passer*
reconcile: *concilier*
weigh the pros and cons: *peser le pour et le contre*

Get ready for the Oral Exam

To what extent can telecommuting be considered an improvement of working conditions?

3 New Jobs

1 Computers need help!

a. Get ready

Observe the pictures on the left and choose an ending for each sentence:
The picture shows a recent scene • a scene from the 18th century • a scene from the beginning of the 20th century.
The character in it is in fact an automaton. Because of the turban he looks like an African • an Englishman • a Turk.
In front of him there is a desk on which we can see dice *(dés)* • a game of chess • a game of cards.

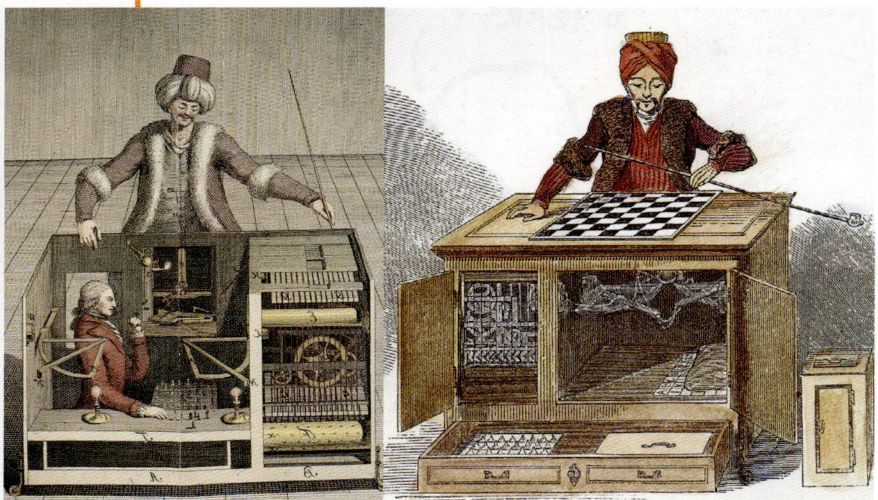

CD 2 PISTE 8

b. Now listen to the report.
- Listen once without taking notes. What is the report about?
- Listen again and organise your notes. Pick out as many words and phrases as you can to answer the following questions:

What does the job consist in? • How much can you earn? • Why this name? • Where do people work from? • Reasons for taking this job? • Opinions?

➜ **Recap** with the help of the recording and the pictures.
- Copy the following definition and replace each number with a word from the following list:

chess • 18th • robots • guiding • man • humans • playing • Turk (x2)

Mechanical (1) gets its name from an (2)-century (3)-playing "machine" that was designed to make people believe the device[1] was capable of (4) and beating (5) at the game. In fact, a (6) was (7) the machine from a secret compartment where he was hiding. Amazon chose the name Mechanical (8) for their web service because real people do tasks that (9) can't do.

1. *(ici) machine*

- Sum up what you have learnt with the help of the following words.

gets its name from • consists in • for example • pay • as little as • per minute • per hour • per day • reasons • choice • bills *(factures)* • mixed feelings • slave • exploit

2 A job opportunity

PREPARE YOUR TASK

Your American friend has started to work as a "Turker" and tries to convince you to do the same. React in an email.

3 Take a stand

PREPARE YOUR TASK

a. Post a comment on a social network on the money "Turkers" get for each task.
b. Group work: The other members of your team will read your comment and react in turn.

Get ready for the **Oral Exam**

Are the jobs created by the rise of new technologies a form of progress?

4 Should We Fear Robots?

video

WORKSHEET 25

PREPARE YOUR TASK

1 Watch a video

Humans need not apply

a. React to the picture and the title of the video.
b. Turn to yout worksheet for help.
c. Write an article for *Time for Kids* in which you explain how the progress in technology has affected the workplace over the years. (150 words)

2 From fiction to reality

a. Get ready: Match the words from list A with their synonym from list B.
List A worry • start to • give control to • in the direction of
List B take the first steps • concern • toward • hand over the keys to
b. Read and understand.

Science fiction authors have predicted it for years. Movies and video games have made references to it, and companies like Google have even taken the first steps toward making it a reality. And now it's starting to happen for real: We're handing over the keys to robots. [...]
For hundreds, if not thousands of years, robotics and artificial intelligence were an unfathomable[1] idea. Now, the idea of artificial intelligence has transformed from the friendly "buddy" type seen in sci-fi movies in the 1950s, to a more genuine[2] concern among the working-class public: Robots are going to take your job. President Obama announced the creation of a program to develop the next generation of artificial workers. When the president of the United States is jumping on board, it's hard to deny[3] that robots are starting to sweep[4] the marketplace.

www.cheatsheet.com

1. mysterious, unexplainable 2. *véritable* 3. *nier* 4. invade

Paragraph 1
– Observe the pronoun in blue. In the text, find what "it" refers to.
– On a separate paper, classify into two columns the words referring to: fiction • reality.
– Rephrase what the journalist explains with the help of the following words:
robots • replace • humans • fiction • become • reality.

Paragraph 2
Classify the information given about the robots in chronological order. Copy the following grid and fill it in with key words from the text.

Time references	For hundreds of years	In the 1950s	Now
People's idea of artificial intelligence (AI)			

➜ **Recap:** Choose the correct option in each statement and justify with words from the text:

For a long time, we knew • didn't know a lot about robotics. In the middle of the 20th century, artificial intelligence was often presented as harmless *(inoffensive)* • dangerous in movies. Now, people are more and more worried • hopeful, because robots can make their job easier • might take their jobs.

Paragraph 3
– Find the words for: *se joint au mouvement* • *marché*.
– Organise the information: Who? What? Opinion on the project? Journalist's conclusion?

3 You are a journalist

Write a headline and a subheading *(sous-titre)* for the article p. 100. The subheading shculd sum up the key idea in one sentence.

4 An alarming report

a. Before listening: Observe the pictures and associate each of them with a word in the bubble:

increase
sportswear
factory

CD 2 PISTE 9

b. Listen to the report once without taking notes. Explain what the recording is about in one or two sentences.

c. Listen again and pick out as many stressed words as possible (names • numbers • countries • feelings • words repeated).

d. Copy the mind map below on a separate piece of paper and classify the information you have found.

Name of the company: …
→ **Turnover *(chiffre d'affaires)*: …**
→ **Product they sell: …**
→ **Employees**
- **In the past**
  - Who?
  - Working conditions?
  - People's reactions?
- **Now**
  - What?
  - Working conditions?
  - → **Consequences?**
    Pick out two numbers:
    … = number of … who have been replaced by …
    … = number of … the company closed down
    Result: the company's profits have …

e. Third listening: complete your notes and try to answer the following questions:
– Which jobs are particularly threatened? Pick out an adjective.
– Find two words describing the employees' feelings. Explain why they feel this way.

f. Use your notes in the mind map to present what you have understood to the class.

5 Writing workshop

PREPARE YOUR TASK

Write a short article using the headline below (150 words). Turn to page 187 for help.

Tomorrow's workplace: should we fear robots?

Help!

Robots /rəʊbɒts/

labor (US)/labour (GB) force = workforce: *main-d'œuvre*

tireless: *infatigable*
mechanised, automated

improve: *améliorer*

Reactions

threat /θret/: *menace*

concerned = worried: *inquiet*
harmful ≠ harmless: *inoffensif*
threatened by: *menacé par*

Get ready for the Oral Exam

Are robots becoming a help or a threat in the workplace?

5 Video Corner — Kiva Robots

1 Watch the first 20 seconds of the video

a. Where does the scene take place?
• a warehouse *(entrepôt)* • a library
• a supermarket

b. Which sentences best describe what is happening?
• Lots of orange robots are moving shelves *(étagères)* around.
• More robots seem to work for this company than people.
• More people seem to work for this company than robots.

2 In the list below, match each word with its synonym:

associate • purchase • stock • client • spokesperson • buy • co-worker • representative • inventory • customer

USEFUL WORDS
- factory (GB) = plant (US): *usine*
- fork truck: *chariot élévateur*
- screw: *visser*

3 Part 1

Pick out as many key words as possible. Copy the grid opposite and classify the information you have heard.

MANUFACTURING ROBOTS	KIVA ROBOTS

Place of work: ... Physical description: ... Only action: ...	Description: ... Actions: ... and ...

4 Part 2

a. Pick out as many key words as possible.

b. Which of these sentences best describes the situation in the company?
• Workers in this company take orders from robots.
• Robots are treated like human beings by the associates.
• Robots are not different from any other working tools *(outils)* in the company.

c. Justify with the words and phrases you picked out.

5 Part 3

a. Complete the sentences below:

The associates working with the robots realise that our Kiva bots just ... .
They're not having to ... , looking for ... that our ... are purchasing.
The robots ... , they make us more accurate *(précis)*, **which ultimately helps ... to ... .**

➜ **Recap:** What is the man's opinion of the Kiva bots? Choose the correct statement(s):
• He believes they only offer advantages.
• He thinks a human employee would work faster than a robot.
• Kiva robots boost the American economy because they help employees be more productive.
• He thinks robots save his employees' time and energy.

6 React

PREPARE YOUR TASK

After watching the video, write a comment on Dailymotion. Would you like to work for this company? Why? Why not? What do you think of the way they consider robots?

Get ready for the Oral Exam

To what extent can robots be an advantage in a company?

Play with words

MP3 N° 10 — CD 2 PISTE 10

WORK

Apply (for a job): *postuler*
application: *candidature*
CV (GB)/resumé (US) /ˈrezʊmeɪ/
cover letter: *lettre de motivation*
recruiter /rɪˈkruːtəʳ/
job interview: *entretien d'embauche*
HR (Human Resources /rɪˈsɔːsɪz/
vacancy /ˈveɪkənsi/: *poste à pourvoir*
hire /haɪəʳ/: *embaucher*

Positions: *postes*
manager
executive: *cadre*
CEO (Chief Executive Officer): *P-DG*
employer
employee
a blue collar: a worker who does a manual job
a white collar: a person who works in an office
skilled ≠ unskilled: *qualifié ≠ non-qualifié*

Career path: *parcours professionnel*
competition: *concurrence*
internship (GB)/work placement (US): *stage*
training: *formation*
job mobility
lay (laid, laid) off: *licencier*
fire sb: *virer qqn (familier)*
quit (quit, quit) one's job: *démissionner*
retire /rɪˈtaɪəʳ/: *prendre sa retraite*

Working for a living: *gagner sa vie*
income: *revenu*
salary
minimum wage: *salaire minimum*
get a rise (GB), a raise (US)
earn = make money
perks: *avantages en nature en plus du salaire*
before tax, gross ≠ after tax: *brut ≠ net*

A **Choisissez parmi les mots ci-dessus et complétez les phrases suivantes sur papier libre.**
a. Your job ... should be sent to the department of Human Resources. Don't forget to write a ... ... explaining why you are interested in the position.
b. Does this company provide ... such as a company car?
c. Work experience is often valued on a CV. That's why many students apply for ... ... before graduating.
d. During the job ... , I asked the ... if I could telecommute once a week.
e. Walmart employees are protesting in order to be paid more than the ... .

B **Associez un mot de la liste A à un mot de la liste B pour retrouver des expressions courantes lorsque l'on postule pour un emploi.**
List A: email • contact • hobbies • work • clean driving • salary • application
List B: expectations • experience • form • address • details • licence • and interests
Traduisez les expressions trouvées. Utilisez un dictionnaire si nécessaire.

C **Parmi les mots ci-dessous, retrouvez lesquels sont synonymes.**
unemployed • work overtime • jobless • job • do extra hours • occupation • out of work

D **Dictée**
Observez l'image ci-contre puis, sur papier libre, notez les phrases que vous allez entendre.

LANGUAGE AT WORK

« Apprendre à Apprendre »
Téléchargez la fiche n°7
www.editions-hatier.fr/langues-eleves

Corrigés p. 216-221

A L'expression du conditionnel

(Précis grammatical 10 p. 197)

1. Lisez les hypothèses suivantes et classez-les en deux colonnes :
hypothèse possible • hypothèse peu probable ou irréelle

a. If robots become more intelligent, they will be able to do more complex jobs.
b. If robots could do any job, all humans would be unemployed.
c. If companies use more robots, many people will lose their jobs.
d. Some people think that there would be fewer accidents if we all used driverless cars.
e. If companies used more robots, there would be more unemployment.

2. Associez chaque début de phrase à sa fin logique.

a. If robots were less expensive,
b. If I could telecommute,
c. If robots become less expensive,
d. Companies would not need as many offices
e. If my boss agreed,
f. I will certainly work from home

1. I would choose to work from home.
2. more companies would invest in them.
3. if I am given the opportunity.
4. more companies will invest in them.
5. I would save a lot of money on transport.
6. if more employees worked from home.

B L'accroissement parallèle

(Précis grammatical 9 p. 196)

3. Faites le plus de phrases possible en associant chaque début de phrase à une fin logique.

The less time employees spend commuting,
The more productive employees are,
The happier employees are at work,
The more time employees spend commuting,

the less efficient they are.
the better for the employer.
the less tired they are.
the more stressed they are.
the more efficient they are.

4. Traduisez les phrases suivantes.
a. The more often employees work from home, the less they can exchange ideas with colleagues.
b. The farther they live from work, the more convenient it is to telecommute.
c. The less time employees spend at the office, the more difficult it is to organise meetings.

5. Utilisez les structures de l'accroissement parallèle pour commenter ce dessin.
Utilisez les mots suivants :
- *numerous*
- *efficient*
- *fire*
- *few*
- *blue-collar worker*
- *unskilled jobs:* emplois non qualifiés
- *humans*
- *unemployment*
- *intelligent*
- *job*

YOUR TASK

SCENARIO 1

You work for *The Economist*. Write the article corresponding to the headline and subheading on the cover.

► **Step 1: Before writing your article, work in groups to explain the message. Use the words below.**

Cover	Message/Impact
tornado /tɔːˈneɪdəʊ/ blockbuster film	scary = frightening devastating
destroy escape = run away from	stand for = represent threaten/endanger

► **Step 2: Go over your notes from the unit.**

a. Think about:
- new ways of working
- the impact of technology (benefits, drawbacks)
- people's reactions to artificial intelligence

b. Turn to p. 187 for help.

SCENARIO 2

The company you work for wants to invest in robots. To convince the workers, they organised a meeting where they showed examples of working robots doing different jobs, in different countries:

receptionist • security guard • order picker *(préparateur de commandes)*

After the meeting, discuss with your colleagues the pros and cons of introducing robots in the company.

► Watch the Video Corner again. You teacher will give you two more videos to watch.
► List all arguments for and against introducing robots in your company.
► Get ready to defend your point of view. Don't forget to use p. 178-179 for help.

Compréhension écrite et expression écrite

WORKSHEET
BAC N° 7

Answer the questions on the worksheet the teacher will give you.

DOCUMENT A

When robots inherit the workplace – and humans' jobs

By Adam Satariano and Dina Bass and Jack Clarck, Bloomberg

May 22, 2015

Willie McTuggie looks like a photocopier on wheels. But he — it, actually — has the engineered brain of a reasonably smart human, and acts like one when he rolls up to a nurse's station, opens a drawer, retrieves[1] a dose of pills and glides off to make a delivery.

Packed with more than 30 motion-detecting and other sensors, Willie and his automated buddies at the UCSF Medical Center can open doors, avoid collisions with doctors on rounds and perceive when to wait for a free elevator.

The machines perform duties once handled by nurses, orderlies,[2] cafeteria staff and maintenance crews. So far, no people have lost jobs to the bot corps.[3]

The human-brain mimics are becoming so clever that, according to a study by the Oxford Martin Program on Technology, 47 per cent of all U.S. jobs are at risk over the next two decades of being given over to computers. They're already writing sports stories, milking cows and reviewing X-ray results.

The artificial intelligence revolution is writing a new chapter in the age-old debate over whether machines are putting people out of work or opening up new opportunities for them. "The idea of technology destroying jobs has been going on for two centuries," says Richard Cooper, an economist at Harvard University who has studied the impact of technological advancements on employment. "Certain jobs get destroyed but other jobs get created."

www.vancouversun.com

1. *récupère* 2. *aide-soignant-es* 3. *(ici) équipe de robots*

DOCUMENT B

WELCOME TO THE ROBOT GENERATION

April 9, 2014 Klaus Æ. Mogensen

The technology that more than any will come to shape the next few decades is robot technology, and children will grow up with robots at home and in the street as something quite natural. Even now, many homes have robot vacuum cleaners,[1] and the robot dog Aibo hit the stores 15 years ago. Like we today develop robots to help with eldercare, we will almost certainly also invent robots and other intelligent technology to aid in childcare. We will attempt to imagine the childhood and youth of Maria, born 2020 in a European suburb. [...]

It is 2024, and Maria is in kindergarten[2] while her parents are at work. Her parents can't always make it home from work before the kindergarten closes, but that isn't a problem. They just send their robot car with instructions to pick up Maria and tell the teachers to follow the girl to the car when it arrives. The car lets Maria off right in front of the door at home when there are no strangers nearby. The door recognises Maria and lets her in and makes sure she gets safely inside.

At kindergarten, there are many robots for playing and learning, from the ball that returns on its own when Maria throws it, to the robots in the kindergarten's rooms and courtyard[3] that look after the kids and can answer all sorts of questions like "Why is the sky blue?", "What kind of butterfly is that?", and "What's for lunch today?" The robots have cameras covering 360 degrees, and Maria's parents can at any time log in to see what's she's doing – face recognition is used to find the right child. [...]

Robot cars remain a minority on the streets, so it is still necessary to look out for[4] the kids, but the teachers hope that the street in front of the kindergarten in time will be closed to human-driven cars – then they will be able to let the children play outside without worry

www.scenariomagazine.com

1. *aspirateurs* 2. *école maternelle* 3. *cour de récréation* 4. stay vigilant

DOCUMENT C

Compréhension de l'oral

CD 2
PISTE 11

Working from Montana

→ Écoutez l'enregistrement trois fois.
→ Prenez des notes puis faites en dix minutes le compte rendu de ce que vous avez compris en français.
→ Utilisez les expressions données p. 183.

USEFUL WORDS

- Eric Whitney, David Blackburn
- real estate: *immobilier*
- six-figure income: $100,000 a year or over

Expression orale

THE IDEA OF PROGRESS { What is the impact of technology on the workplace?

What is the impact of technology on the workplace?

How do the changes to the workspace affect the way we work?

collaborate
multitask
work on the move

To what extent can telecommuting be considered an improvement of working conditions?

remote worker/telecommuter
convenient *(pratique)*
weigh the pros and cons

Are the new jobs created by the rise of technologies a form of progress?

exploit
perform tasks

Robots

What advantages can they represent for a company?

productive
improve
boost the economy

Are they becoming a threat to our jobs?

automated workforce
concerned = worried
be threatened by

1. Définissez le mot « progrès ». Reportez-vous à la page 4.
2. Pour répondre à la problématique, recopiez le schéma ci-dessus sur papier libre et complétez-le avec les documents étudiés en classe.
3. Utilisez le vocabulaire donné p. 5 et dans l'unité pour enrichir votre expression.
4. Ne rédigez pas votre présentation, notez les idées clés, les mots importants.

Unit 8

THE IDEA OF PROGRESS
Why is fighting prejudice a step towards progress?

More Than Meets the Eye

1 Tune In!

1 Too good to be true!

Help!

Situation/Story

ponytail: *queue de cheval*
shadow
spiked club: *massue hérissée de pointes*

hide (hid, hidden): *cacher*
hit (hit, hit): *frapper*
take revenge on sb
forgive (forgave, forgiven): *pardonner*

Goal

deceive = mislead = fool: *tromper*
expect sb to + BV: *s'attendre à ce que qqn*
trust sb: *se fier à qqn*

a. Group work

PREPARE YOUR TASK

- React to the document: colours, people, possible relationship.
- Concentrate on the situation: What does each character plan to do?
- What happened before? Imagine a story and compare it with those of the other groups.
- The artist's goal: What does the viewer realise?

b. Classwork

Compare your reactions with the other groups'.

YOUR FINAL TASK

Create a short video to fight prejudices. (p. 117)

OR

Write a short text to introduce the video you have posted. (p. 117)

2 The power of appearances

a. Get ready

- Look at the photo: What are the people doing? Imagine the reason they are acting this way.
- In your opinion, what is the text about?

b. Read and understand.

"I had photographers follow me around and act as paparazzi. There were 15 people in total that were actually in on it." [...]
Cohen and his entourage began their walk toward Times Square. It didn't take long before crowds began to surround him on every block. [...] One little boy was particularly excited to meet the fake[1] celebrity. Cohen said the boy went so far as to make an international call home on his cell phone, and was overheard screaming, "I just met Brett Cohen!" [...]
From beginning to end, the whole thing took about three hours to shoot.[2] Cohen said the hardest thing about the entire experience was stopping the frenzy,[3] literally.
"It was really hard to end the shoot. How the hell do you stop when there's so many people following you? We actually had to walk away from Times Square and into a small hotel," Cohen said. "One of my bouncers[4] blocked off the door to the bar to keep the public from going in. It was the only way we were able to stop it."

ABC News Blogs, August 23, 2012

1. false 2. film 3. *agitation, frénésie* 4. *videur (fam.), garde du corps (ici)*

- List the places mentioned in the text. Name the city where the scene takes place.
- List the different people present in the scene and identify them using the words from the following list, when possible:

so many people • his entourage • paparazzi • the fake celebrity

- Pick out the verbs describing actions. Associate them with the people you listed.
- Sum up the situation in one or two sentences.
- What does *"three"* (l. 9) correspond to?
- Pick out the sentence that best corresponds to Brett Cohen's goal. Justify with a quote.

He wants to promote a new brand of camera.

He wants to show it is difficult to attract attention.

He wants to show people are influenced by what they see/appearances.

PREPARE YOUR TASK

- Imagine the phone conversation between the boy and his father. Include the following points: place, people, actions, reactions.

3 Watch a video

Looks aren't everything

WORKSHEET 26

a. Go on the Internet and type: Cameron Russell, Looks aren't everything, English. Watch the young model talking about her job (from 5:44 to 6:20).

b. Turn to your worksheet for help.

4 Writing workshop

After watching Cameron Russell's video, you post an article on her blog to support her. Your article is entitled: You are easily fooled *(trompé.e)* by appearances. (100 words)

2 The Real "Me"

1 My true self

Help!

Photo

lipstick

flashy
spiked hair

Text and slogan

guess: *deviner*
judge sb by: *juger qqn d'après/sur*

Target and message

cliché = stereotype = fixed (often wrong idea about sth or sb)
skill = ability

be considered
be discriminated against
be prejudiced against: *avoir des préjugés contre/envers*

a. React to the photo: What immediately catches your eye?
b. Read the text: Who does "you" refer to? How would you answer the question?
c. Focus on the slogan. Go on this website: www.oxforddictionaries.com/definition/english/
and check the meaning of this phrase.
d. Find the target of this campaign (several possible answers): employers • prejudiced people • average people • doctors • employees • conservative people • open-minded people.

e. Pick out the title that best corresponds to the message:

Take care of your appearance!
Be yourself!
Don't trust appearances!
Fight clichés!

f. Do you find this campaign effective? Justfy your choice.
– It forces us to question ourselves.
– The advertiser addresses us directly.
– It's not informative.
– It gives you no solutions.

2 Tattoos or no tattoos?

a. Get ready

Look at the photo. Which words do you expect to find in the article?

metro • holiday • relaxed • job • visit • career • creativity • shocked • different • non-conformist • concert

b. Read the text and find out about the lady in the picture.

On a crowded subway train one morning, a young woman stands out.[1] She is wearing shorts and a tank top. However, it is not her clothes that make her look different from her fellow commuters.[2] It's her arm. She has a large, brightly colored tattoo of a beautiful woman with long dark hair, wearing a red scarf and jewels. The tattoo covers the top of her left arm.

Her name is Erin DeRosa. She is a 26-year-old hair stylist. Ms. DeRosa says her college friends warned her to not get such large tattoos. They told her the tattoos – or "tats" for short – would make it hard for her to get a job.

Not so, says Ms. DeRosa. She says the hair industry puts importance on creativity and individuality. So, showing her tattoos actually helps her career. She says that her clients do not get "freaked out" or are not upset[3] by her tattoos. She says that her salon is a modern one, suggesting that perhaps in a more conservative salon, customers might be freaked out by her tattoos. [...]

www.learningenglish.voanews.com

1. *se distingue* **2.** somebody taking the metro from the suburb to the city every day **3.** disturbed

– Identify the main character: name, age, occupation, looks.

– Concentrate on her friends' reaction and choose the sentence corresponding to what they think:

They encouraged Erin not to hide her tattoos.

They encouraged Erin to get a new job.

They encouraged Erin to be discreet.

– True or False? Justify by quoting the text.

Her friends thought it would be difficult for Erin to find a job.

She didn't agree with them.

– You are Erin. Tell your college friends your experience about finding a job.

CD 2
PISTE 12

3 Look good, feel good!

WORKSHEET 27

a. Listen to hiring managers telling people about how to dress and groom *(s'apprêter)* before a job interview.

b. Turn to your worksheet for help.

c. Your best friend has his/her first job interview tomorrow. He/She is nervous. Give him/her advice about dressing and grooming.

PREPARE YOUR TASK

4 School survey

PREPARE YOUR TASK

Ask at least five students what they think about tattoos and piercing in the workplace.

Get ready for the Oral Exam

How important are appearances in a job interview?

3 Never Judge a Book by its Cover!

© Joel Parés

CEO = Chief Executive Officer: *Président-Directeur Général*

1 Get ready

a. React to the photos: What immediately strikes you?

b. Compare the man in the photos: name, origin, clothes, occupation, expression on his face.

c. Complete this sentence: The same man ... different in the two photos. The impression we get depends on the ... he is wearing.

d. What is the photographer's message? (several possible answers)

Only the rich get credit. Only the rich go on holiday. Don't judge people by their ethnic origin.
Hispanics are not necessarily working class people. People should think twice before judging someone.

e. In your opinion, what is the text below about?

2 Read the text and check your answers to e.

I stepped off[1] the Marta rail at Five Points Station a little past eight o'clock on a Saturday evening. I had noticed previously on the train an older woman, perhaps in her mid sixties, staring at me[2] with a look that suggested she was anything but content with my presence in the seat across from hers. As we exited the train she continued to make glances[3] in my direction. [...] It was obvious that she was uncomfortable with me walking the same path[4] as her. [...]

The entire experience was nothing new for me; in fact it has become somewhat of the norm, however it is something I could never completely get used to.[5] For those who have never experienced a stereotype, I would be glad to lend my shoes for a day and let them experience one first hand.

Since the founding of this country, American society has been filled with stereotypes that label[6] individuals based on physical appearance rather than personality or intellect. [...]

For nearly three hundred years it was believed that African-Americans were inferior to Caucasians[7] due to the color of their skin. Here I stand a young African-American male in the 21st century, still categorized by a society that knows nothing about me. I encounter atrocious stares from strangers who cannot seem to see past the baggy pants and dreadlocks. I am a sixteen-year-old student who will next year graduate with not only a high school diploma, but with an associates degree as well, yet I am labeled a criminal by so many due to the apparel I choose to wear.

www.helium.com

1. got off 2. *qui me regardait fixement* 3. *coups d'œil* 4. way 5. *je n'ai jamais pu m'habituer complètement* 6. *étiquettent* 7. white people

a. Find the following information about the narrator: age, origin, nationality, appearance.
b. Find three different places. Where does the scene take place?
c. Is the lady he meets old or young? Pleased or displeased? Embarrassed or comfortable? Quote from the text to justify your answers.
d. "*make glances*" (l. 4), "*staring at*" (l. 2), "*atrocious stares*" (l. 13). The lady looks at the narrator because:

he looks like her grandson — he looks suspicious — he is on the wrong train.

Find an adjective to qualify the lady's attitude towards the young man.
e. From "*The entire experience*" (l. 6) to the end
- Read the definition opposite.
- Pick out the sentence(s) that correspond(s) to the old lady's prejudices, preconceived ideas.

DEFINITION

Stereotype: preconceived idea about a group of people with a particular characteristic.

The narrator is a dangerous man because he wears dreadlocks and baggy pants.

The narrator is a brilliant young man because he wears glasses.

The narrator is not judged by his intellect and personality because of his physical appearance.

f. Pick out the adjective that best describes the narrator's feeling at the end of the text:

hopeful — discouraged/hopeless — surprised — terrified — friendly — understanding

CD 2 PISTE 13

WORKSHEET 28

3 Testimony

a. Listen to Rosa Chen speaking about how the Chinese community is perceived in the US.
b. Turn to your worksheet for help.
c. Prepare an account of what you have understood.

PREPARE YOUR TASK

4 Get up, stand up!

a. You are Edgar Gonzalez. You are invited as a successful CEO to make a speech at the Equal Opportunities Commission. You support anti-discriminatory attitude. Give precise examples.
b. Go on Joel Pares's website (Judging America). Look at all the photos and select one. Write a short paragraph under the photo. The person photographed explains why he/she is the victim of prejudices and argues against using stereotypes. Vote for the best text.

Help!

Photos	Article	Fight
gardener working clothes suit: *costume* smiling	(look) suspicious: *louche* narrow-minded ≠ open-minded: *large ≠ ouvert d'esprit* worried = anxious be prejudiced against	cliché = stereotype eradicate prejudices be discriminated against underline judge sb by: *juger qqn d'après/sur*

Get ready for the **Oral Exam**

How do appearances influence our perception of people?

4 Video Corner Beyond Appearances

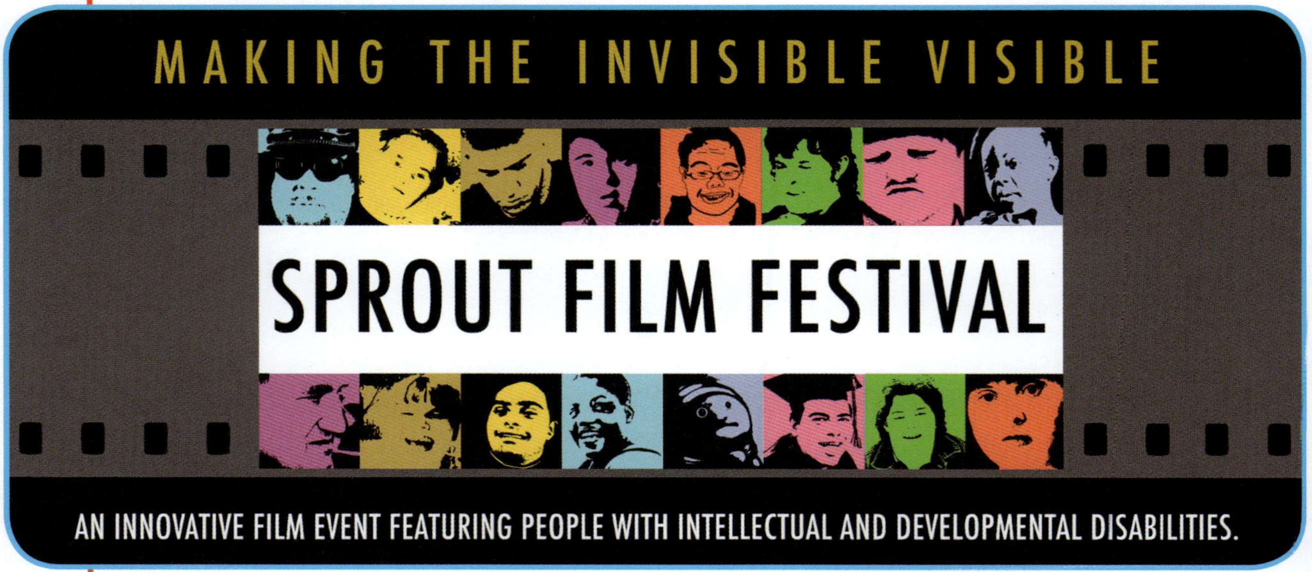

USEFUL WORDS

- Down's Syndrome: *trisomie*
- disability = handicap
- merry-go-round/carousel: *manège*
- homeless: *sans-abri, sans domicile fixe*

1 Get ready

a. Observe the poster and read the useful expressions and words for one minute.
b. Close your books. Which words can you remember?
c. What is people's general attitude to people with intellectual and developmental disabilities?
embarrassed = ill-at-ease • sympathetic • compassionate • laugh at = make fun of

2 Watch the video

PART 1: from the beginning to 1:20

a. Where does the scene take place?
b. Look at the two boys: What do you notice *(remarquez)* about them? How do they feel?
c. Focus on their activities. What are they doing now? What are Jimmy's other activities?
d. In your opinion, which of the two boys is Jimmy? Justify your answer.

PART 2: from 1:21 to the end

e. What do you realise about Jimmy and his everyday life? What about the other boy?
f. Read the sentences on the screen. Pick out the sentence(s) that best correspond(s) to them:

Children with Down's Syndrome must be treated the same as other children.
Children with Down's Syndrome cannot live a normal life.
Children with Down's Syndrome must be treated with dignity.

Homeless children do not live a normal life.
Homeless children must be helped.
Homeless children must be discriminated against.

g. Do you find the video effective? Why or why not?

Get ready for the Oral Exam

To what extent do stereotypes influence our judgement of people?

Play with words

MP 3 N° 11 · CD 2 PISTE 14

A **Look at the word cloud and match the words with the corresponding picture.**

trousers/pants
hooded sweatshirt
swimsuit
half-sleeve
shorts
tank-top
suit
tie
skirt
cap
gloves
shirt

B **Find the odd one out and justify your choice by giving a title for the remaining *(restants)* words in each list.**

List A knee • arm • leg • head • ear • cleavage: *décolleté* • lips • bonnet • hair • cheek • eyebrow

List B respect • tolerance • open-mindedness • discrimination • consideration • esteem

C **Copy the following paragraph and complete it with words from the unit. Check your answers with the recording.**

a. This awareness campaign, which denounces ... , must have been inspired by Martin Luther King's famous "I have a dream" speech.
b. In the photo, the young boy is not white and he is ... ... appearances.
c. He is ... ... become a street cleaner when he is older.
d. The campaign shows how strong ... can be.
e. He is ... ... although he is just a few months old.
f. But ... do not reveal the true nature of people, their personality, intellect and abilities.
g. People should be more ...-... .

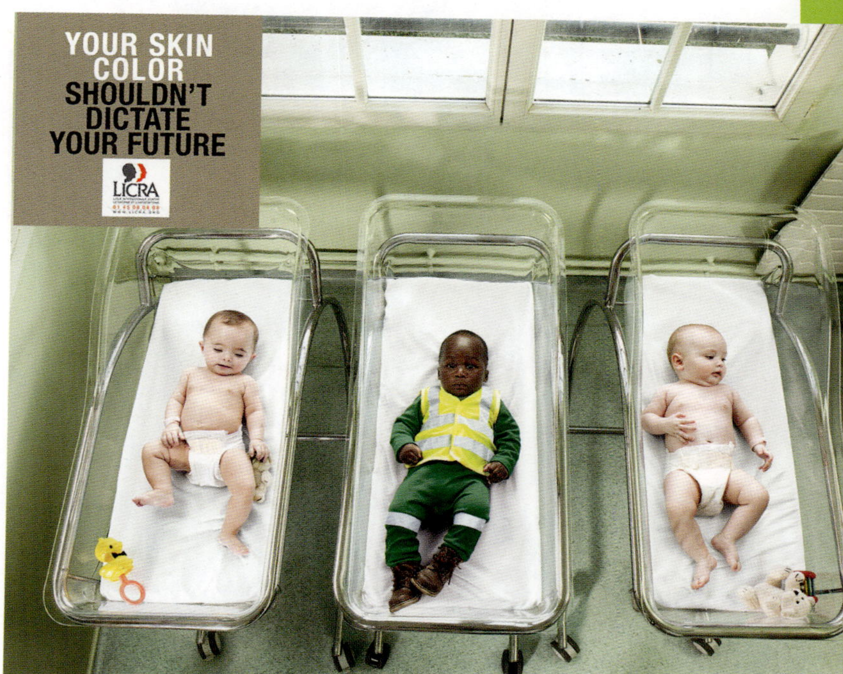

LANGUAGE AT WORK

«Apprendre à Apprendre»
Téléchargez la fiche n°8
www.editions-hatier.fr/langues-eleves

Corrigés p. 216-221

A L'expression d'un souhait, d'une réalité imaginaire (Précis grammatical 10 p. 197)

1. Que signifient ces phrases ?

– I wish people could get rid of their prejudices and we could all live in harmony.
– If only prejudices were not so deeep-rooted, life would be easier.

2. Traduisez les phrases suivantes.

a. Si seulement les gens ne jugeaient pas sur l'apparence physique !
b. Je souhaite que les gens changent et jugent moins vite.
c. Cameron Russell souhaite que les jeunes filles aient plus confiance en elles.
d. Si seulement les gens étaient plus intéressés par notre personalité que par notre physique !

B L'utilisation des prépositions après les adjectifs

3. Complétez ces phrases avec la préposition qui convient. Utilisez un dictionnaire si nécessaire.

a. Givonte Latimore is fed up ... the narrow-minded old lady.
b. Edgar Gonzalez feels different ... the man dressed as a gardener.
c. The old lady is suspicious ... young men with dreadlocks and baggy pants.
d. Rosa Chen must be proud ... her successful results at school.
e. The blonde girl is ashamed ... herself because she offended the young man.
f. The punk girl is really aware ... prejudices against people having eccentric hairstyles!
g. The old lady is scared ... him because of his physical appearance.

ON YOUR OWN!

Imagine you work for an advertising agency in the 60s. You defend your campaign based on prejudices between generations. Explain what the women and the three girls think of each other:

They wish they... | If only...

Help!

Women	Girls
traditional /trəˈdɪʃənl/ discreet conform ≠ rebel change	mini-skirt daring: *audacieux* fashionable = trendy provocative self-assured /selfəˈʃʊəd/

YOUR TASK

SCENARIO 1

You are a member of the UNICEF group in your school. You have decided to create a short video to fight prejudices. Work in groups.

video

► Step 1: **Watch the video *Don't be too quick to judge* by Maaz Khan and answer the following questions.**

a. Explain what the problem is.

b. What happens in the end? What are the characters' feelings?

c. What is the film director's message?

► Step 2: **Create a short video to fight prejudice and stereotypes, to make people aware appearances can be deceiving.**

a. Read the notes you took on this unit again (vocabulary, grammar, themes, etc.).

b. Prepare your scenario: setting *(décor)*, time, characters, situation, problem, characters' feelings, hopeful or hopeless conclusion, soundtrack if possible.

c. Write a short dialogue between the characters.

d. Shoot the scene then vote for the best one.

The jury (formed by the rest of the class) will vote for the best performance based on the following criteria:

The staging location • costumes • props *(accessoires)*	0 1 2 3 4 5
The actors • Their voice was clear and understandable. • The key words were stressed. • The pronunciation was correct.	0 1 2 3 4 5
The dialogue was original • yes • not really • not at all	0 1 2 3 4 5
Film techniques	0 1 2 3 4 5
Final mark	/20

SCENARIO 2

Write a short text to introduce the video you have posted. (about 100 to 150 words)

► **Use the following guidelines for help.**

- Sum up the video: setting *(décor)*, time, characters, situation, problem, characters' feelings.
- Say why the problem raised is important to you.
- Write a punchy text to attract viewers.

Compréhension écrite et expression écrite

WORKSHEET BAC N° 8

Answer the questions on the worksheet the teacher will give you.

DOCUMENT A

The first time I taught a writing class in graduate school, I was worried. Not about the teaching material, because I was well prepared and I was teaching what I enjoyed. Instead I was worried about what to wear. I wanted to be taken seriously.

I knew that because I was female, I would automatically have to prove my worth. And I was worried that if I looked too feminine, I would not be taken seriously. I really wanted to wear my shiny lip gloss and my girly skirt, but I decided not to. I wore a very serious, very manly, and very ugly suit. The sad truth of the matter is that when it comes to appearance, we start off with men as the standard, as the norm. Many of us think that the less feminine a woman appears, the more likely she is to be taken seriously. A man going to a business meeting doesn't wonder about being taken seriously based on what he is wearing—but a woman does.

I wish I had not worn that ugly suit that day. Had I then the confidence I have now to be myself,[1] my students would have benefited even more from my teaching. Because I would have been more comfortable and more fully and truly myself.

Chimamanda Ngozi Adichie, *We Should All Be Feminists*, 2014

1. *si, à l'époque, j'avais eu l'assurance que j'ai maintenant pour assumer ce que je suis*

DOCUMENT B

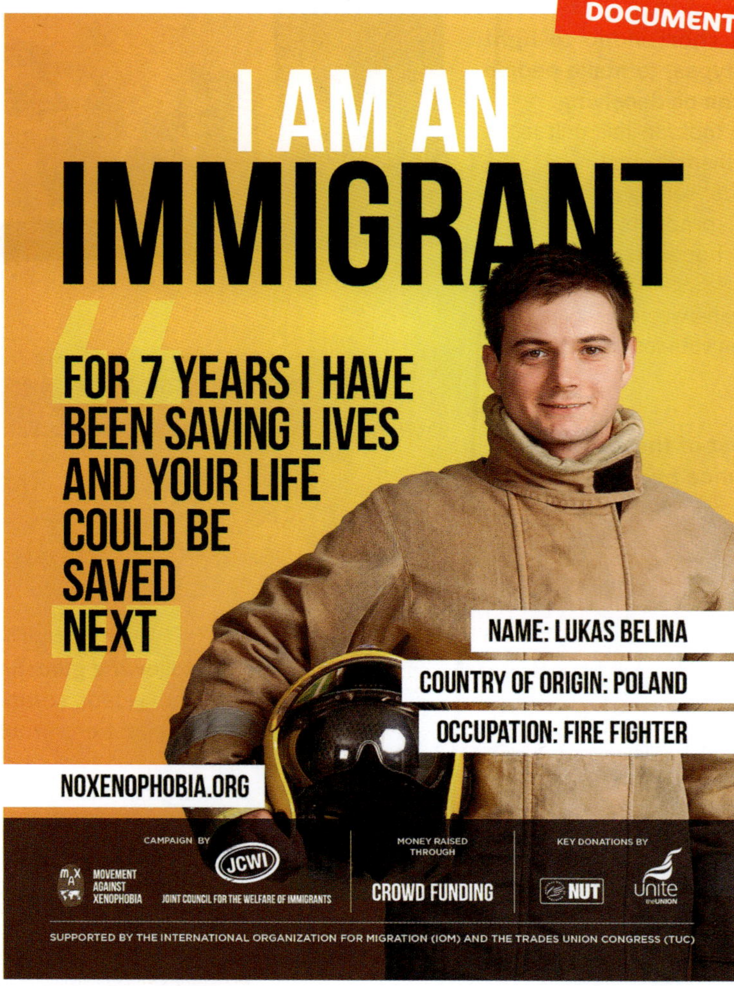

DOCUMENT C

× +

I was promised a promotion when I turned 18. I was waiting on this promotion from a buser—a person who buses tables,[1] washes dishes, serves food and stocks coolers[2]—to a server at a bar and grill for five months. On my 18th birthday I got a half-sleeve[3] and my boss immediately denied me the promotion he promised me even though some of my co-workers had much more visible tattoos and piercings.

I quit a month later. He didn't say directly that it was because of my tattoo, but the comments he made toward me made it clear he didn't like it. He asked me if I was crazy for getting it and why my parents would let me do this to myself. He also said it's very dark (I don't really know if he meant dark as in black or dark as in creepy) and that I'm better for in the kitchen rather then being a waitress.

■ "I missed out on a promotion", Emily, Wisconsin, USA, www.bbc.com

1. *qui débarrasse les tables* **2.** *qui gère les stocks de nourriture dans les réfrigérateurs* **3.** a tattoo that takes up half an arm

Compréhension de l'oral

CD 2 PISTE 15

video

A mother's fight

→ Écoutez l'enregistrement trois fois.

→ Prenez des notes puis faites en dix minutes le compte rendu de ce que vous avez compris en français.

→ Utilisez les expressions données p. 183.

USEFUL WORDS

- achondroplasia: dwarfism: *nanisme (insuffisance de croissance)*
- Strong and Mighty Max: a story book

Expression orale

THE IDEA OF PROGRESS { **Why is fighting prejudice a step towards progress?**

Comment parler de la notion ?

Ne rédigez pas votre présentation, contentez-vous de noter les idées-clés, les mots importants.

❶ Définissez les mots **préjugé** et **progrès**.

❷ Sélectionnez les documents qui vous permettent de répondre à la problématique.
Sur papier libre, classez-les dans la grille suivante :

Documents (titre / nature)	Idée(s) principale(s) (1 ou 2 phrases maximum)	Mots-clés pour rendre compte du document

❸ Pour dégager les idées essentielles contenues dans les documents, appuyez-vous sur les questions suivantes :

- Quels sont les préjugés, les stéréotypes ?
- Quels sont les problèmes rencontrés ?
- Comment ont réagi les divers personnages impliqués ?
- Quels sont les moyens utilisés pour dénoncer les préjugés ?
- Quelles sont les solutions possibles ?
- Quels sont les progrès notés ?

❹ Illustrez vos propos à l'aide d'exemples précis. Utilisez le vocabulaire donné p. 115 pour enrichir votre expression.

❺ N'oubliez pas une conclusion personnelle.

Unit 9

THE IDEA OF PROGRESS
Is gender inequality a thing of the past in developed countries?

Wind of Change for Women?

1 Tune In!

Angelina Jolie

Serena Williams

Hillary Clinton

1 Influential women

CD 2 PISTE 16

a. In pairs, share what you know about each of these women.
b. Listen to their biographies and complete your notes (key words only).
c. Use your notes to present them to the rest of the class.
d. Why are these women considered influential?

2 QUIZ

a. In groups, give as many answers as possible to the following questions. You have 15 seconds for each one.
- How many men/women presidents or prime ministers can you think of?
- Which films showing a man/woman as the main character come to your mind?
- How many male/female singers can you name?
- Which male/female football players do you know?

b. Draw your conclusions:
- Did you find more male or female names?
- What do your results say about the place of women in politics, sport and entertainment?

Help

CEO (Chief Executive Officer): *P.-D.G., Président.e Directeur.rice Général.e*
role model: *exemple à suivre*

ambitious
determined /dɪˈtɜːmɪnd/
successful
influential /ɪnflʊˈenʃəl/
powerful

succeed in V-ING ≠ fail to + BV
reach the top = make it (to the top)
get involved in: *s'engager dans*
stand for = represent
embody: *incarner*

YOUR FINAL TASK OR

- Write an article about gender equality. (p. 129)
- Design a poster and prepare an oral presentation to promote gender equality. (p. 129)

3 Reaching the top

a. Learn more about...

Sheryl SANDBERG
Born: 28 August 1969
Birthplace: Washington, D.C.
Education: economic studies at Harvard, graduation in 1991 – MBA at Harvard Business School in 1995
Current position:
- 2008-present: Chief Operating Officer of Facebook
- 2012: first female Facebook board member

Previous experience: the World Bank, the US Treasury, Google (2001-2008)

b. In the order of the text, find the equivalents of: *obtention d'un diplôme* • *école de commerce* • *Directrice Générale* • *membre du conseil d'administration* • *ministère des Finances*

c. Observe the picture opposite.
- What kind of document is it?
- Which word do you immediately notice?
- Find a verb expressing a feeling. Is it positive or negative?
- What does it reveal about other people's attitude towards Sandberg? Choose the correct answers: They are: envious • proud *(fiers)* • jealous • impressed.
- In your opinion, who is the headline addressed to: men • women • businessmen?

PREPARE YOUR TASK

d. You are the editor of *Time* magazine. Write a short introduction explaining why Sheryl Sandberg was chosen for the front cover.

4 Websearch

Mary Barra - General Motors

Ginni Rometty - IBM

Indra Nooyi - PepsiCo

In groups, go on the Internet and find information about one of the CEOs (Chief Executive Officers) above. Take notes only and get ready to give a one-minute presentation to the class.

Get ready for the Oral Exam
- **What do the women on this double page represent?**
- **Do you believe it was easy for them to make it to the top?**

2 Women's Battles: Past and Present

1 Get ready

a. Read the introduction below. Fill in each blank with one word from the following list on a seperate sheet of paper:

employers • pay discrimination • underpaid • strike • work • 1968

In ... , the Ford car factory in Dagenham, east London, was one of the largest private ... in the United Kingdom. 187 ... women led by Rita O'Grady, a machinist, decided to stop ... and go on ... in protest against ... .

CD 2 PISTE 17

b. Listen and check your answers.

2 Read and understand

In the passage, Rita and some of her co-workers are meeting Barbara Castle, the Secretary of State for Employment.

Barbara Castle: I've been following your dispute very closely. And I want to say how proud I am of the battle you've fought. I fully support the struggle[1] for equal pay. And you *will* have it... But in time. [...] Return to work, get back to your machines and then you have my word that I will push forward with your fight.
Rita: No!
Barbara Castle: Mrs O'Grady—
Rita: That ain't[2] good enough—We want somethin' now! Somethin' solid—
Barbara Castle: But...
Rita: You got the authority, you—We thought... seein' you, we'd—
Barbara Castle: In politics you sometimes have to play the long game...
Rita: We ain't[3] politicians! We're workin' women. And so are you!
Barbara Castle: Very well. What would it take...? To get you back. [...]
Rita: We'd need a guarantee that we're gonna get equal pay. And in the meantime, we need to move much closer to the male rate. Now. At Ford.
Barbara Castle: Seventy five per cent?
Rita: Ninety.

Made in Dagenham, directed by William Ivory, 2010

1. fight **2.** = isn't (incorrect English often used by working-class people) **3.** = aren't

a. Give the French equivalent of "Secretary of State for Employment" (introduction).
b. Use the context to guess the meaning of:
– dispute (l. 1): *dispute* • *député* • *conflit*
– I support (l. 3): *je supporte difficilement* • *je soutiens* • *je compte sur*
– male rate (l. 24): *taux de natalité pour les hommes* • *taux salarial des hommes* • *taux de chômage*
c. – What does "your dispute" (l. 1) refer to?
– "And you *will* have it... But in time." (l. 4-5) What does "it" refer to? Give a synonym of "in time".
d. What does Barbara Castle promise, on what condition?
e. Pick out three sentences showing Rita's answer.
f. What do the following numbers refer to? 75 • 90
g. What do Rita's answers to Mrs Castle show about her personality? Pick the correct adjectives. Is she: submissive: *soumise* • intimidated • determined /dɪ'tɜːmɪnd/ • shy: *timide* • straightforward = direct • strong-willed: *résolue* • independent • fearless?

3 A note to the Prime Minister

PREPARE YOUR TASK

After the workers left, Barbara Castle writes a note to the Prime Minister, Harold Wilson, to tell him what happened and what she thinks of Rita's arguments and her personality.

– See how to write a formal letter (→ p. 189).

– Give an account of the meeting (who? what? final decision, difficulties). Don't forget to mention Barbara Castle's reactions.

Help!

Barbara Castle	Rita	Results
supportive patient /peɪʃənt/ advise sb to do sth: *conseiller à qqn de faire qqch* negotiate /nɪ'gəʊʃieɪt/ at first... but then...	obey sb: *obéir à qqn* fight (fought, fought) discuss demand (changes): *exiger* stand strong/firm	wage equality: *égalité de salaires* agreement pay rise: *augmentation de salaire* compromise /kɒmprəmaɪz/ promise /prɒmɪs/

4 A call to action

Read what Patricia Arquette declared at the Hollywood Oscar ceremony in 2015.

a. Who does "we" refer to?

b. What does the actress denounce?

c. What do Patricia Arquette and Rita O'Grady have in common? What are their goals?

5 Watch a video

video

WORKSHEET 29

Fast facts about gender equality

Turn to your worksheet for help.

USEFUL EXPRESSIONS

• **OECD**: Organisation for Economic Co-operation and Development (an organisation of industrial countries that encourages trade and economic growth)

• **glass ceiling**: An unjust system acting like an invisible barrier that stops some people (like women) from having access to the most powerful jobs.

→ **Recap:** What do all the documents on this double page show about the situation of women today?

Get ready for the Oral Exam

How has the fight for equal pay evolved over the years?

3 The Influence of the Media

1 Read and understand

A "In our society [...] women are still being presented in the media as being there for decoration. Women are held up to[1] an impossible airbrushed[2] beauty ideal where how they look becomes more important than what they do, think or say. One gender is allowed to be fully clothed, look old and be overweight while the other isn't. The impact this has on girls and young women is sad and unfair. It's far more difficult to be brave change makers in the world, when the world repeatedly tells you that you're only here to look pretty! The media needs to be far more responsible and respectful in how it represents women."

■ Lucy-Anne Holmes, a female activist

1. *doivent être à la hauteur de* **2.** (here) artificial

a. **A** Observe the words highlighted in purple. How are they built? Match each word with its translation: *constamment* • *en surpoids* • *injuste* • *tout habillé*.

b. Pick out all the words related to appearances.

c. Who do the words in orange refer to?

d. Observe the word in blue. How is it built? Complete the following definition: it means people who... .

e. **B** Who speaks? What was the mother's message to her sons? Why?

B "My mom brought me up to be a feminist. She would always point out to my brother and me that our culture does often portray women like objects... She wanted me and my brother to be aware of it because we see these images on TV, in the movies and on magazines all the time. And if you don't stop and think about it, it just sort of seeps into your brain[1] and that becomes the way you perceive reality."

■ Joseph Gordon-Levitt, an American actor

1. *(ici) s'insinue dans votre cerveau*

➜ Recap

Use the words below to say what you have understood in both texts.

objects women judgement media conform pressure men ideal impact appearances

2 Am I ugly?

WORKSHEET 30

a. Go on the Internet and type: Ted • Meaghan Ramsay • Am I ugly.

b. Listen to the speech (from 4:18 to 5:23) and turn to your worksheet for help.

Get ready for the **Oral Exam**

To what extent do the media influence teenagers?

4 Because You're Worth It!

1 Assert yourself

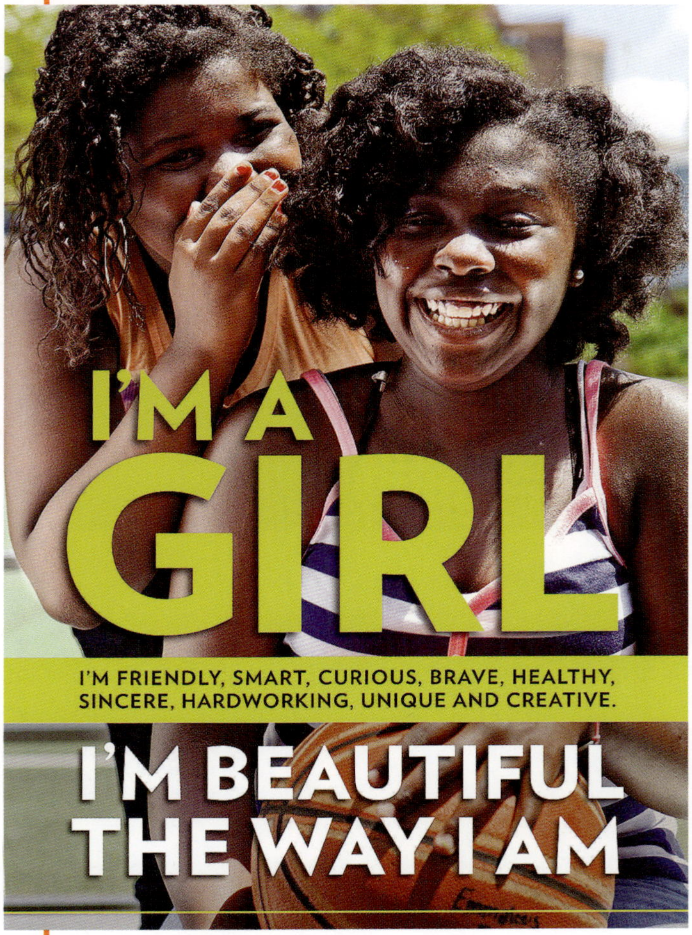

Help!

beauty ideal /aɪˈdɪəl/
self-esteem: *estime de soi*
prejudices: *préjugés*

self-confident: *sûr de soi*
proud of: *fier de*

put pressure on sb
conform to sth
boost sb's confidence
believe in sb's capacities

a. Describe the poster (who? age? attitude?).
b. Focus on what is written.
– Which words are similar to French words? Translate them.
– Observe these words:
friendly • healthy • hardworking.
How are they built? Translate them.
– Find a synonym for:
intelligent • courageous.
c. Conclude: what is the message in the poster? (Several possible answers.)
– Girls are pretty but are not intelligent.
– Girls have a lot of qualities and should feel self-confident.
– Girls need to make a lot of effort to be beautiful.
– Beauty comes from the inside, not from the way you look.

2 Watch a video

USEFUL WORD
4th grade = 9 or 10-year-old pupils

Teach your children well
a. Get ready. Classify the following activities in two columns:
activities usually connected with boys • activities usually connected with girls.

walk in the mud *(boue)* | wear nail varnish *(vernis à ongles)* | build a rocket | learn astronomy | use a drill *(perceuse)* | wear lipstick *(rouge à lèvres)*

b. Go to www.verizon.com/about/responsibility/girls-in-stem. Watch the advert "Inspire her mind".
At the beginning, find an adjective associated with "girl".
c. Pick out key words pronounced by the parents. Would you say they are: encouraging the girl to discover new things • stopping her from doing boys' activities?
d. Focus on the end of the video: What does the girl see? Where? What does she decide to do?

3 Be the judge!

PREPARE YOUR TASK

One of the two campaigns above will be released on Women's Day. You must choose the more effective one. Justify your choice.

Get ready for the Oral Exam

How can girls become more self-confident?

5 Video Corner How to Get a Raise?

1 Get ready

a. Observe the still opposite. What strikes you (character and clothes)?

b. Associate each word from list A with its French equivalent from list B.

List A earn money • work for free • get a raise • at the current pace

List B *obtenir une augmentation* • *travailler gratuitement* • *au rythme où vont les choses* • *gagner de l'argent*

c. Observe the expression: a gender-equal country. How is it built? How would you translate it? *Un pays où…*

d. What do you think the video is about?

2 Watch the video

a. First viewing: Pick out the name of a country and the figures *(nombres)* given. What do they refer to?

b. Second and third viewings:

Copy the mind map on a separate paper and organise your notes.

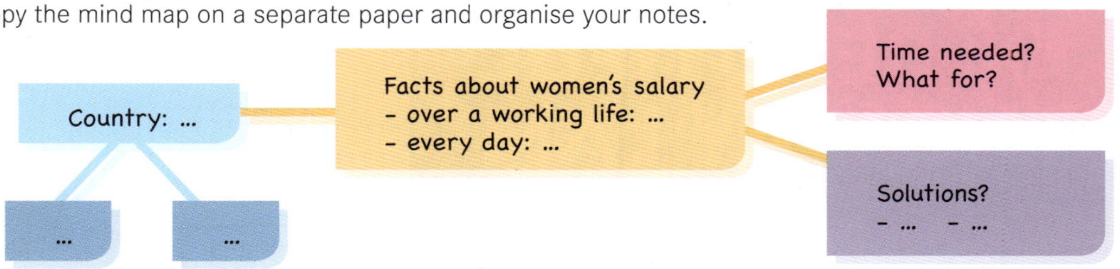

c. What are the goals of this campaign?

d. Which of the solutions given is the more effective? Why?

3 Go further

a. Go on the Internet and watch this video: #LeanInTogether: NBA & WNBA Stars Are In–Are You?

b. Complete the two definitions given for "lean in":

– "Support women... ."

– "... aim high *(viser haut)*."

c. What happens when men lean in? Pick out key words.

Help!

turn into: *(se) transformer en*

be on an equal footing: *être sur un pied d'égalité*

be discriminated against

protest/rebel against

denounce = condemn

make people aware of

4 Express yourself

PREPARE YOUR TASK

Imagine a tweet with one of these hashtags. Tell what you think about the campaigns. (140 characters)

#GenderEqualityNow

#BeAMan

#LeanInTogether

Get ready for the Oral Exam

To what extent can awareness campaigns have an impact on gender equality?

Play with words

MP3 N° 12 — CD 2 PISTE 18

A **Replace the words in bold letters with a word of similar meaning given below. Make the necessary changes.**

a. Today, women generally earn a lower **salary** than men. Many people consider it **unjust**.
b. Women in Dagenham **fought** for equal pay. Their **success** was remarkable.
c. It is important to **make** this situation **better** for the generations to come.
d. Many women would like to **reach a higher position** in a company but they often hit a glass ceiling.

WORK
wages/income: *salaire*
career
apply (for a job): *postuler*

SUCCESS
achievement: *réalisation*
opportunity
successful
succeed in V-ING
reach the top/make it to the top
climb the social ladder: *gravir l'échelle sociale*

PROTEST
struggle/fight for ≠ against
go on strike: *faire grève*
speak up against
denounce

OBSTACLES
prejudice: *préjugé*
glass ceiling: *plafond de verre*
be discriminated against
be denied access to: *se voir refuser l'accès à*

RESULTS
equal ≠ unequal
fair: *juste* ≠ unfair: *injuste*
dominant ≠ submissive
improve: *améliorer*
be on an equal footing: *être sur un pied d'égalité*

B **In the unit, find the adjectives corresponding to the following nouns.**

a. influence ➜ ... **b.** support ➜ ... **c.** determination ➜ ... **d.** success ➜ ... **e.** ambition ➜ ... **f.** independence ➜ ... **g.** inequality ➜ ... **h.** power ➜ ...

C **Dictation**
Listen to three sentences and write down what you have heard on a separate paper.

D **On a separate sheet of paper, complete the following paragraph with words from the list. Check your answers with the recording.**

opportunities • prejudices • aware • believe • equal • conform • self-confident • advise

This campaign makes people ... of the ... that exist between boys and girls at an early age. Parents should ... their children to play with the same toys, to give them equal ... , and encourage them not to ... to society's stereotypes. If young girls and boys are on an ... footing, girls will ... in their capacities and be more ... when they apply for a job.

image via Shutterstock

LANGUAGE AT WORK

« Apprendre à Apprendre »
Téléchargez la fiche n°9
www.editions-hatier.fr/langues-eleves

Corrigés p. 216-221

A Prétérit simple ou *present perfect* ?

(Précis grammatical 32 p. 206)

– On utilise le prétérit pour parler d'un fait passé non relié au présent.
– On utilise le *present perfect* (*have/has* + participe passé) pour parler du résultat dans le présent d'un événement passé ou d'un événement qui dure encore au moment présent.

1. a. Lisez les phrases suivantes. Les marqueurs de temps sont soulignés.
– Women (start) the fight for equality a long time ago.
– Many organisations (launch) campaigns for women's rights over the last few years.
– In the sixties, female workers in Dagenham (stop) work and (go) on strike.
– So far, equal pay between men and women (not become) a reality.

b. Choisissez la traduction appropriée pour chaque marqueur de temps :
dans les années soixante • jusqu'à présent • il y a longtemps • au cours des dernières années.

c. Réécrivez chaque phrase en utilisant le prétérit ou le *present perfect*.

2. Mettez le verbe entre parenthèses au prétérit simple ou au *present perfect*.
a. The situation of women (improve) over the years, but there is still a lot to do.
b. During the 1950s, the role of women (begin) to change: they (become) an important part of the workforce.
c. Hillary Clinton (deliver) a speech in 1995 in which she (defend) the cause of women.
d. In recent years, more and more men (join) the fight for gender equality.
e. Men (realise) they can help the cause of women by fighting against gender stereotypes.
f. In a UN speech Emma Watson (encourage) men to get involved.

B Équivalents anglais de « depuis » : *for, since* et le *present perfect*

(Précis grammatical 13 p. 198)

3. Mettez les verbes entre parenthèses à la forme qui convient. Complétez avec *for* ou *since*.
a. ... 1909, the USA (celebrate) Women's Day, that is to say ... more than a hundred years.
b. UN Women (organise) campaigns to promote gender equality ... a few years now.
c. In Great Britain, women (have) the right to vote ... 1918.
d. Women (fight) for their rights ... many years.
e. ... WWII, women's role (change).

C Prononciation de la terminaison *-ed*

4. Mettez le verbe entre parenthèses au prétérit simple.
In 1903, Emmeline Pankhurst (launch) a campaign because she (want) equal voting rights for women. She (refuse) to be treated differently. She (use) militant tactics to influence politicians. Suffragettes (demonstrate) even if the police (arrest) and (imprison) them. Emmeline (die) in 1928, shortly before women were given full voting rights.

▲ *Suffragette*, a film by Sarah Gavron (2015)

MP3 N° 13 — CD 2 PISTE 19

5. Prononcez les formes verbales ci-dessus et classez-les en trois colonnes selon la prononciation de leur suffixe *-ed*. Vérifiez à l'écoute.

/d/	/t/	/ɪd/

YOUR TASK

SCENARIO 1

As a journalist, you have been investigating gender equality and the condition of women in developed countries. Write an article based on your findings. (150-200 words)

▶ **Include some of the following points:**
- examples of successful women and how they reached their position;
- the obstacles women still face at work;
- the vision of women given in the media;
- the campaigns launched to promote gender equality;
- the role men have in the fight.

▶ **See method p. 187: *Écrire un article de journal*.**
- A catchy headline will make the readers want to read further.
- The subheading should sum up the main contents of your article in one or two sentences.

▶ **Don't forget to date and sign your article.**

▶ **Avoid basic mistakes → *Relire son devoir p. 7.***

SCENARIO 2

You have been asked to prepare a new campaign to promote gender equality. Design a poster and prepare an oral presentation for the selection committee.

▶ **Create your poster.**
- What do you want to show? Women who have succeeded? The obstacles women are still faced with?
- Don't forget a logo and a website name and address, which media you will use to promote your cause (Facebook page, Twitter).
- Include some eye-catching elements, which will attract people's attention (images, words in capital letters...).

▶ **Get ready for the presentation.**
- Give the reasons why you decided to launch a campaign (situation today, problems you want to denounce...).
- Explain why your campaign is effective.
- Suggest solutions for things to change for women at work and at home, to help women evolve...
- How do you plan to involve men?

▶ **Be prepared to answer the committee's questions.**

Tips
- Take notes only, don't read.
- Keep eye contact with your audience.
- Look and sound convincing.

Get ready for the Exam BAC

Compréhension écrite et expression écrite

Answer the questions on the worksheet the teacher will give you.

WORKSHEET BAC N° 9

DOCUMENT A

THE SUNDAY TIMES

Sunday 6 July 2014

Indra Nooyi, 58, is chief executive of PepsiCo – as in, you know, Pepsi. She has been a feature[1] of Forbes magazine's "most powerful women" list since 2006; this year she is ranked at No 13. Her pay package last year was £7.3m. [...]

She was "working late" when she got a call from the chairman[2] saying they were going to announce her appointment.[3] "I was overwhelmed, because look at my background and where I came from – to be president of an iconic American company and to be on the board of directors, I thought something special had happened to me," she said, not unreasonably. So rather than "stay and work until midnight, which I normally would have done" she decided to go home at 10pm and tell her family.

She found her mother waiting for her at the top of the stairs. "I said, 'Mom, I've got great news for you.' She said, 'Let the news wait. Can you go out and get some milk?' [...]

So like a dutiful[4] daughter I went out and got the milk."

When she came back with the milk she told her mother about her stellar promotion. Her mother's reply was as follows: "Let me explain something to you. You might be president of PepsiCo. You might be on the board of directors. But when you enter this house you're the wife, you're the daughter, you're the daughter-in-law, you're the mother. You're all of that. Nobody else can take that place. So leave that damned crown[5] in the garage, and don't bring it into the house."

1. (ici) a fait l'objet d'un article spécial 2. président de la société 3. (ici) nomination 4. obéissante 5. couronne

DOCUMENT B

"Can't believe our baby's going to be four," mused Ned, running his thick fingers through his thinning but still full head of mid-brown hair. "I don't want her to grow up, do you?"

She looked at Ned, his face filled with pleasure at the homeliness of the scene. He loved the world she had created within the walls of this stunning home. He was a good, hard-working, family-oriented man and she knew she should be grateful for that. How could she tell him that the life she led here in this beautiful home, with their three adorable children, was killing her? She'd tried to explain to him before how she felt but he didn't hear it–didn't *want* to hear it. Once she'd actually been offered a part-time job–working in a friend's coffee shop–and he managed to talk her out of it. But this time, she thought with uncertain resolve, she was going to stick to her guns.[1] [...]

"Come over here and sit down a minute," she said, untying her apron[2] and laying it on the work surface. She'd been through this conversation with Ned a hundred times in her head. It was now or never. [...]

"I was thinking of going back to work."

"Right," he said thoughtfully, rubbing his chin as though checking for bristles. Bridget held her breath until he said, "Do you think you'll have time what with running the house and all?"

"I'll have from nine to three every day, except Fridays," she said defensively. "It should be possible to fit in a part-time job."

"Finding something to fit in with those hours could be a problem," he said doubtfully, "especially round here."

Erin Kaye, *Closer to Home*, 2006

1. not to change one's opinion 2. *tablier*

DOCUMENT C

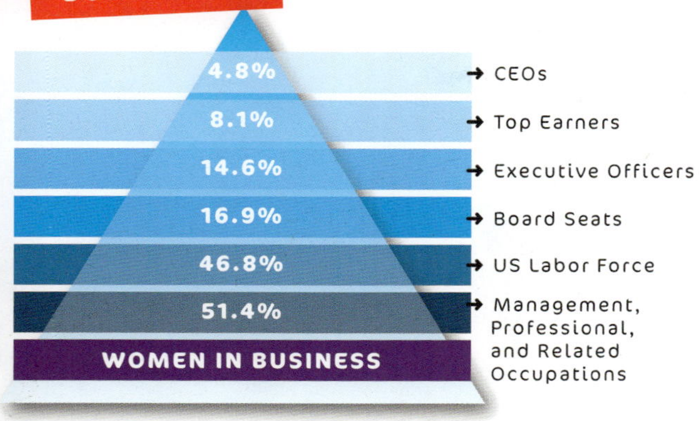

Compréhension de l'oral

CD 2 PISTE 20

A new doll

→ Écoutez l'enregistrement trois fois.
→ Prenez des notes puis faites en dix minutes le compte rendu de ce que vous avez compris en français.
→ Utilisez les expressions données p. 183.

Expression orale

THE IDEA OF PROGRESS { **Is gender inequality a thing of the past in developed countries?**

Comment parler de la notion ?

❶ Définissez le mot « progrès » et notamment le progrès social. Reportez-vous à la page 4.
❷ Recopiez le schéma ci-dessous sur papier libre et complétez-le avec les documents étudiés en classe.

Is gender inequality a thing of the past in developed countries?

Successful women
Do you believe it was easy for them to make it to the top?

CEO, glass ceiling, determined, influential, powerful, succeed in V-ING

Obstacles?

At work
How has the fight for equal pay evolved over the years?

wage equality, pay rise, demand changes, prevent sb from V-ING

In the media
To what extent do the media influence teenagers?

prejudice, put pressure on sb, conform to

Solutions?
How can girls become more self-confident?
To what extent can awareness campaigns have an impact on gender equality?

be on an equal footing with sb, support, make people aware of, improve

❸ Utilisez le vocabulaire donné p. 5 et dans l'unité pour enrichir votre expression.
❹ Ne rédigez pas votre présentation, notez les idées clés, les mots importants.
❺ Anticipez les questions qui pourront être posées (points à approfondir, exemples pour illustrer un argument, opinion personnelle...).
❻ N'oubliez pas une conclusion personnelle.

▲ *Game of Thrones*, season 3, a series by David Benioff et D.B. Weiss (2013)

Myths and Heroes

Unit 10

Dreamers

THE AMERICAN DREAM, A MYTH OR REALITY FOR IMMIGRANTS TO THE USA?

YOUR FINAL TASK

- Interview an illegal teenager. (p. 143)

OR

- Write emails about immigration plans. (p. 143)

p. 134-145

Unit 11

Sports Heroes

ARE SPORTS CHAMPIONS TRUE HEROES?

YOUR FINAL TASK

- Write an article about an athlete you admire or hate. (p. 155)

OR

- Defend your choice for a new mural in your school. (p. 155)

p. 146-157

Unit 12

Ambassadors of Conscience

ARE WHISTLEBLOWERS THE HEROES OF MODERN TIMES?

YOUR FINAL TASK

- Introduce an Ambassador of Conscience at an award ceremony. (p. 167)

OR

- Record the voice-over for a video. (p. 167)

p. 158-169

À la fin de chaque unité, vous trouverez un entraînement type bac complet (compréhension et production écrite, compréhension et expression orale).

Dreamers

1 Tune In!

1 Crossing the border

a. In groups, discuss where the scenes take place, who the people are and what they are doing. Justify your answers.
b. Compare with the other groups.

Help!

Obstacles	Immigrants	Border patrol
fence: *barrière*	climb: *grimper, escalader*	check: *vérifier*
border: *frontière*	emigrate to	forbid sb to do sth: *interdire à qqn de*
		prevent from V-ING: *empêcher de*

YOUR FINAL TASK OR
- Interview an undocumented teenager. (p. 143)
- Write emails about immigration plans. (p. 143)

2 Explain the situation

Why do people decide to emigrate from Mexico or Central America to the USA?
Classify the reasons into two groups: **push factors** or **pull factors**.

- poor medical facilities
- good education prospects
- 40% of the population unemployed
- well-paid jobs
- excellent hospitals
- higher life expectancy
- many jobs available for unskilled workers
- violence
- fear
- low-paid jobs

DEFINITION

Pull factor and push factor
The push factor is what drives people away from a place and the pull factor is what draws them to a new location.

3 The wall

CD 2 PISTE 21

A Train your ears

a. Copy the words on a sheet of paper and listen to the recording. Underline the ones you can hear: barrier • through • sensor • militia • desert • climb • virtual • entire.
b. Which French words do the words "barrier" and "virtual" remind you of?
c. Which of the words you have heard correspond to the following translations: *capteurs* • *à travers* • *désert?*

WORKSHEET 31

B QUIZ How much do you know about the Mexico-United States barrier?

Answer the questions on the worksheet your teacher will give you.

USEFUL WORDS
- trafficking cartel = drug criminal organisation
- smuggler: *passeur, trafiquant*

CD 2 PISTE 22

C Listen and check if you guessed correctly.

Then report to the class what you remember about the Mexico-United States barrier.

video

4 Watch a video

A trip to hell

a. Observe the word cloud opposite and imagine what the video is about.
b. Watch the video and pick out more information. Give an account of what you have understood.

immigrants Rio Grande smugglers abused border robbed trouble bodies lost undocumented patrol die trafficking

2 The Journey

1 Get ready

Match each word in list A with its equivalent in list B. Use a dictionary if necessary.

List A: rob • seek • search • chase

List B: look for • try to find • steal • run after

2 Observe and react

a. What are these young people doing? attacking the train • playing a foolish game • trying to leave their country • getting on the train without paying

b. Pick out the adjectives that you believe correspond best to the boys' attitude. Justify.

courageous | stupid | heroic | reckless *(téméraire)* | risky | careless

3 Now read the text to check your answer to question a.

Text A

Enrique wades chest-deep across a river. He is 5 feet tall, stoop-shouldered and cannot swim. The logo on his cap boasts hollowly, "No Fear."
The river, the Rio Suchiate, forms the border. Behind him is Guatemala. Ahead is Mexico, with its southernmost state of Chiapas. "Ahora nos enfrentamos a la bestia," immigrants say when they enter Chiapas. "Now we face the beast."
Painfully, Enrique, 17, has learned a lot about "the beast." In Chiapas, bandits will be out to rob him, police will try to shake him down, and street gangs might kill him. But he will take those risks, because he needs to find his mother.
When he was 5 years old, she left him in Honduras and joined hundreds of thousands of women from Central America and Mexico seeking work in the United States. An estimated 48,000 youngsters go north alone every year, many to search for their mothers.
This is Enrique's eighth attempt to reach El Norte.

▲ "The beast"

Text B

I began to understand just how dangerous this journey was for young migrants. They travel alone—cold, hungry, and helpless, with little or no money. Thousands make their way through Mexico, clinging to the sides and tops of freight trains[1]. They are chased and hunted like animals. Gangsters control the train tops, bandits rule the tracks, and the Mexican police who patrol the train stations rape and rob. Most migrant children are attacked at one point, sometimes several times along the way. Some are killed.

■ Sonia Nazario, *Enrique's Journey*, 2007

1. *trains de marchandises*

4 Read for details

Text A

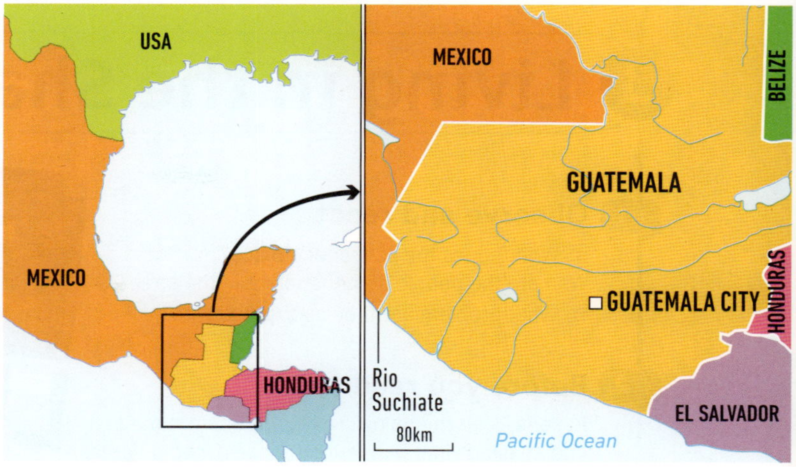

a. Find information about the main character: name, age, physical description.
b. Where is the main character? Locate the place on the map. Which is the country of origin and the final destination?
c. Use photo 2 p. 136 and the map to explain what the beast is.
d. List the dangers emigrants face when they are on the beast.
e. What does "48,000" (l. 10) correspond to?
f. Why did the boy want to leave his native country?

Text B

a. Find in the text information illustrating photo 2 on p. 136.
b. Choose the correct statement(s) and justify.
The police help the immigrants. • The police are criminals. • The police kill them.
c. List the dangers faced by migrants.
d. What do you learn about the journey?
e. Look at the following words carefully. Which ones can apply to Enrique?

daring | courageous | determined | selfless | fearless
generous | brave | strong | adventurous | invulnerable | clever

5 Watch a video

video

WORKSHEET 32

PREPARE YOUR TASK

Nelson Omar's journey

a. Watch the video. What do you learn about Nelson Omar and his journey?
Fill in the worksheet your teacher will give you.
b. What are the common points and differences between Enrique and Omar?
c. With the help of the text and the video, write a short article about children migrating illegally from Central America to the USA. (100 words

Help!

Dangers
robber: *voleur*
smuggler: *passeur / trafiquant*
thief (pl: thieves): *voleur*
steal (stole, stolen): *voler, dérober*

Personality
brave = courageous
daring: *audacieux*
fearless: *intrépide*
selfish: *égoïste*
wilful: *volontaire*

Get ready for the Oral Exam

Can Enrique and Omar be called heroes?

3 Living in the Shadows?

1 Observe and react

a. Where does the scene take place?
Who are the people demonstrating in the street?
b. What problem are they confronted with?

2 Before you read

In pairs, read the following key words from the text and imagine what happened to Jose Antonio Vargas. Then compare your stories to the real story.

permit
citizenship proof driver's
undocumented fake card
immigrant grandparent
green US residency
purchased journalist

Tip

Before you start try to link the words together, for example "green card".

3 Read and understand

One day when I was 16, I rode my bike to the nearby D.M.V.[1] office to get my driver's permit. Some of my friends already had their licenses, so I figured it was time. But when I handed the clerk[2] my green card as proof of U.S. residency, she flipped it around, examining it. "This is fake," she whispered. "Don't come back here again."
Confused and scared, I pedaled home and confronted Lolo. I remember him sitting in the garage, cutting coupons. I dropped my bike and ran over to him, showing him the green card. "*Peke ba ito?*" I asked in Tagalog.[3] ("Is this fake?") My grandparents were naturalized American citizens – he worked as a security guard, she as a food server – and they had begun supporting my mother and me financially when I was 3, after my father's wandering eye and inability to properly provide for us led to my parents' separation. Lolo was a proud man, and I saw the shame on his face as he told me he purchased[4] the card, along with other fake documents, for me. "Don't show it to other people," he warned.
I decided then that I could never give anyone reason to doubt I was an American. I convinced myself that if I worked enough, if I achieved enough, I would be rewarded with citizenship. I felt I could earn it.
I've tried. Over the past 14 years, I've graduated from high school and college and built a career as a journalist, interviewing some of the most famous people in the country. On the surface, I've created a good life. I've lived the American dream.
But I am still an undocumented immigrant.

Jose Antonio Vargas, *The New York Times*, June 2011

1. Division of Motor Vehicles **2.** *employée*
3. principal language of the Philippines **4.** bought

WORKSHEET 33

Read the text and fill in the worksheet.

→ Recap

- What did the narrator find out one day? How did he react?
- What decision did he make?

Culture Tip

The American Dream is the opportunity for all citizens to achieve their goals and become rich and famous if they work hard enough.

PREPARE YOUR TASK

4 Role play

The narrator is talking to a friend and explains why he thinks he should be awarded American citizenship.

CD 2 PISTE 23

5 Testimony

Maricela Aguilar, an undocumented college student.

a. Use words from the list below to say what you can see in the picture.

school
proud
high
successful
diploma
Hispanic
Latino
graduation
university
college
succeed
success

b. Before you listen, read the title of the recording at the top and the following words. In pairs, decide which ones you are likely to hear in the audio:

Mexico • crossed illegally • came by car • graduated top 5 percent • didn't do well at school • degree • waitress • unemployment • work hard • easy life • paid cash • horrible • fear • deported • great experience • delighted • American dream

c. Now listen and check.

d. Listen again and try to get Maricela's story: who she is (date and place of birth) • education: first diploma, achievements at school • jobs she can have • main obstacle in her life and consequences.

➜ **Recap** what you have understood.

Help!

Incident

confident: *confiant*
amazed at/by = astonished at/by: *étonné par*

Narrator

disappointed with

deport sb: *expulser qqn*
integrate into = fit into

Lolo

tell lies ≠ tell the truth
hide the truth from sb: *cacher la vérité à qqn*
catch, caught, caught

Get ready for the Oral Exam

- What are the common points and differences between Jose Vargas and Maricela?
- Has the American Dream come true for them?

4 Video Corner — Between two Countries

1 Get ready

Look at the photo above.
- Where does the scene take place?
- What are the children doing?

USEFUL WORDS
• El Paso • Ciudad Juàrez • visa • register: *(ici) s'enregistrer*

2 Watch and understand

a. Watch the report once and write down as many elements as possible on a sheet of paper:

Groups of people involved • Numbers • Countries • Other elements

b. Watch again, organise your notes and give an account of what you have understood.

Groups of people the report is about:

- **First group: ...** How many? Activities? Time of day?
- **Second group: ...** How many? Activities?
- **Third group: ...** How many? Activities? Legal status? Consequence?
  - **New rules:** What?

c. Write a short newspaper article.
- Recap what you have understood in the report.
- Use this still to illustrate your article and write a caption.
- What is the impact of immigration laws on immigrants?

Play with words

MP3 n° 14 · CD 2 PISTE 24

A

1. Replace the words in bold type with synonyms from the list.

a. They go to the USA to have a **better salary**.
b. After their journey they are **extremely tired** because it is very **dangerous**.
c. They just want to **realise** their dream.
d. Many companies are ready to employ **illegal** immigrants.

2. Complete with words from the list.

a. He works in the USA without a green card, he is … .
b. They go to the USA in an … to … poverty.
c. They pay … a lot of money to cross the … .
d. The border patrol try to … them … crossing the … .
e. Some of them … of … when they cross the desert.

WORD LIST

Nouns
attempt (to): *tentative*
border: *frontière*
journey: *voyage*
smuggler: *passeur*
wages: *salaire*
hardship: *difficulté*

Adjectives
desperate: *désespéré*
exhausted: *épuisé*
risky: *risqué*
undocumented: *sans papiers*

Verbs
die of thirst: *mourir de soif*
escape: *fuir, s'échapper*
fulfil one's dream
prevent from V-ING: *empêcher de*
cross the desert: *traverser le désert*

B

Match each word in List A with its opposite in List B. Use a dictionary if necessary.

List A: hopeful • optimistic • manage to • succeed • wealth • make it • skilled

List B: fail • pessimistic • poverty • hopeless • unskilled

C

Traduisez les mots soulignés en utilisant la liste suivante :
améliorer • atteindre ses buts • conditions de vie • gravir l'échelle sociale • niveau de vie • réaliser ses rêves • recommencer à zéro

a. Most immigrants have to <u>start from scratch</u> because they left everything behind.
b. They want to have a better life and <u>climb the social ladder</u>.
c. They are ready to work very hard to <u>achieve</u> their <u>goals</u> and fulfil their dreams.
d. They dream of having a higher <u>standard of living</u> and <u>improving</u> their <u>living conditions</u>.

D

Copy the following paragraph and complete it with words from the unit. Check your answers with the recording.

The two immigrants have reached the **1**. The scene takes place at night, so they must be **2**. They are **3** from entering the US and they must be very **4**. They **5** of a better life, a higher **6** **7** **8**. They want to **9** their **10** **11**. After a long **12** they expect to find a **13** job and **14**. They thought they would **15** and escape **16**. Will they **17** their goals or **18** ?

LANGUAGE AT WORK

« Apprendre à Apprendre »
Téléchargez la fiche n°10
www.editions-hatier.fr/langues-eleves

Corrigés p. 216-221

A L'expression du but et de la cause

(Précis Grammatical 6 p. 195)

1. Associez chaque question à sa ou ses réponse(s).

a. Why does Alejandro want his son to come to the US?
b. What do Mexicans migrate for?
c. Why did they go to the USA?

1. Because they dreamt of a better life.
2. Because he knows he'll get a better education.
3. So as to get away from poverty.
4. In order to get a job.

2. Rédigez des énoncés dans lesquels vous exprimerez le but. Faites les ajustements nécessaires.

a. Mexicans • go • the USA • run away from • poverty in their country
b. Hondurans • flee • escape • gangs in their country
c. Mexicans • try to cross the border • enjoy • a better standard of living
d. They are ready to do everything • not • be killed • in their country
e. Immigrants • give smugglers money • take • across the desert

B Les mots interrogatifs

(Précis grammatical 22 p. 202)

3. Trouvez les questions qui ont provoqué ces réponses.

...? Lourdes lived Tegucigalpa, in Honduras.
...? In a factory.
...? She is 24.
...? Because she couldn't afford food for her family.
...? She will stay in the United States.
...? To make money and send it home.
...? She will be gone for one year.
...? She will try to bring her children with her.

ON YOUR OWN!

The cartoonist is interviewed and explains his goals when he/she drew this portrait of Uncle Sam. He/She describes the cartoon for the listeners and explains his/her intentions. Record a two-minute programme.

Help!

Uncle Sam	People
bent over: *plié* weak: *faible*	manual job odd jobs: *petits boulots*
become aware of = realize	take care of sewing /səʊiŋ/: *coudre* shine (shoes): *cirer*

Culture Tip

Uncle Sam is the personification of the US government.

YOUR TASK

SCENARIO 1

A journalist for NPR interviews an undocumented teenage immigrant he/she has met in a detention center.

You will be either the teenager or the journalist. Prepare your dialogue.

▶ Include questions and answers about:
- the teenager's identity: full name, age, country of origin;
- route taken, countries crossed, means of transportation, people who helped him/her, smugglers, incidents/difficulties;
- number of months;
- travel companions;
- arrival in the United States: where was the child caught? Time of day?
- hopes and dreams, plans for the future.

▶ Use the preterit and the future tense (will + BV).

▶ Use link words: first • then • after a while • a few minutes/months later • finally • before • after • as soon as • when • until.

▶ Mind the word order in questions *(→ précis grammatical 22 p. 202).*

Tips

- Don't read. Talk. Use notes only.
- Make eye contact with the person you are speaking to.
- Speak loud and clear.
- If you hesitate, use gap fillers *(→ p. 178).*

You can play the interview in front of the class or film the interview (1:30 or 2 minutes).

SCENARIO 2

A teenager wants to migrate to the US and manages to exchange emails with his cousin who has lived in the US since he was two. They talk about his plans.

▶ Include the following points:
- the teenager's plans: possible route, countries crossed, means of transportation, travel companions;
- hopes and dreams of a new life, plans for the future;
- cousin's reactions, questions and fears;
- cousin's warnings (difficulties, dangers);
- the teenager's final decision.

Get ready for the Exam BAC

Compréhension écrite et expression écrite

WORKSHEET BAC N° 10

Answer the questions on the worksheet the teacher will give you.

DOCUMENT A

The eighteen wetbacks[1] were led to a miserable truck[2], which had bounced over these roads many times, but before they were allowed to climb in, a man named Hanson growled: "Fifteen bucks, and I put you back on a back road to Fort Stockton." He stood in the shaded glare of the headlights, verifying the payments, and when all were accounted for, he piled the Mexicans and started north, but as he drove, a cohort[3] rode atop the cab of the truck, keeping a shotgun aimed at the passengers.

"Don't no one try to jump off," he warned. "We don't want to show La Migra[4] how we move about." [...]

At four in the morning, when they were far from the river, the driver, seeing a chance to earn a lot of money with no responsibility, made the engine cough and then conk out.[5] "Damnit," he cried, "we've got to fix this," and he ordered the Mexicans to leave the truck and stand well back while he worked in it. To their delight, the engine began to sputter, caught, and then purred nicely. [But] to their horror, the two Anglos revved[6] the motor and took off across the desert, leaving the wetbacks stranded, with no guide, no food and, worst of all, no water.

It was a trip into hell. At ten in the morning of the second day when the sun was blazing high, the first Mexican died, a man in his forties whose swollen tongue filled his mouth.

An hour later, six others were dead, but the two Guzmans still survived. "Manuela," Candido whispered, "we must look for plants, anything".

■ James A. Michener, *Texas*, 1985

1. (slang) Mexican illegal immigrants **2.** *camion* **3.** *acolyte*
4. the US Border Patrol **5.** *tomber en panne* **6.** *(ici) ont accéléré*

DOCUMENT B

theguardian

For the children of undocumented Mexican migrants in the United States, life demands secrecy. They learn to navigate between the two cultures while hiding their illegal status – all the while praying for immigration reform. Their Mexican memories – if they remember at all – are replaced by American dreams. After a few years, they often feel, look and sound so American, they can forget that, in the eyes of the law, they are aliens.

But they are, and they can be arrested at any moment. At least 500,000 young adults who grew up in the US have been deported or have decided to return to Mexico in the past decade. For many it is akin to[1] arriving in a foreign country for the second time, but this time they lack a child's ability to acclimatise. For years, little was known about what happened to these youngsters, but a picture is now emerging of a well-educated, bilingual, bicultural group whose traumas and talents are being ignored.

■ www.theguardian.com, May 17, 2015

1. similar to

DOCUMENT C

I wish my teacher knew how much I miss my DaD because he got deported to Mexico when I was 3 years old and I haven't seen him in 6 years.

■ www.dailymail.co.uk, an elementary school pupil from Colorado

Compréhension de l'oral

CD 2 PISTE 25

An extract from Obama's speech to the nation (2014)

→ Écoutez l'enregistrement trois fois.
→ Prenez des notes puis faites en dix minutes le compte rendu de ce que vous avez compris en français.
→ Utilisez les expressions données p. 183.

USEFUL WORDS

- Technology magnet school: *IUT du secteur*
- Astrid Silva

Expression orale

MYTHS AND HEROES — The American Dream, a myth or reality for immigrants to the USA?

Comment parler de la notion ?

1. Quel sens du mot « mythe » allez-vous retenir ? Définissez ensuite le rêve américain.
2. Sélectionnez les documents qui vous permettent de répondre à cette question. Sur papier libre, classez-les dans la grille suivante :

Documents (titre / nature)	Idée(s) principale(s) (1 ou 2 phrases maximum)	Mots-clés pour rendre compte du document

3. Pour dégager les idées essentielles contenues dans les documents, appuyez-vous sur les questions suivantes : Quel était le rêve ? Que s'est-il passé ? Quels ont été les succès ? Les limites et les obstacles ?
4. Illustrez vos propos à l'aide d'exemples précis. Utilisez le vocabulaire donné dans l'unité et p. 141 pour enrichir votre expression.
5. Vous pourrez conclure en vous appuyant sur un film, un reportage ou vos connaissances personnelles.
6. Préparez-vous à prendre la parole à partir de notes : ne rédigez pas votre présentation, contentez-vous de noter les idées clés, les mots importants.

Unit 11

MYTHS AND HEROES
Are sports champions true heroes?

Sports Heroes

1 Tune In!

1 Who's this?

a. Work in groups. Can you name the athlete painted on this mural? How much do you know about him and his performances?
b. What strikes you about this mural? What is the athlete compared to?

Go on the Internet and find more about this athlete: www.tinyurl.com/pxwovsd

Help!

Achievements	Reactions	Opinion
gold-medal winner record holder impressive achieve sth break a record surpass oneself	proud of identify with look up to = admire idealise worship: *vénérer*	hero(es) /hɪərəʊ/ ≠ villain /vɪlən/ icon /aɪkɒn/ role model I believe/I reckon/I think I agree ≠ I don't agree

OR
Write an article about an athlete you admire or hate. (p. 155)
Defend your choice for a new mural in your school. (p. 155)

2 Hall of fame

Group work

a. Select a picture of a world sports champion you admire. What has he/she achieved?
b. Present him/her to the class and say why he/she is remarkable.

3 What is a sporting hero made of?

a. Read the following quotes and find the English equivalents of:
force • *atteindre* • *insurmontable* • *malgré.*

"A hero is an ordinary individual who finds the strength to persevere and endure in spite of overwhelming obstacles."
Christopher Reeve, actor, film director and activist

"The hero shows us what we ought to be,[1] and we make him a hero because we wish to be what he is."
Professor Richard C. Crepeau, *Sport, Heroes and Myth* (1981)

1. *devrions être*

"You don't have to be a fantastic hero to do certain things – to compete. You can be just an ordinary chap,[1] sufficiently motivated to reach challenging goals."
Sir Edmund Hillary, mountaineer and explorer

1. *gars, bonhomme*

b. Use the word cloud to say which qualities characterise a hero in each quote.
c. Do any of the quotes apply to the champion(s) you chose in question **2**?

4 myhero.com

PREPARE YOUR TASK

Post an article on the site about your favourite sports hero. What are his/her achievements and which qualities do you admire most in him/her? (100 words)

Help!

Sports	Athletes	Actions
the Olympics	sportsperson (sportsman/sportswoman)	compete
athletics: *athlétisme*	amateur/professional athlete /æθli:t/	defeat an opponent = beat: *vaincre un adversaire*
field events (jumping, throwing)	champion	perform well
track events (races)	competitor	score a goal
world cup	title holder: *détenteur d'un titre*	challenge
tournament: *tournoi*		train hard

Get ready for the Oral Exam

- **What is expected from an athlete for him/her to be called a hero?**
- **Which qualities are necessary?**

2 Overcoming Obstacles

1 Wonder Woman

In groups, react to the two photos.

a. Which questions come to your mind?

b. What does the phrase "Wonder Woman" make you think of?

c. Share with the class.

2 Aimee Mullins

a. Read the article and check your answer(s) to question **1. b**.

I grew up in America, the child of an immigrant father from Ireland. [...] And the idea of getting an education and then using that education was paramount[1] in our family. [...] Thanks to an academic scholarship[2] from the Department of Defense, I got to attend Georgetown University, which I wouldn't have been able to afford even with student loans.[3] While at college, my sports career took off, and I was sprinting at the Division 1 level (the first college athlete amputee to compete against non-amputees) and flying around the world, representing our country in sporting and speaking events. Then because of the revolutionary carbon-fiber prosthetic legs I wore in athletic competitions, I was being invited to speak at design conferences. I was asked to walk the runways[4] with supermodels, doing fashion shoots with the best photographers in the world. All of that was because I was open to adventure and followed my curiosity into everything that challenged my comfort zone. [...]
I've turned down film, television and theater roles with people I hugely admire, because they weren't coming to me as an actor, but as a novelty. [...] It's taken a little while for casting directors to stop seeing me as just someone who wears prosthetic legs. I love that I now get to play characters. That's why I was drawn to acting in the first place: To not be Aimee Mullins. To stretch and push and pull myself to the farthest reaches of[5] my emotional, intellectual and physical capacity.

■ www.yahoo.com, April 14, 2015

1. extremely important **2.** *bourse* **3.** *prêt* **4.** *défiler* **5.** *jusqu'à la limite de*

WORKSHEET 34

b. Turn to your worksheet for help.

c. Prepare a two-minute podcast entitled "Aimee Mullins: An inspirational woman". Include the following points:

- Her social background
- Her careers and achievements
- Her personality
- Give your point of view

3 Video Corner

America Strong

1 Get ready

a. Look at the photo and imagine what the video is about.
b. Read the following words.

athletics · pole vault · run a lane · leap · track · sight
steps · high school · jump over · struggle · obstacle
guide dog · high jump · race

c. In the list above, find the English equivalents of:
bondir • *piste* • *saut à la perche* • *saut en hauteur* • *lutter* • *pas*
d. Which of these words and what kind of information do you expect to hear in the video?

2 Charlotte Brown

a. Watch the video once. Is it: a talk show • a film trailer • a news bulletin • a commercial • a report?
b. How many speakers are there? Who are they?

3 Watch the video again.

Part 1: from the beginning to 00:58

a. Pick out numbers and as many key words as you can.
b. Organise your notes.

- Her age
- When she was a baby
- Her disability
- Her decision

Part 2: from 0:59 to 1:29

USEFUL WORDS

- blur: *se brouiller* • a sighted ≠ blind person
- turf: *gazon (de stade)* • a straw: *une paille*

c. What words did you hear?
light • lane • blurry: *flou* • straight • count • calm • steps
d. Explain what method she uses.

Part 3: from 1:30 to the end

USEFUL WORD

11 feet, 6 inches = 3.5 meters

e. List her supporters and pick out as many key words as you can.
f. Why is she admired and considered a role model?

4 An amazing teen

PREPARE YOUR TASK

Write a short article about Charlotte Brown for a sports magazine. (150 words) (→ *Écrire un article de presse,* p. 187)

Get ready for the Oral Exam

To what extent do disabled athletes deserve to be called heroes?

Help!

Disability

amputee
disability = handicap
prosthetic legs = artificial legs

disabled ≠ able-bodied
blind: *aveugle*
visually impaired: *déficient visuel*

Surpassing oneself

determined
iron-willed: *qui a une volonté de fer*

accomplish
manage to = succeed in + V-ING
deserve to (win): *mériter de*
break a record

Enthusiasm

awe-inspiring: *qui inspire le respect et l'admiration*
incredible = unbelievable
stunning: *stupéfiant*

embody: *incarner*
command admiration: *forcer l'admiration*

4 From Champion to Spokesperson

1 Silent gesture

a. In groups, look at the book cover:
- What is the author's name? What sort of book is it?
- What are the two athletes doing? What is unusual about their attitude?

b. Which questions come to your mind when you see this cover?

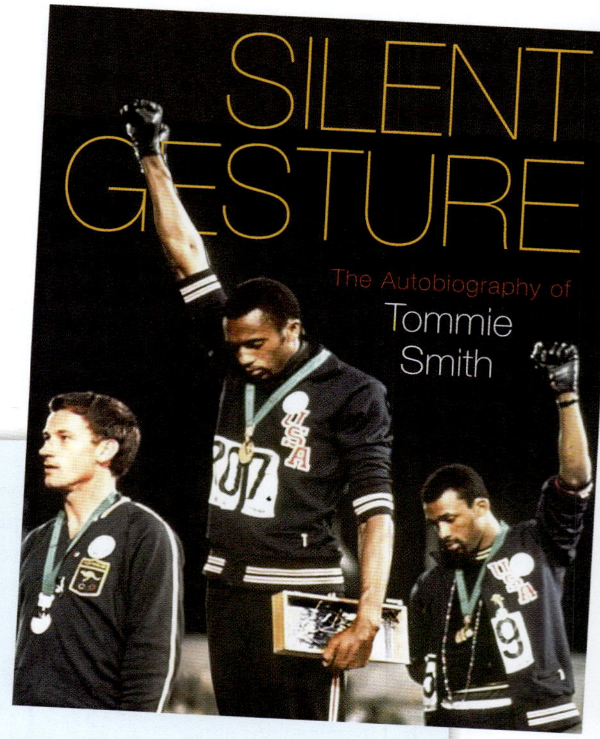

2 A victory stand

In the text, find the information corresponding to each box. Then sum up briefly what happened and why.

a. When the story took place

b. Places mentioned
Place where the main action took place

c. The narrator's clothes and attitude

d. The audience: number and attitude

e. The narrator's achievements

f. Words related to danger

g. The narrator's motivations

Thirty-five years earlier, I had thought I would never see the city of San Jose, the campus of San Jose State College, my home on the west edge of campus, or my wife and son ever again. On the night of October 16, 1968, I had stood on a platform on the infield[1] of the Olympic Stadium in Mexico City, with a gold medal around my neck, black socks on my feet, and a glove on the right fist I had thrust[2] in the air. My head was bowed,[3] and inside that bowed head, I prayed—prayed that the next sound I would hear, in the middle of the Star-Spangled Banner,[4] would not be a gunshot, and prayed that the next thing I felt would not be the darkness of sudden death. I knew there were people, a lot of people, who wanted to kill me for what I was doing. It would take only one of them to put a bullet through me, from somewhere in the crowd[5] of some 100,000, to end my life because I had dared to make my presence—as a black man, as a representative of oppressed people all over America, as a spokesman for the ambitious goals of the Olympic Project for Human Rights—known to the world.
That was my victory stand. Not only because I had won the gold medal in the 200-meter final a half hour earlier, in world-record time. This was my platform,[6] the one I had earned by years of training my body and my mind for the ultimate achievement. The athletic achievement paved a road toward my quest for a social victory, where everyone would be listening to and watching my statement about the conditions in which my people and I were living in the greatest country in the world. I never said a word as the national anthem was playing. My silent gesture was designed to speak volumes. [...] This victory stand represented more than just a place to accept a medal.

Tommie Smith, *Silent Gesture*, 2008

1. *terre-plein central* **2.** *brandi* **3.** /baʊd/ *baissée* **4.** the national anthem (*hymne*) **5.** *foule* **6.** *tribune*

CD 3
PISTE 1
WORKSHEET 35
PREPARE YOUR TASK

3 The price to pay

a. Listen to a reporter telling what happened to the two athletes after the Olympic Games. Turn to your worksheet for help.

b. Prepare a two-minute radio report about the event and its consequences for Black History Month.

4 Little Big Man

a. Get ready: observe the film poster. Pick out the key elements and try to guess as much as you can about the film hero.

b. Haile Gebrselassie /ˈhaɪli gebrɪsəˈlæsi/
Skim through *(parcourez rapidement)* the following sites to find the answers to the questions below.

www.tinyurl.com/p3oyut9
www.tinyurl.com/net6vd5
www.tinyurl.com/o6e2bxw

➜ Who is the man?

- Date of birth • country of origin • difficulty he had to face as a child and consequence(s) this had.
- How and when did his career begin?
- In the following list, choose sports that he specialised in: middle-distance • long-distance • relays • hurdles *(haies)* • road running (= marathon) • cross country running.

➜ His achievements

- How many Olympic gold medals has he won?
- How many world champion titles does he hold?
- When did he switch to road running?
- How many world records has he set?

➜ Beyond sports

- Where does he invest his money? What for?
- How many people does he employ?

Go to the following site: www.tinyurl.com/qcmwjaw
What other causes has Haile Gebrselassie been involved in?

PREPARE YOUR TASK

c. Write a comment on the champion's fan club website. Explain why you admire him and think he deserves to be called a hero. (100 words)

Help!

Qualities

committed: *engagé*
courageous, bold: *audacieux*
determined /dɪˈtɜːmɪnd/
persevering /pɜːsɪˈvɪərɪŋ/

Fighting for a cause

involvement: *implication*

dedicated: *qui se donne à fond*
involved in: *impliqué dans*

defend a fair cause = fight for what is right
protest against

Get ready for the Oral Exam

Can athletes' involvement outside their sport transform the idea we have of them?

5 Fallen Champions

1 Lance

a. Look at the cartoon.
Who is represented? What do you know about him?
Choose the correct statement(s):
- He lied about his health. • He cheated.
- He won the Tour de France seven times.
- He took performance-enhancing drugs.
- He stole a medal. • He forced athletes in his team to take performance-enhancing drugs.

b. What does the cartoonist want to denounce?
– Look at the champion's face and attitude and choose the adjectives that correspond best:

smug/arrogant | scared | triumphant | self-satisfied | ashamed: *honteux* | careless: *insouciant* | insecure | self-confident

– Complete the following sentences:

The bike spokes *(rayons)* are represented as ... , so the cartoonist wants to denounce the use of ... to help ... athletes' performances. The champion looks ... because he knows that thanks to ... , he is certain to ... .

2 *The Program*

a. Watch the trailer of Steven Frear's film (2015) without the sound.

The Program →
- Places, moments and objects shown on screen
- People's reactions (fans, athletes in his team, coach and friends)
- Lance Armstrong's actions and attitude

b. From what you have seen, is the champion guilty of doping? Why?
c. Watch the video with the sound and pick out key words.
– Organise your notes into two parts:
The champion (Lance Armstrong's ambition and personality, a disease he recovered from, what his medals brought him)
The liar *(menteur)*
– Note down sentences Lance Armstrong repeats several times.
– Explain the catchphrase of the film: "Winning was in his blood."
d. The person in charge of writing the synopsis of the film for the DVD jacket has made six mistakes. Correct them. Turn to your worksheet.
e. Give your opinion.
– Does this trailer make you feel like watching the film? Explain.
– Is Lance Armstrong a fallen hero? Why? Why not?

WORKSHEET 36
PREPARE YOUR TASK

Help!

Doping
performance-enhancing drugs
sample: *échantillon*
syringe: *seringue*
drug test = doping test

avoid detection
jeopardise: *mettre en danger*
test positive for drugs/doping

Reactions
trustworthy = honest
outrageous: *scandaleux*
shameful: *honteux*
dishonest

deceive sb: *tromper qqn*
pretend to V: *faire semblant de*

Get ready for the Oral Exam

Can champions still be considered heroes in spite of their wrongdoings *(écarts de conduite)*?

Play with words

MP 3 N° 15 · CD 3 PISTE 2

SPORT

Champion

courage
motivation
skills

persevering

compete
train
achieve a goal
mount the podium
win a medal
endure pain
persevere
break records
overcome obstacles

Hero

example
outstanding results: *résultats remarquables*

extraordinary
honest

play by the rules: *respecter les règles*
inspire respect

Reactions ⊕

admiration
respect

look up to = admire

Villain

bribe: *pot-de-vin*
bribery: *corruption*
lie (tell a): *mensonge*
performance-enhancing drugs

dishonest
shameful

bribe: *corrompre, acheter*
cheat: *tricher*
corrupt
deceive: *tromper*
lie: *mentir*

Reactions ⊖

disappointment
contempt

look down on = despise

A **Barrez l'intrus et donnez un titre à chaque liste.**

a. dishonest • shameful • exemplary • outrageous
b. deceive • cheat • corrupt • defeat
c. long jump • pole vaulting • cycling • hurdles
d. determined • courageous • blind • persevering

B **Complétez ces phrases avec des mots de la carte mentale ci-dessus.**

Champions have to … , … obstacles, … pain before they … records and … the podium. They should not spoil *(gâcher)* everything by not playing by the … . It is always a great … when you are an athlete's fan to discover that the athlete you admire has taken … … drugs. When an athlete … , the fans feel … . Athletes are role models and their behaviour should be irreproachable.

C **Entourez la voyelle accentuée de ces mots. Vérifiez à l'écoute.**

performance-enhancing • outstanding • persevere • dishonest • unbelievable • opponent • distrustful • reliable • admire • admirable

D **Classez ces mots selon la prononciation de la terminaison *-ed*. Vérifiez à l'écoute.**

achieved • committed • dedicated • determined • iron-willed • disabled • defeated • accomplished • handicapped

E **Complétez les phrases suivantes et vérifiez à l'écoute.**

If drug tests were done more systematically, it would be more difficult for athletes to … and for teams or coaches to … doctors or authorities. In the cartoon the athletes are trying to escape the tests. If they test positive they will lose their … and they will certainly not be regarded as … by their fans anymore because their fans will feel they have been … .

LANGUAGE AT WORK

«Apprendre à Apprendre»
Téléchargez la fiche n°11
www.editions-hatier.fr/langues-eleves

Corrigés p. 216-221

Équivalents anglais de « que »

(Précis grammatical 40 p. 210)

1. Complétez ces phrases à l'aide de *as*, *than*, *that* ou *Ø*.

a. Until today Usain Bolt is the fastest 100 metre sprinter ... the world has ever known.
b. Lance Armstrong has won more *Tours de France* ... any other bike rider.
c. Michael Jordan and Magic Johnson are among *(parmi)* the best basketball players ... I've seen.
d. Arthur Ashe is as well known for being the first African-American tennis player to win the US Open and Wimbledon ... for his political activism and his awareness campaigns about AIDS, a disease ... he contracted via a blood transfusion.
e. There was perhaps no greater cultural icon from the world of sport in 20th century America ... Muhammad Ali.

2. Reliez les deux membres de phrase en utilisant *who/whom/Ø* ou *which/that/Ø*. Plusieurs choix sont parfois possibles.

a. The drugs... he took were never detected.
b. Marion Jones was forced to return the five medals ... she won at the Sydney Olympics because she tested positive for drugs.
c. Oscar Pistorius, ... the world also knows as the Blade Runner, fell into disgrace when he was accused of killing his girlfriend.
d. Arthur Ashe is a great African-American tennis player ... many consider a hero.
e. The film ... we saw about Lance Armstrong does not provide new revelations.
f. Now ... athletes are also celebrities, they can become international heroes of the modern age.
g. Terry Fox, ... Canada considers a national hero, should be considered a hero in the sports world at large *(dans son ensemble)* after finishing the "Marathon of Hope", a cross-country run across Canada, on an artificial leg, in 1980.

3. Complétez les phrases suivantes à l'aide de *which*, *that*, *who*, *Ø* ou *than*.

a. The man .... we can see in the photo is a lacrosse champion who belongs to the Canadian paralympic team.
b. We can see ... he is disabled because he is sitting on a special skate ... enables him to play in spite of his handicap.
c. Many people admire ... the courage he has because of all the obstacles ... he had to overcome. Lacrosse is a sport ... is physically very demanding.
d. The man here is certainly more persevering, more courageous, more deserving ... many able-bodied athletes.
e. Disabled athletes are certainly people ... we should call heroes.

YOUR TASK

SCENARIO 1

Choose an athlete you consider a hero or one you consider a villain and write one of the articles published in a sports magazine's special issue entitled *50 athletes we admire or hate*.

- Decide on an athlete you would like to write about.
- List your arguments:
  qualities • flaws *(défauts)* • attitude • commitment
- Prepare a punchy title and a subheading.
- Prepare your introduction carefully (make the reader feel like reading more). Don't forget to write a conclusion.
- Do not forget to proofread your article.

Tips

- Go to page 187 and check how to write a newspaper article.
- Use superlative and comparative forms (→ p. 196).

SCENARIO 2

A wall of the gym in your school is going to be decorated with the portrait of a sporting hero. Choose a champion and defend your choice in front of the class.

- In groups, **decide** on an athlete you would like to see on the mural and why.
- **List all the arguments** in favour of your choice.
- **Be ready to compare** the athlete you have chosen with other athletes who will be suggested. (Use comparative and superlative forms, think of which records the athlete of your choice has broken, what he/she may do outside his/her sport that makes him/her exceptional.)
- **Justify your choice** in front of the class and try to **convince** them it is the best choice.
- **Vote** for the athlete who deserves *(mérite)* most to be painted on the mural.

Get ready for the Exam BAC

Compréhension écrite et expression écrite

WORKSHEET BAC N° 11

Answer the questions on the worksheet the teacher will give you.

DOCUMENT A

Ellis Paul - The Hero In You, 2012

Everybody's got a story, of all their troubles, all their glories
Tell me yours, you cannot bore me, I love to listen to you
All your bumps[1] and all your scratches[2], all your holes and all your patches[3]
It's you, it's true, I hope it sunk in, there's a hero in you

You can make the hero you are
With your brains, your aim, and your battle scars
Everybody's got a tale, of how they chase the great white whale[4]
Some succeeded, some just failed, trying's what you gotta do
Cause in the trying you feel you're flying
The whole wide world's beneath you lying
It's you, it's true, there's no denying
There's a hero in you

You can make the hero you are
With your brains, your aim, and your battle scars
Everybody's got a story, of all their troubles, all their glories
Tell me yours you cannot bore me, there's a hero in you

So use your brain and do some thinking
You could be the next Abe Lincoln[5]
Use your muscle, try to hustle
You could be Mohammed Ali[6]
Use your toes and dance on pumpkins
You can be Isadora Duncan[7]
It's you, it's true, I hope it sunk in, there's a hero in you

You can make the hero you are
With your brains, your aim, and your battle scars
Everybody's got a story, of all their troubles, all their glories
Tell me yours you cannot bore me, there's a hero in you

1. *bosses*
2. *égratignures*
3. *pansements*
4. *baleine blanche (référence à Moby Dick où le capitaine Achab rêve de capturer la baleine blanche car cela le rendrait célèbre)*
5. Lincoln abolished slavery.
6. professional boxer
7. American dancer

DOCUMENT B

JUL 8, 2015 @ 06:36 PM **624** VIEWS

Imperfect Heroes

Heroes are an endangered species. Yet heroes are important in every walk of life, from athletics to politics to the arts. When they achieve the extraordinary, they spur us to higher expectations for ourselves. Heroes embody courage, determination, and superb abilities—though they are human beings, just like us. So why are they scarce[1] and how can the trend be reversed?

We now demand perfection from our heroes.

And when they then fail, [...] we reject them with disdain. When we see that they have feet of clay,[2] we not only push them off their pedestals, we fail to heed[3] the lessons that can be learned from flaws and mistakes.

We often ask our heroes in one arena to be heroes in all aspects of life. A few may meet that mark, but most will fail. [...] The public should not expect from those with remarkable talent in one arena more than a display of prowess in that arena. We should hail them as heroes in their fields, while recognizing that they are human.

www.forbes.com

1. rare **2.** hidden faults **3.** pay careful attention to

DOCUMENT C

Compréhension de l'oral

CD 3 PISTE 3

Doping Charges and Sports Giants

→ Écoutez l'enregistrement trois fois.

→ Prenez des notes puis faites en dix minutes le compte rendu de ce que vous avez compris en français.

→ Utilisez les expressions données p. 183.

USEFUL WORDS
- legacy: *héritage*
- charges: *accusations pénales*
- Bill Strickland
- Neal Conan

Expression orale

MYTHS AND HEROES { **Are sports champions true heroes?**

Comment parler de la notion ?

Are sports champions true heroes?

- What is expected from an athlete for him/her to be called a hero?
- Which qualities are necessary?

achievements
role model
hard-working
persevering
remarkable
extraordinary

Why do disabled athletes deserve to be called heroes?

awe-inspiring
overcome obstacles
challenge

Can athletes' involvement outside their sport change the idea we have of them?

fund-raising
involvement
human rights
spokesman/spokesperson
defend/fight for a cause

Can champions still be considered heroes in spite of their wrongdoings (*méfaits*)?

fallen hero
villain
legacy
shameful
unforgivable
deceive: *tromper*

1. Which documents did you study in the unit?
2. In each document, select appropriate elements to illustrate the notion.
3. Use the mindmap above to organise your ideas.
4. Don't forget a personal conclusion.

Ambassadors of Conscience

1 Tune In!

1 Little big man

a. Look at the document and read the catchphrase. Who can this human rights defender be? What do you know about this icon?

b. Listen to the recording and organise your notes:

CD 3 PISTE 4

- date of birth and death;
- social background;
- education/studies;
- cause supported;
- major achievements *(succès)*;
- awards.

Give an oral account of what you have understood.

c. You are going to hear the definition of an "Ambassador of Conscience" for Amnesty International. Listen, write down key words and sum up what you have understood.

CD 3 PISTE 5

2 An icon

PREPARE YOUR TASK

Amnesty International wants to create a gallery of portraits of all its past Ambassadors of Conscience. You are in charge of this icon's article. (120 words)

2 One Voice

WORKSHEET 37

a. Before reading the text, turn to your worksheet for help. Then read the text and answer the questions.

a. Who is the narrator?

b. Identify the different places.

c. Who are the people mentioned? Classify them in three categories: allies • opponents • people she fights for.

d. List the time references. Match them with the narrator's different activities.

e. Focus on line 21 to line 27: find the narrator's final decision.

When I was twelve, my family in Dhaka, Bangladesh, fell into poverty, and I started working in a garment[1] factory. The life I had then is difficult to remember and nearly impossible to describe. For years, I worked day and night among other exhausted[2] children, some as young as eight. I earned less than $7 a month, yet often worked eighteen-hour days in chaotic, unhygienic, and unsafe environment. Becoming an activist has taken[3] finding my voice and learning to speak up about my experience: the opposite of what women are taught in my country. Just a couple of years after I started working at the garment factory, I spoke up to my bosses because my co-workers and I were denied overtime pay we were owed.[4] Some of my co-workers and I decided to strike[5] in protest. I was fired,[6] but I kept speaking up. [...] As an adult, I've traveled around the globe, and I've spoken to audiences of thousands about the working conditions in my home country. I've spoken up to multinational corporations like Walmart[7] and my own government, and my name has been in newspapers around the world. Even after I was jailed and tortured by agents of the state, and even after my friend and colleague was assassinated for standing up for workers' basic rights, I kept raising my voice.

It was hard for me to tell my story for this book and to make my life so public. But I ask myself: How do I want to live? Suffer in silence from the trauma I have faced and the stories I hear from workers every day? Or speak out, be passionate, love and celebrate the beauty in life, believe in the goodness of humanity, and do what I can to inspire others to act? If my story touches someone's heart–maybe yours–if it lets another woman who has faced exploitation and repression feel that she is not alone, and even encourages her to speak up, then it is worth it.

Invisible Hands, foreword by Kalpona Akter, 2014

1. *vêtements* **2.** very tired **3.** *a demandé (que)* **4.** *qu'on nous devait* **5.** *de nous mettre en grève* **6.** = laid off: *licenciée* **7.** a US discount supermarket

PREPARE YOUR TASK

b. You are Kalpona Akter. You meet the head of Walmart to denounce the awful working conditions in Bangladesh. Imagine the dialogue.

DEFINITION

A whistleblower is a person who tells police, reporters, etc., about something (such as a crime) that has been kept secret.

Get ready for the Oral Exam

- **To what extent can Kalpona Akter be called a whistleblower?**
- **What makes her a hero?**

3 Wanted

1 Before you read

a. Read the following definition and the headline of the article below:

DEFINITION

The National Security Agency (NSA) **is an independent agency within the US Department of Defense. It directs specialized activities to protect US information systems and collects information about secret communications in foreign countries.**

b. In pairs, use the words opposite and guess what Edward Snowden did and why.

2 Read and understand to find out what Snowden did

Edward Snowden: the whistleblower behind the NSA surveillance revelations

[While he was working for the NSA, Snowden] learned just how all-consuming the NSA's surveillance activities were, claiming "they are intent on making every conversation and every form of behaviour in the world known to them."

He described how he once viewed the Internet as "the most important invention in all of human history." As an adolescent, he spent days at a time "speaking to people with all sorts of views that I would never have encountered on my own".

But he believed that the value of the Internet, along with basic privacy, is being rapidly destroyed by ubiquitous[1] surveillance. "I don't see myself as a hero," he said, "because what I'm doing is self-interested: I don't want to live in a world where there's no privacy and therefore no room for intellectual exploration and creativity."

Once he reached the conclusion that the NSA's surveillance net would soon be irrevocable,[2] he said it was just a matter[3] of time before he chose to act. "What they're doing" poses "an existential threat[4] to democracy," he said.

A matter of principle

As strong as those beliefs are, there still remains[5] the question: why did he do it? Giving up his freedom and a privileged lifestyle? "There are more important things than money. If I were motivated by money, I could have sold these documents to any number of countries and gotten[6] very rich."

For him, it is a matter of principle. "The government has granted itself power[7] it is not entitled to.[8] There is no public oversight.[9] The result is people like myself have the latitude to go further than they are allowed to," he said.

■ *The Guardian*, June 11, 2013

1. /juːˈbɪkwɪtəs/ *omniprésente* **2.** *définitive* **3.** question **4.** *menace* **5.** *reste* **6.** = got (US)
7. *s'est arrogé un pouvoir* **8.** *(ici) auquel il n'a pas droit* **9.** supervision

WORKSHEET 38

What does Snowden denounce? What does he want to defend? Turn to your worksheet for help.

CD 3
PISTE 6

WORKSHEET 39

3 More about Edward Snowden

Listen to an extract from Snowden's interview with *The Guardian*.
Turn to your worksheet for help.

WORKSHEET 40

4 Make a choice

You are a journalist and you want to illustrate the article on Snowden. Which of these cartoons would you choose? Use the article and the interview to explain your reasons to the editor.
Turn to your worksheet.

DEFINITION

Counter-powers are opposing powers which question absolute authority, aim at limiting its excesses and resist it.

Help!

Revelations

reveal abuse /əˈbjuːs/: *révéler des abus*
disclose = unveil: *divulguer*
release /rɪˈliːs/: *publier*
accuse sb of sth/V-ING

Goals

question: *mettre en cause*
limit excesses
keep sb informed
attract sb's attention
violate sb's privacy /prɪvəsi/

Consequences

break the law
risk one's life
fear/dread sb might + BV: *craindre que*
defy/challenge (authority...)
bring about change

Get ready for the Oral Exam

- To what extent does Edward Snowden represent a counter-power?
- Would you call him a hero? Why? Why not?

4 Rebel With a Cause

1 Get ready

Look at the cartoon. What is the cartoonist's goal? Pick out the correct answer(s) and justify your choice.

- He denounces the hunting of wild animals.
- He denounces the dangers of gas drilling and hydraulic fracturing.
- He denounces the abusive exploitation of natural resources.
- He denounces the excessive use of pesticides.

fracking: *technique pour exploiter le gaz de schiste*

WORKSHEET 41

2 Read the text.

Turn to your worksheet for help.

Offshore fracking fight washes up on the pristine[1] shores of Arnhem Land

The first Alice Eather knew of Paltar Petroleum's plans for her ancestral land was when she read a square-inch[2] notice buried[3] in the back pages of the NT News. The August 2012 announcement detailed an application by the resource giant for a license for exploratory oil and gas drilling. If successful, it planned to carry out[4] hydraulic fracturing, or fracking, around the coastline of Maningrida in West Arnhem Land.

"It was the most horrible day of my life," says 24-year-old Eather. "No one was told a thing. There had been no consultation and the ad said we would be given two months to object."[5]

Objections from the region's myriad Aboriginal clans and some 13 language groups have since been vocal[6] and persistent. Almost two years on, leaders from the Protect Arnhem Land campaign say they will take their battle as far as the high court if necessary.

"I had never done any of this in my life," says Queensland-raised[7] Eather, whose mother is from the Kunibidji people of Maningrida. "But our job is to protect our country. If we don't do this, we are not doing our duty."

The 10-million hectares of Arnhem Land represent a fraction of the some 80% of the Northern Territory which is currently under application for unconventional oil and gas exploration. But the local campaign to halt[8] fracking by Paltar highlights the complexity of trying to protect land in this resource-rich territory.

The Guardian, June 13, 2014

1. /prɪstaɪn/ in its natural state 2. *d'environ 2,5 cm²* 3. (*ici*) hidden 4. execute 5. protest 6. *font désormais entendre leur voix* 7. *qui a été élevée dans le Queensland (État du nord de l'Australie)* 8. stop

PREPARE YOUR TASK

3 Counter-strike

You are a Greenpeace activist. You help Alice Eather prepare the speech she will deliver in the high court. You tell her what you know about the dangers of fracking and drilling and you give her some advice.

Help

Alice's land	Fracking and drilling	Reactions
heritage	greedy	dejected = discouraged
harmonious way of life	damage	devote oneself to + V-ING: *se consacrer à*
pure /pjʊəʳ/ = unspoilt	pollute	resist ≠ give up

5 Video Corner — Alice Eather's Story

1 Get ready

a. Which English word does each illustration correspond to:
wave • seabed • storm • dust • chest • leaves ? Use a dictionary if necessary.

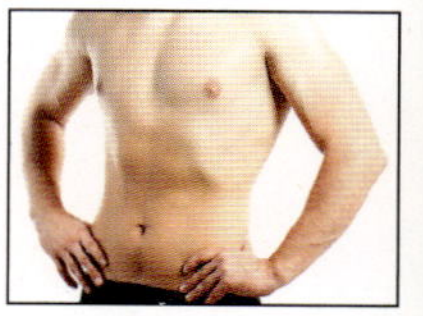

CD 3 PISTE 7

b. Train your ears. Write down the words that you hear, then say them aloud.
c. Find the French equivalent of "seabed".

2 Watch and understand

Part 1: from the beginning to 0:58

a. Pick out as many words as you can that are related to nature.
b. Focus on the messages Alice gets: Who are they from? What do they tell her to do?

Part 2: from 0:59 to 1:32

USEFUL WORDS
fantasy: *(ici) rêves* • three digits: *nombre à trois chiffres*

c. Who does "they" refer to?
d. On a separate piece of paper, organise your notes:

Their vision | Alice's vision

Part 3: from 1:33 to 2:07

USEFUL WORDS
tide: *marée* • dig deep: *creuser profondément* • shallow: *superficiel* • sweat /swet/: *sueur*

e. What are "they" only interested in? Pick out one sentence.

→ **Recap**

Use these two stills and the following words to give an account of what you have understood.
heritage • money-oriented • greedy: *avide* • damage /dæmɪdʒ/ • destroy • respect • close /kləʊs/ to: *proche de* • steal • impose on

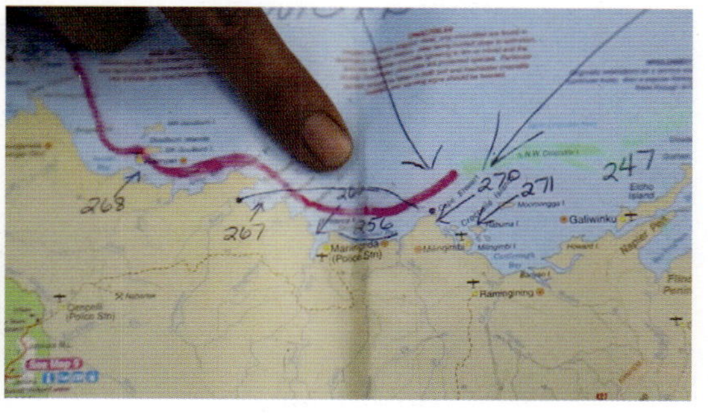

Get ready for the **Oral Exam**

- What qualities do indigenous Australians need to resist the oil company?
- To what extent is the Aborigines' fight against fracking heroic?

6 Face to Face

1 The myth

a. How much do you know about the story of David and Goliath?
b. Compare your answers then read more about it either on the Internet or in an encyclopaedia. Then report to the class.

2 Group work A
Observe the top half of the ad

a. What is represented?
b. What impressions does it give?

3 Group work B
Focus on the bottom half and the catchphrase

a. Who is it? What is he trying to do?
b. Who does he symbolise?
c. What is the message?
d. What makes him a hero?

Help!

Goliath /ɡəʊˈlaɪəθ/	David /deɪvɪd/	Greenpeace
oil platform/rig black fumes huge, gigantic ≠ tiny be based /beɪst/ on a contrast	dinghy /dɪŋɡi/: *canot* sling: *lance-pierres* target an opponent: *viser un adversaire*	grass-roots citizen: *citoyen de base* spokesperson: *porte-parole* urge people to: *inciter fortement les gens à* denounce = expose

Get ready for the Oral Exam

- **What are the common points between David and the Aborigines in Arnhem Land?**
- **Why is the myth of David and Goliath still relevant today?**

Play with words

MP 3 N° 16 · CD 3 PISTE 8

A Lisez les mots suivants. Puis écoutez-les.

Whistleblowers
spokesperson: *porte-parole*
revolted = outraged
determined = strong-willed
daring = bold: *audacieux*
reckless/fearless: *téméraire*
selfless: *altruiste*

Protest
opponent to: *adversaire de*
lack of: *manque de*
accuse sb of V-ING
resist = stand up against
fight for one's rights
violate basic rights
infringe on: *porter atteinte à*
rule = dominate

Goals
question: *remettre en cause*
expose = denounce
challenge = defy
assert one's rights: *affirmer ses droits*
condemn
urge sb to: *inciter fortement qqn à*
empower: *donner du pouvoir à*

Risks
risk V-ING: *risquer de*
intimidate
threaten: *menacer*
spy on sb: *espionner qqn*

B

1. Trouvez la racine de ces mots :
revolted · daring · fearless · selfless · threaten · empower.
2. Quels sont les contraires de ces mots ?
ally · intimidate · hide · agree with
3. Comment se prononce la voyelle soulignée dans les mots suivants ? Sur papier libre, classez-la dans la colonne correspondante et vérifiez à l'écoute.
urge · determined · assert · stand · lack · challenge · dominate · violate · intimidate · empower · outraged

/ɜː/ (bird)	/eɪ/ (cake)	/æ/ (cat)	/aʊ/ (cow)

4. Sur papier libre, recopiez ce paragraphe. Utilisez les mots dans les bulles ci-dessus pour compléter les blancs, conjuguez les verbes. Vérifiez à l'écoute.

Two men are sitting on a bench. The man working for the NSA already knows what his neighbour thinks and says. The cartoonist wants to ... the role of the NSA. The agency ... ... people's private lives and ... their ... . The artist wants to ... the methods used by the NSA. People must ... ... their rights. He ... the NSA ... spying on people. He ... the ... of freedom. He is ... because people don't realise they are being watched. Our freedom of speech and thought are ... .

LANGUAGE AT WORK

« Apprendre à Apprendre »
Téléchargez la fiche n°12
www.editions-hatier.fr/langues-eleves

Corrigés p. 216-221

Le style indirect

(Précis grammatical 15 p. 199)

1. Récrivez les phrases suivantes au style direct. N'oubliez pas les guillemets.
Attention aux changements des mots en gras : le temps des formes verbales • les pronoms • l'ordre des mots en c. • les auxiliaires modaux en d. • *if* en d.

a. Snowden **said that he was** convinced that our freedom of speech and thought **was** threatened (in danger).

b. Snowden **explained that/Ø he didn't see himself** as a hero, because what **he was doing was** self-interested.

c. A Greenpeace activist **asked why it was so difficult** to take measures to protect the environment.

d. Kalpona Akter **asked** international companies **if** the safety rules **could** be respected, **if** workers **would** be protected in the future.

2. Récrivez ces phrases au style indirect. Faites les transformations nécessaires.

a. Alice Eather asked the Australian government: "Why did you allow oil and gas drilling?"

b. "I want workers to be protected," Kalpona Akter declared.

c. "I do not want to live in a society where everything I do or say is recorded," Snowden insisted.

d. "Why can't American people have a debate about surveillance?" Snowden wondered.

e. "I have cherished the ideal of a democratic and free society," Mandela asserted.

f. "One day, people will live together in harmony," he said hopefully.

g. The journalist asked Edward Snowden: "Do you believe things can change in the future? Do you feel democracy is threatened?"

ON YOUR OWN!

Imagine you are the father. You report to your wife the conversation you had with your son.
Use different verbs: declare • add • reply • explain • tell.

YOUR TASK

SCENARIO 1

Who would you give the title of Ambassador of Conscience?
Draw his/her portrait. Say what he/she has fought against, list his/her qualities.
In groups, decide who you will choose.

Introduce an Ambassador of Conscience at an award ceremony. Prepare a speech to welcome the new nominee at the award ceremony. Deliver it in front of the class or film it. (2 minutes maximum)

Tips

- **Look at your audience.** As you begin your oral presentation, select two or three students at different places in the room, and look them in the eye.
- **Hold your head high and smile**, even if you feel tense and stressed! Relax your shoulders.
- **Speak clearly**, loud enough and not too fast.
- **Make short, punchy sentences.**
- **Just look at your notes for help** but do not read them, only if necessary.
- **Stress the key words** to sound more convincing.
- **Use gap fillers** if you hesitate (→ p. 178).

SCENARIO 2

Become a whistleblower. Go on the Internet and watch the video: "Lego: Everything is NOT awesome." You are in charge of recording the voice-over to explain the phenomenon and denounce the situation.

▶ **Focus on the following points:**
- device *(procédé)* used, setting, place, inhabitants, landscapes *(paysages)*;
- name of the company, installations;
- what happens and the impact on people and nature;
- target of the ad.

▶ **In groups, prepare your recording.**
Use the vocabulary you studied in this unit.

▶ **The class will select the best recording.**

Get ready for the **Exam** BAC

Compréhension écrite et expression écrite

Answer the questions on the worksheet the teacher will give you.

WORKSHEET
BAC N° 12

DOCUMENT A

Colonel Nyathi tells a policewoman, Captain Mbali Kaleni, and two other policemen, that the State Security Agency is going to replace them on the case they are investigating.

"I am sorry, sir, but I am not going to stop investigating this case." [...]
"Mbali, do you want to be suspended? Do you want to get the whole of us fired?"
"Let them try."
There was still no confrontation in Mbali's voice. It confused Nyathi. "Captain, you are very close to insubordination. What the hell has got into you?"
"Sir, I am wondering the same thing about you and the brigadier..."
"Captain, I am now officially warning you that you are going too far. One word and you are suspended."
"Sir, you can suspend me or you can fire me, I don't care..."
Nyathi's eyes narrowed and he drew a breath to respond, but Captain Mbali spoke with a passion and conviction that none of them had heard before. "My father used to tell me stories of how he did not dare use his phone, because the security police was listening. He was part of the Struggle,[1] Colonel. Back when the secret services conducted all the important criminal cases, when they told the police what to do. When everybody was spying on each other. And everything was hushed up by the media. And the public knew nothing. Today it is happening again. Now Parliament is passing a Security Bill.[2] Why? Because they want to hide things. Now this. State Security eavesdropping on us,[3] and taking over a criminal case. Just like in the apartheid times. We are destroying our democracy, and I will not stand by and let it happen. And it will, if we let it. I owe[4] it to my parents' struggle, and I owe it to my country. You and the brigadier too. You owe it to all the comrades who gave their lives for the cause. So, no, I will not stop. And if you try to stop me, I will go to the press and I will tell them everything."

■ Deon Meyer, *Cobra*, 2014

1. the fight against apartheid **2.** *(projet de) loi visant à renforcer la surveillance de la population pour déjouer d'éventuels crimes* **3.** *nous met sur écoute* **4.** *dois*

DOCUMENT B

Dear Future Generations,

I think I speak for the rest of us when I say,
sorry, sorry we left you our mess[1] of a planet.
I hope you forgive[2] us,
we just didn't realize how special the Earth
was, [...]
we didn't know what we had until it was
gone. [...]
You know what, cut the beat, I'm not sorry.
This future I do not accept it,
because an error does not become a mistake,
until you refuse to correct it.

We can redirect this, how?
Let me suggest that if a farmer sees a tree that
is unhealthy,
they don't look at the branches to diagnose it,
they look at the root, so like that farmer,
we must look at the root,
and not to the branches of the government,
not to the politicians run by corporations.
We are the root, we are the foundation, this
generation,
it is up to us to take care of this planet. [...]
And to betray[3] nature is to betray us,
to save nature, is to save us. [...]
Because if we don't all work together to save
the environment,
we will be equally extinct.
Sorry.

■ *Dear Future Generations: Sorry*, Prince Ea, 2015

1. *(ici) dans un état lamentable* **2.** *(ici) pardonnerez* **3.** *trahir*

Compréhension de l'oral

CD 3 PISTE 9

How to react to a surveillance society?

→ Écoutez l'enregistrement trois fois.
→ Prenez des notes puis faites en dix minutes le compte rendu en français de ce que vous avez compris.
→ Utilisez les expressions données p. 183.

Expression orale

MYTHS AND HEROES { **Are whistleblowers the heroes of modern times?**

Comment parler de la notion ?

1 Définissez la notion ***Myths and Heroes***. Revoyez la définition d'***Ambassador of Conscience*** (p. 158), de ***whistleblower*** (p. 159) et de ***counter-power*** (p. 161). Relisez vos notes sur David et Goliath.
2 Sélectionnez les documents qui vous permettront de répondre à la problématique posée. Appuyez-vous sur la carte mentale ci-dessous pour organiser votre prise de parole.

Are whistleblowers the heroes of modern times?

What do they stand up against?
– Big corporations
→ Kalpona Akter and Alice Eather
– Governments and official organisations
→ Edward Snowden

accuse sb of V-ING
expose = denounce
dominate

• Who and what do they stand for? Why?
• Who supports them?

resist
fight for one's rights
violate basic rights
urge sb to: *inciter fortement qqn à*

• Which qualities are required?
• Do you consider whistleblowers heroes? Why? Why not?

reckless = fearless: *téméraire*
risk V-ING: *risquer de*

• Are counter-powers necessary in today's society? Why?
• To what extent can they change the world?
• Which episode in the Bible do they remind you of?

spokesperson: *porte-parole*
defy
assert: *affirmer*
empower: *donner du pouvoir*

3 Utilisez le vocabulaire donné p. 5 et 165 pour enrichir votre expression.
4 Préparez-vous à prendre la parole à partir de notes : ne rédigez pas votre présentation, notez les idées clés, les mots importants.
5 Anticipez les questions qui pourront être posées par l'examinateur (points à approfondir, exemples pour illustrer un argument, opinion personnelle...).

Fast Facts: The United Kingdom

The United Kingdom
Capital city: London

- **Currency: Pound Sterling (£)**
- **Great Britain**
  - England (English)
  - Scotland (Scottish)
  - Wales (Welsh)
- \+ **Northern Ireland or Ulster**
- **National emblems**
  - Leek (Wales)
  - Rose (England)
  - Thistle (Scotland)
  - Shamrock (Northern Ireland)
- **National anthem:** *God Save the Queen*
- **The British Flag: The Union Jack**
  - St Patrick's Cross (Ireland)
  - St George's Cross (England)
  - St Andrew's Cross (Scotland)

British institutions

- **Head of the state: Queen or King.** Has mainly a representative role. (a constitutional monarchy)
- **The Houses of Parliament (Legislative power)**
  - **The House of Commons** (650 elected members)
  - **The House of Lords**

- **Executive power**
  - **Prime Minister** = Head of the government
  - **The Cabinet**

Major political parties

Labour Party	Liberal Democrats	Conservative Party

The UK: a timeline

1066 AD*

William, Duke of Normandy, invades Britain and becomes King of England

1509-1547
During the reign of Henry VIII, the Church of England becomes independent from the Roman Catholic Church

1558-1603
Elizabeth I (Tudor)

1837-1901
Queen Victoria's reign sees the expansion and prosperity of the British Empire

*AD: after Christ
(BC: before Christ)

Fast Facts: The United Kingdom

Landmarks

Iconic places

Big Ben

Stonehenge

Tower Bridge

Trafalgar Square

Stratford-upon-Avon: Shakespeare's birthplace

Education

University of Oxford

University of Cambridge

Places of power

Economy

The City of London (historical centre of London: banks and the Stock Exchange)

Government and institutions

10, Downing Street (Residence of the Prime Minister)

Buckingham Palace

Scotland Yard

Arts

Tate Modern Gallery (Museum of Modern Art)

National Gallery

British Museum

British media

TV and Radio

- BBC (British Broadcasting Corporation) — BBC
- Independent channels (ITV, Sky...)

The press

- Popular press (tabloids): The Sun, Daily Mail
- Quality papers (broadsheets): The Times, the guardian, The Independent, The Daily Telegraph

Timeline

1914-1918 World War I

1940-45 and **1951-55** Winston Churchill, Prime Minister

1939-1945 World War II (the Blitz)

1979-1990 Margaret Thatcher, Prime Minister, was nicknamed "The Iron Lady"

1918 Women get the right to vote in the UK

1952

Elizabeth II's coronation

1961

The Beatles' first performance

1973

The UK joins the European Community

1994 The Channel Tunnel is officially inaugurated

2014 Referendum: Scotland remains in the UK

Fast Facts: The United States of America

The United States
Capital city: Washington, D.C.

National emblems

The American Great Seal

Bald Eagle

Uncle Sam personifies the country

50 white stars representing the 50 States

13 red and white stripes representing the 13 original colonies

The American Flag: The Star Spangled Banner or Stars and Stripes

National anthem: *Star Splangled Banner*

The Statue of Liberty

Mottos

"E Pluribus Unum" (Out of many, one)

"In God We Trust"

Currency : US Dollar ($)

Public holidays

3rd Monday of January: Martin Luther King Day

4th July: Independence Day

1st Monday of September: Labour Day

12th October: Columbus Day

4th Thursday of November: Thanksgiving

American institutions

Federal Government

Legislative power – Congress

Congress

The Senate (100 members)

The House of Representatives (435 members)

Executive power

The President – Elected for 4 years. Lives in the White House

The Cabinet – 15 heads of department

Judicial power

The Supreme Court – Ensures that the law is not against the Constitution

Political parties

The Democrats (emblem = donkey) They favour stronger federal control

The Republicans (emblem = elephant) They favour restriction on central power

The Constitution 1787

13th Amendment – **1865**: abolition of slavery

15th Amendment – **1870**: Right of vote for all men (prohibits the denial of suffrage based on skin colour) (1870)

19th Amendment – **1919**: right of vote for women

The Bill of Rights (1789: first 10 Amendments)

1st Amendment – Freedom of speech, thought and religion

2nd Amendment – The right to bear arms

The USA: a timeline

1492

Discovery of America by Christopher Colombus

1620

The Pilgrims arrive aboard the Mayflower

1849

The California Gold Rush

1861-1865 US Civil War

1863

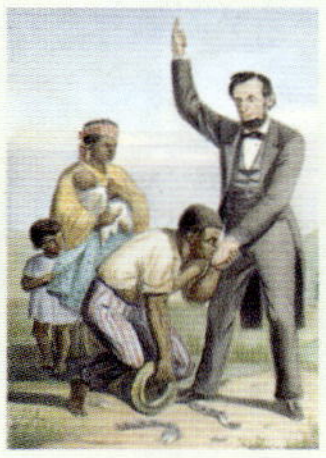

President Abraham Lincoln abolishes slavery

1914-1918 World War I

1920 Women get the right to vote

1929

Wall Street Crash (beginning of the Great Depression)

Fast Facts: The United States of America

Cultural Landmarks

Iconic places

Liberty Bell (symbol of American Independence)

Ellis Island (where European immigrants arrived in New York from 1892 to 1954)

Freedom Tower (where the Twin Towers of the World Trade Center stood before the 2001 terrorist attack)

Mount Rushmore South Dakota

Plymouth Rock Massachusetts where the Pilgrims landed

Concepts

Work ethic
A belief in the importance of hard work to climb the social ladder

Melting pot
The image of the USA as a pot in which immigrants will be americanized (now considered a myth and replaced by the expression "salad bowl").

The Frontier
The moving line between "civilization" (settled territories) and the wilderness (Indian territories). It often refers to the American expansion westward.

Places of power

Silicon Valley (close to San Francisco, is the home to the computer industry)

The White House

The Pentagon

New York Stock Exchange (Wall Street)

The Ivy League (a group of long-established eastern universities of high academic and social prestige)

American media

Cinema industry

- Warner Bros
- Columbia Pictures
- Universal
- Metro Goldwyn Mayer

Television (more than 1,500 channels)

- abc
- CBS
- NBC
- CNN

The press

Newspapers (more than 10,000)

- The Wall Street Journal Interactive Edition
- USA Today
- Chicago Tribune
- The New York Times — Expect the World®
- The Washington Post

Magazines (more than 11,000)

- TIME

Radio

National Public Radio (NPR)

Timeline

1939-1945 World War II

1954-1975 Vietnam War

1941

Attack on Pearl Harbor

1954 Beginning of the Civil Rights Movements

1963 Martin Luther King delivers famous speech *"I have a dream"*

1964 Civil Rights Act

1969

First man on the moon (Neil Armstrong)

1991 @ The World Wide Web is launched

9/11/2001 World Trade Center is destroyed by largest terrorist attack in US history

2009

Barack Obama becomes the 1st black president of the USA (44th)

Commenter une image

I. Parler d'une image fixe

MP3 n° 17 — CD 3 piste 10

1. Les types d'images

advertisement/advert/ad: *publicité*
cartoon: *dessin humoristique*
comic strip: *bande dessinée*
drawing: *dessin*
map: *carte*
painting
photograph: *une photograhie*
photography: *la photographie (l'art de)*
poster
still from a film: *image de film*

2. Situer les différents éléments de l'image

MP 3
N° 17
CD 3
PISTE 10

3. Nommer les éléments de l'image

character: *personnage*
a person *(singulier)*/people *(pluriel)*
setting: *décor*
title, headline
balloon: *bulle*
caption: *légende*

I can see…
There is/are…
The woman is sleeping (V-ING) and her children are playing.
The children **look** stupid (look + *adjectif*).
They **look like** monsters (look + *nom*).
The focus is on…

II. Les prépositions

1. Position

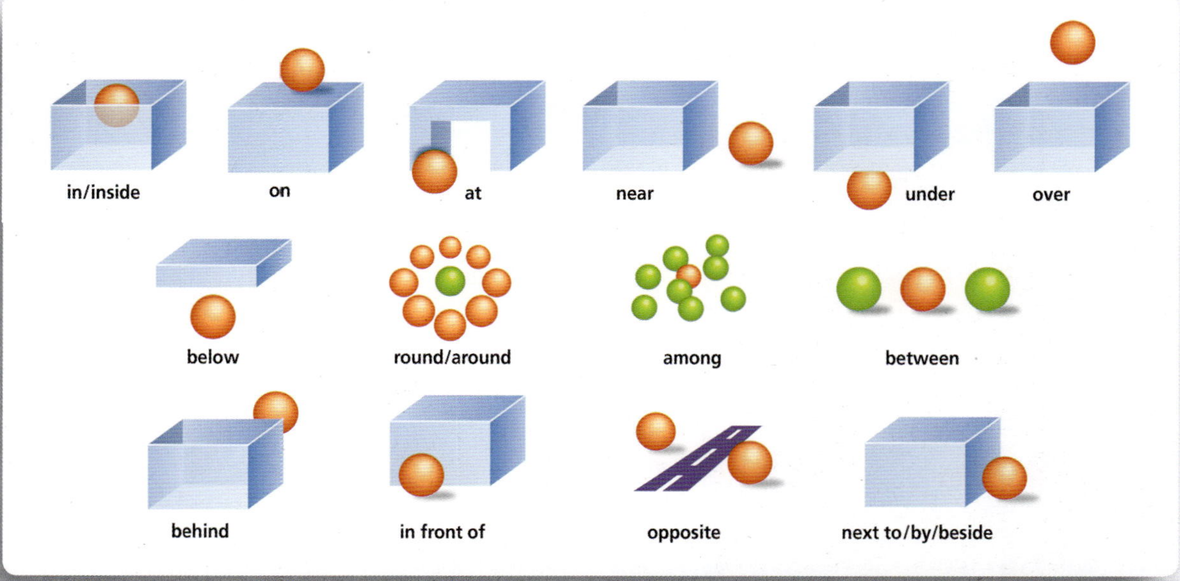

2. Mouvement

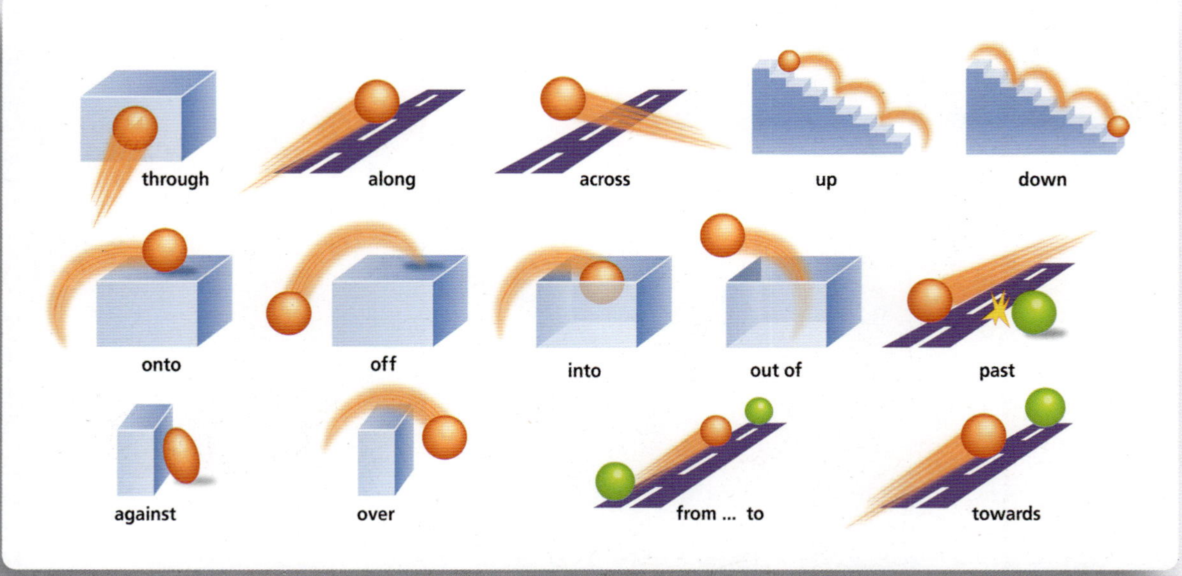

III. Parler d'une image animée

1. Les plans et les angles

A. Medium shot
The camera focuses on the character's head and shoulders.

B. High-angle shot
The shot makes the character look smaller and the viewer dominates the scene.

C. Low-angle shot
The character is seen from below and the viewer feels dominated.

D. Full shot
The camera shows the characters standing.

E. Long shot
The camera shows a distant object or landscape.

F. Close-up
The viewer can see details on a face or an object. This shot is used to express emotions.

2. Les types d'image animée

black and white movie
blockbuster film: *film à grand succès*
commercial: *publicité à la télévision*
disaster film
detective film
documentary
report: *reportage*

comedy
musical
trailer: *bande-annonce*
war/adventure film
thriller
cartoon: *dessin animé*

3. Parler d'une scène

Who?
The people involved are…
What?
The document is about…
The document deals with…
Where?
The scene takes place in a station.
The scene is taken from…
The setting is a house, a street, an airport.
shoot, shot, shot: *tourner*
It was shot in a studio.
When?
The incident took place during the day/at night.

First reactions
What strikes me (the) most in/about this is…
I think it is surprising/funny to see…
It is incredible: *incroyable*
interesting
ridiculous
impressive
scary: *effrayant*
unusual: *inhabituel*
disturbing: *troublant / dérangeant*
moving: *émouvant*
humorous /ˈhjuːmərəs/
We get a feeling of suspense/danger/threat *(menace)*.

4. Les bruits et les sons

soundtrack: *bande-son*
sound effect: *bruitage*
film score: *musique*
voice-over: *voix off*
male/female voice

lively/cheerful
dramatic
spooky: *qui fait froid dans le dos*
deafening: *assourdissant*
dull/muffled: *étouffé*

MP3 n°18
CD 3 PISTE 11

5. Interpréter

The director's aim/goal is to…
It makes me think of…
It reminds me of…: *cela me rappelle*
It illustrates/represents…

It is a symbol of…/It symbolises…
The director wants to make us aware of…: *le réalisateur veut nous faire prendre conscience de…*
It criticises/It denounces…

Enrichir sa prise de parole

Get started

- To start with, …
- First of all, I would like to say that…

Gap fillers

- Well, …
- I mean, …
- Well, you see…/you know, …
- Um…
- What I am trying to say is that…
- It's an interesting question…

How to check that you understood correctly

- What do you mean by that?
- So, if I understand correctly, you mean that…
- I'm not quite sure I understand what you mean here.

How to check somebody has understood you

- Did you get my point?
- Do you see what I mean?
- Does it make sense?

When something is not quite clear

- Could you say that again, please?
- Could you repeat what you said?
- Would you mind repeating, please?
- I'm sorry, what did you say?
- Excuse me, what did you say?
- Are you saying that…?
- What do you mean by…?

How to introduce your opinion

- To me, …
- In my view, …
- It seems to me that…
- To my mind, …
- In my opinion, …
- I have the feeling that…
- I believe that…

How to present different ideas

- To begin with, …
- Well, first of all, …
- Firstly, … Secondly, … Lastly/Finally, …
- I also think that…
- Besides, …
- I'd like to add that…

How to agree strongly

- Exactly!
- Absolutely true!
- That's a very good point.
- Sure!
- That's right!
- That's exactly what I think.

How to half agree

- Yes, I suppose so. However…
- Yes, sure, but…
- Do you really think so?
- Well in a way, but…
- Well, it depends.
- Well, yes, up to a certain point.
- I've got mixed feelings about that.

How to disagree politely

- Um, … I'm not sure.
- Don't you think that…?
- Do you really believe that…?
- Well, I think it depends on…

How to disagree strongly

- I totally disagree with you.
- I really can't agree.
- You can't be serious!
- No, you're wrong!
- You must be joking/kidding! *(informal)*
- Nonsense! *(informal)*

How to interrupt

- I'm sorry, but…
- Actually, …
- Yes, but…

How to counter an argument

- Yes, but remember that…
- That may be true but…
- Don't you think…?
- Contrary to you, I think…
- On the contrary, I believe…

How to give an example

- For example, …
- Take… for instance.
- For instance, …
- That is to say…

How to show different aspects of a question

- Generally…
- At first sight, …
- On the one hand, … On the other hand, …
- On second thoughts, …

How to add something

- What's more, …
- I'd like to add that…
- On top of that, …
- By the way, …
- In addition, …
- Besides, …
- I'd also like to say that…
- I'd like to make another point.

How to conclude

- In conclusion, …
- Lastly, …
- In that case…
- In short, …
- To sum up, …
- Finally, …

Mots de liaison pour structurer son discours

1. Connecteurs chronologiques

Sur papier libre, recopiez le texte qui suit en y insérant les mots ci-dessous.

later on • after that • first (of all) • finally/eventually • then • secondly

Looking for a job

1, you have to look at the ad column in a newspaper or on the Internet.

2, once you have found an interesting ad corresponding to your skills and expectations *(compétences et attentes)*, you will prepare your CV/ resumé presenting your profile, your work experience and qualifications.

3, you will write a cover letter explaining why you are the best candidate for the job and 4, you will email it to the hiring manager.

5, when you get an invitation for the first interview, you will try to show you are the ideal person for the job.

6, on D-day, you will dress appropriately, hide your piercings and tattoos (if you have any), relax and smile!

2. Connecteurs logiques

a. Quelle est l'idée à exprimer ? Sur papier libre, associez chaque mot à un mot de sens proche.

1. opposition / contraste	a. cible / objectif
2. cause	b. résultat / suite
3. conséquence	c. affrontement / contradiction
4. but	d. compromis
5. concession	e. déclencheur

b. Quel connecteur faut-il utiliser ? Sur papier libre, recopiez le tableau ci-dessous et complétez-le à l'aide des connecteurs logiques de la liste suivante.

because • in order to + BV *(pour)* • and yet *(et cependant)* • whereas *(alors que)* • since *(puisque)* • although *(bien que)* • even if • so/that's why

Opposition	Cause	Conséquence	But	Concession

c. Complétez les énoncés suivants en utilisant le connecteur logique qui convient.

1. ... I have only spent a few weeks in England, I speak English quite well.
2. I have applied for a job in Australia ... I'm ready to go abroad and work in a foreign country.
3. ... I'm very good at languages, I think I'm a suitable candidate for this job.
4. I passed my driving test last summer, ... I can take any position offered in the area.
5. I got my driving licence ... be able to take any position offered in the area.
6. I have applied for a job in Chicago ... it's far from home.
7. I have sent many application forms, ... I haven't received any answers.
8. I haven't received my pay check ... my co-workers have! I'm sure it won't be long now.

Nombres et graphiques

1. Dates and numbers

a. Years:

1800	1906	2000	2006	2016
eighteen hundred	nineteen-o-six	the year two thousand	two thousand and six	twenty sixteen

b. Dates:

	1st January 2016	12/06/2000 (GB)	06/12/2000 (US)
On écrit :	1st January 2016	12/06/2000 (GB)	06/12/2000 (US)
On dit :	The first of January twenty sixteen (or two thousand and sixteen)	The twelfth of June two thousand	June the twelfth two thousand

c. Numbers:

- **0** ➞ zero /ˈzɪərəʊ/ • **12** ➞ twelve • **13** ➞ thirteen /θɜːˈtiːn/ • **30** ➞ thirty /ˈθɜːti/ • **14** ➞ fourteen /fɔːˈtiːn/ • **40** ➞ forty /ˈfɔːti/ • **800** ➞ eight hundred *(invariable)* /ˈhʌndrəd/
- **3.6** ➞ three point six *(trois virgule six : le point correspond à la virgule d'un nombre décimal)*
- ***La virgule sert à séparer les groupes de trois chiffres.*** *2,385,942 se lit donc :* two million three hundred and eighty-five thousand nine hundred and forty-two.
- **Hundred**, **thousand** *et* **million** *ne prennent la marque du pluriel que lorsqu'ils renvoient à une quantité indéfinie :* **2,000** ➞ two thousand /ˈθaʊznd/ *(invariable)*

Mais : hundreds of…, thousands of…, millions of…

- *L'ordre des grands nombres est :* thousand *(millier)*, million *(million)*, billion *(milliard)*, trillion *(trillion), etc.*

d. Lengths *(longueurs)*: 1 inch *(pouce)* ➞ 2.54cm • 1 foot ➞ 30.4cm • 1 yard ➞ 91.4cm • 1 mile ➞ 1,609m

e. Phone numbers: (508) 963 – 0021: five-o-eight nine six three-o-o-two one

WORKSHEET 42

f. Practise on your worksheet.

2. Graphs and charts

a. Different graphs:

pie chart

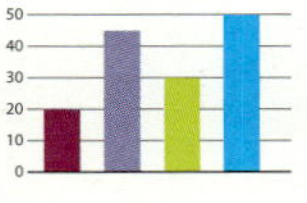

bar chart

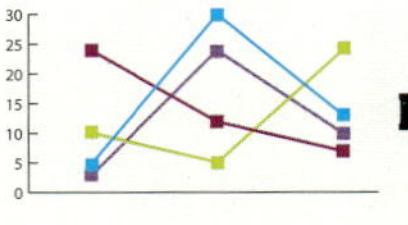

line chart

b. What a graph shows:

- This graph shows/illustrates…
- The bar chart underlines *(souligne)*…
- The pie chart highlights *(met en relief)*…
- The line chart brings out *(fait ressortir)*…

c. Analysing trends *(tendances)*

↗ Verbs	↗ Nouns	↘ Verbs	↘ Nouns
increase (by 3%) rise (to…) reach a peak: *atteindre un sommet*	increase (in + noun): *augmentation de* rise (in): *hausse (de)*	decrease (by 2%) drop (from… to): *chuter* go down/fall (to) collapse: *s'effondrer*	decrease (in + noun): *diminution de* drop (in) = fall (in) decline (in)

d. Describing trends more precisely with adjectives (or adverbs):

dramatic(ally): *(de manière) spectaculaire* • sharp(ly): *fort(ement)* • slight(ly): *léger (légèrement)* • gradual(ly) • rapid(ly) • steady(ily): *régulier (régulièrement)* • slow(ly)

WORKSHEET 42

e. Practise on your worksheet.

Comprendre un document oral

1. Les étapes à suivre

a. J'anticipe à partir du titre.

J'émets des hypothèses sur le contenu, le thème de l'enregistrement ; je mobilise rapidement le lexique que je connais sur ce thème.

b. Première écoute

- J'identifie la nature du document : interview, débat, reportage, témoignage, dialogue…
- Je repère le nombre de voix (masculines / féminines), les lieux mentionnés, les indications de temps (dates, durées…) et les nombres.
- Je note quelques mots-clés pour vérifier mes hypothèses et déterminer le thème du document.

c. Deuxième écoute

- Je repère les informations sur les interlocuteurs (nom, âge, pays d'origine, profession, lien entre eux) et leurs actions.
- Je trouve à quoi correspondent les nombres, les dates et les durées.
- Je note le maximum de mots accentués.
- Avant l'écoute suivante et pendant la minute de pause, j'établis des liens entre les éléments qui vont ensemble (par des traits ou des flèches) et je classe les informations.

d. Troisième écoute

- Je complète mes notes.
- Je me concentre sur l'opinion exprimée par le(s) locuteur(s), s'il y a une note optimiste ou pessimiste, et / ou un message qu'il / elle veut transmettre.

e. Je fais le compte rendu en français de ce que j'ai compris à l'aide des expressions p. 183.

Je m'entraîne MP3 n° 20 — CD 3 piste 13

YOUNG AND UNDOCUMENTED

Appliquez les étapes ci-contre à cet enregistrement.

WORKSHEET 43 Si vous avez besoin d'aide, votre professeur pourra vous distribuer une fiche plus détaillée.

2. Comment comprendre l'implicite d'un message ? (→ B2)

a. Anticipez à l'aide de l'image ci-contre.

Quelles hypothèses pouvez-vous émettre sur le contenu de l'enregistrement (qui parle, à quelle occasion) ?

USEFUL WORDS

- **Harriet Tubman** was an African-American woman who fought against slavery in the USA in the 19th century.
- an **Emmy**: *récompense pour des rôles et émissions de télévision*
- no how: *(ici) peu importe ce que je fais*

MP3 n° 21

b. Écoutez le document en entier.

- De quel type d'enregistrement s'agit-il (interview, extrait de film, discours…) ?
- Repérez le plus de mots connus ou proches du français. Quels mots sont répétés ?

c. Réécoutez du début jusqu'à 00:45.

CD 3 piste 14

- La locutrice cite Harriet Tubman décrivant : une réalité • une scène imaginaire • le lieu où elle était la veille.
- Relevez les mots porteurs de sens et classez-les en trois colonnes :

People mentioned	Place and objects	Problem she faces

- Déduisez : que représente ce qu'elle décrit ?

d. **Concentrez vous sur la fin (à partir de 00:39).**

- Notez un maximum de mots accentués et remplissez cette carte mentale sur papier libre.
- Recopiez et complétez le paragraphe ci-dessous. Expliquez l'implicite du message et les sentiments que la locutrice peut ressentir. Justifiez vos réponses à l'aide des mots que vous avez relevés.

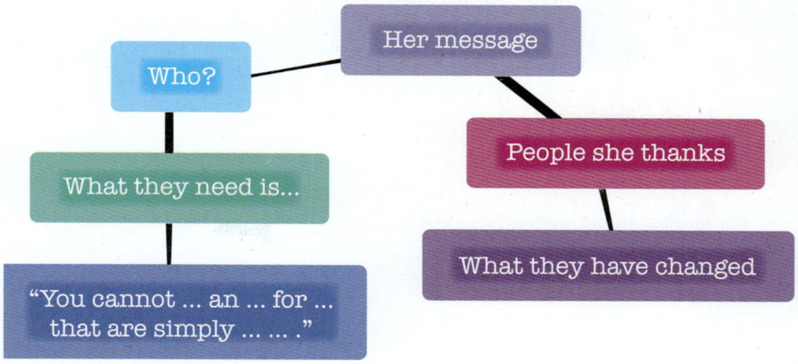

Cette actrice (Viola Davis) cite Harriet Tubman évoquant une ... qui la séparé / rapproche des femmes blanches / de couleur. Encore aujourd'hui, cette ... représente les ... qui existent entre les différentes minorités. Dans son discours, Davis dénonce / approuve le fait que les femmes blanches / de couleur n'aient pas accès aux mêmes ... , notamment à des ... qui leur permettraient d'obtenir un ... . Elle est très ... lors de son discours, et critique / remercie les ... qui l'ont aidée à franchir cette ... . Ils ont redéfini ce qu'être ... , ... et ... veut dire, et prouvé que des femmes ... peuvent aussi avoir des rôles principaux / secondaires.

3. Entraînez-vous

CD 3
PISTE 15
PISTE 16
PISTE 17

Voici plusieurs enregistrements que vous pouvez écouter trois fois en suivant la méthodologie proposée p. 182. Prenez des notes, puis faites le compte rendu en français de ce que vous avez compris.

Utilisez les expressions données ci-dessous.

#1: Information society

#2: A day to remember

#3: Obama: we must act now!

4. Comment rédiger le compte rendu ?

a. **Précisez le type de document.**

Cet enregistrement / Cette vidéo est un extrait d'un discours, une conférence de presse, un journal télévisé, un reportage, un film, un débat...

b. **Qui parle ? Soyez aussi précis que possible.**

Un(e) journaliste, le président de... , ... personnes sont interviewées...

c. **Thème abordé ?**

Cela soulève le problème / traite de... , on y évoque la question de... , le sujet principal est... , le journaliste attire notre attention sur le fait que...

d. **Variez les verbes introducteurs.**

Il / Elle mentionne, évoque, exprime, souligne, rappelle, insiste sur le fait que, présente...

e. **Définissez le ton et l'opinion du narrateur.**

Il / Elle fait l'éloge, la promotion de, dénonce, critique, semble pessimiste, optimiste, a des sentiments ambivalents...

Comprendre un extrait de roman

1. Utilisez les stratégies suivantes

PREMIÈRE LECTURE

- J'identifie la nature du document et sa source (auteur, date de publication).
- Je ne souligne pas les mots inconnus, je m'appuie sur les mots proches du français et les mots que je connais.
- Je lis les questions posées seulement une fois que j'ai lu le texte.

SECONDE LECTURE

- Je surligne le nom des personnes, les lieux, les dates, les marqueurs de temps.
- Je me concentre sur les différents personnages et les relations entre eux.
- Je repère les éléments clés de l'histoire.
- Je m'appuie sur le contexte, la composition et dérivation pour déduire le sens des mots inconnus.

2. Entraînez-vous

I went into the kitchen to turn the heating[1] on, and boil the kettle,[2] and while I was there I glanced at the answering machine mounted on the wall. It blinked a number back at me. "Five." Five phone messages, while I'd been away for almost a month? This was ridiculous. Did I dare[3] to listen to them? [...]

I made a mug of strong tea and took a couple of sips before pressing the "Play" button on the answering machine. But my mood of trembling anticipation was short-lived. There was a message from my employer, reminding me to come in for a final meeting with the Occupational Health Officer in a few days' time. There were two messages from my dentist. [...] Then there were two blank messages, consisting simply of long electronic beeps followed by the noise of somebody hanging up. [...]

So much for the telephone.

Well, maybe Facebook would cheer me up. I had more than seventy friends on Facebook, after all. Surely that must have created some activity while I'd been away. I took my tea upstairs, settled down in front of the computer and logged in to my home page.

Nothing.

I stared at the screen in shock. Not a single friend had sent me a message or posted anything on my wall in the last month. If the evidence was to be believed,[4] in other words, not one of those seventy people had thought of me once during my absence.

■ Jonathan Coe, *The Terrible Privacy of Maxwell Sim*, 2010

1. *(ici) mettais le chauffage en route* 2. *bouilloire* 3. *osais* 4. *(ici) si je devais croire ce que je voyais*

→ Étape 1 : résoudre les problèmes de vocabulaire

1. Utilisez le contexte pour déduire le sens des mots surlignés en jaune.
2. Décomposez les groupes de mots en bleu pour comprendre leur sens.

→ Étape 2 : trouver les informations clés

1. Observez les expressions en gris. Que révèlent-elles sur ce que le narrateur a fait récemment ?
2. a. Où est le narrateur au début et à la fin du texte ? Citez le texte.
b. Que consulte-t-il au début du texte (paragraphes 1 et 2) ? Citez un mot du texte.
c. Que consulte-t-il ensuite (paragraphes 3 et 4) ? Citez un mot du texte.

3. a. À quoi *this* (l. 4) fait-il référence dans le texte ?
b. À quoi *that* (l. 13) fait-il référence dans le texte ?

4. Que trouve le narrateur d'abord (paragraphe 1) ? Que donne sa recherche (des lignes 7 à 16) ? Justifiez votre réponse à l'aide d'une citation du texte.

5. Que s'attendait-il à trouver la seconde fois ? Pourquoi ?
Choisissez les affirmations qui conviennent.
a. Puisqu'il avait un certain nombre d'amis, il devait y avoir quelques messages pour lui.
b. Il imaginait que, dans tout son réseau, quelques personnes auraient pensé à lui.
c. Il ne pensait pas que personne ne lui écrirait.

6. Sélectionnez les adjectifs qui s'appliquent le mieux aux réactions du narrateur et justifiez à l'aide du texte.

frustrated — disappointed — lonely — anxious — indifferent
worried — frightened — astonished (very surprised) — depressed

→ Étape 3 : comprendre l'implicite

1. Quelle conclusion tire-t-il de cette découverte ? Recopiez les bulles qui conviennent le mieux.

"I have no real friends!"

"My computer doesn't work. I must have it repaired!"

"We have a lot of technological devices and yet we don't communicate!"

"I am alone in the world."

"I feel so lonely!"

2. Indiquez en une ou deux phrases en anglais les liens entre le texte et ce dessin humoristique. Utilisez les réponses ci-dessus.

Raptus www.fragocomics.com

Comprendre un article de presse

Should employers pay for women to freeze their eggs[1]?

15 October 2014 | **BUSINESS**

A recent story by NBC news revealed that Facebook helps its female employees in the US to pay for the cost of freezing their eggs, while Apple is planning to introduce the policy in January.

The tech giants are thought to be the first major American companies to offer this benefit.
But does this level the playing field[2] for women, as some have claimed[3] or is it step too far by employers?
The reaction has been mixed – with many applauding the move but some less enthusiastic responses.
"Anything that gives women more control over the timing of fertility is going to be helpful to professional women," Shelley Correll, a sociology professor [...] told the news agency AP. [...]
"Many women are shocked to find that although[4] they are physically fit[5] their egg quality is actually poor, and that if they had frozen their eggs in their early 30s the picture would have been very different," he says. [...]
But some feminists are not completely convinced about the move.
"There's a danger that with this sort of policy companies give a signal – or even promote the idea – that a woman needs to postpone[6] having children in order to succeed in the workplace," says Daisy Sands, head of policy at the Fawcett Society, a group that campaigns for equality for women. [...]
Geraldine Gallacher set up a company, Executive Coaching, that specialises in advising women who return to work after having a baby, particularly at law firms and banks. She also feels that this sort of policy reinforces the message that it is a problem to be a mother.
"It's a high-tech solution to a human problem," she says. [...] This is "a step too far".

www.bbc.com

1. *congeler leurs ovules* 2. *(ici) donne les mêmes chances* 3. *soutiennent* 4. *bien que* 5. *en bonne forme* 6. *remettre à plus tard*

1. Au cours de la lecture

a. Observez les éléments surlignés et associez chaque couleur à une catégorie ci-dessous.

- Source / origine / nom du journal
- Introduction d'un point de vue contraire (quel mot est utilisé ?) et arguments donnés
- Opinion exprimée et arguments donnés
- Idées-clés qui résument le contenu
- Sous-titre *(subheading)* résumant le contenu de l'article
- Titre *(headline)* : sujet de l'article

b. Appuyez-vous sur les mots transparents (mots proches du français).

c. Déduisez le sens des mots inconnus à l'aide de la nature du mot, du contexte ou en les décomposant (dérivation, composition).

2. Après la lecture

a. Faites un compte rendu de l'article (thème abordé, opinions défendues, arguments donnés).

b. Réagissez en écrivant au courrier des lecteurs *(Letter to the editor)*. (120 mots environ)

Écrire un article de presse

American newspapers have organised a contest about the dangers of distracted driving. It is open to all high school students and the best article will be published on the front page of a national newspaper.

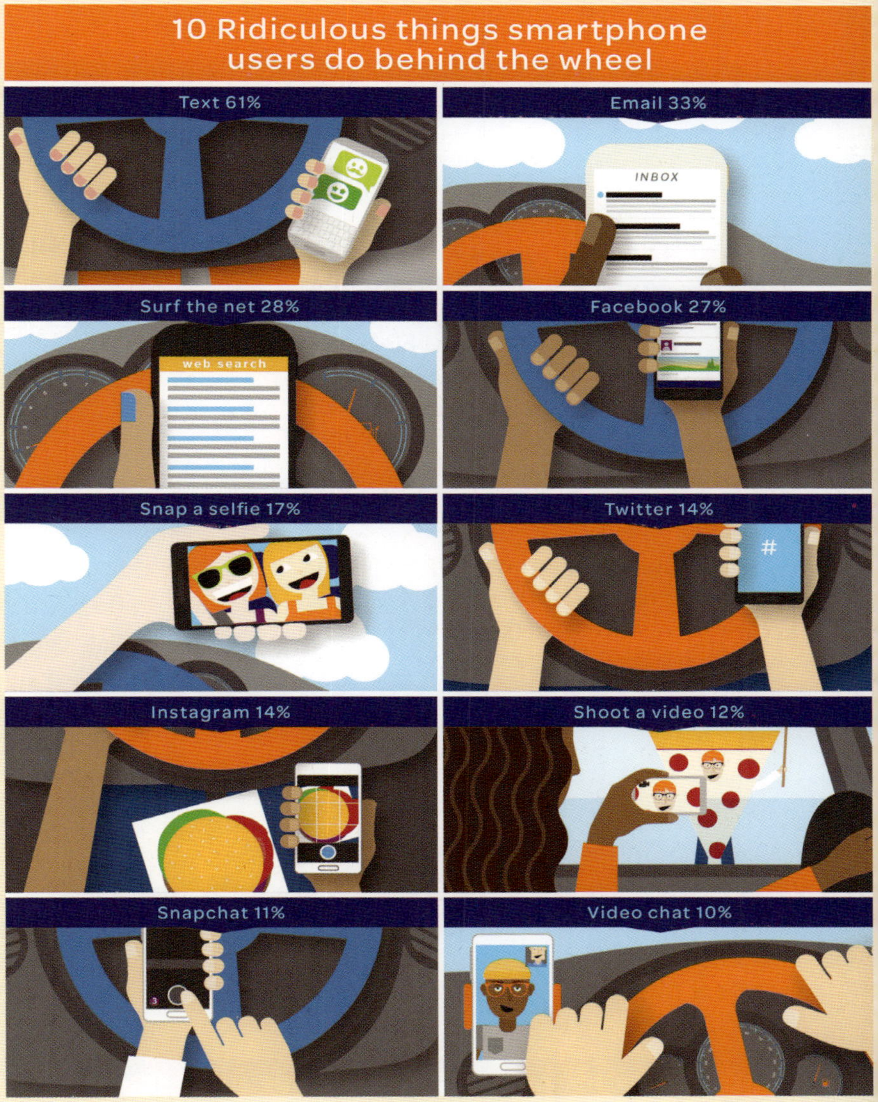

Les étapes à suivre

a. Choisissez le nom du journal, du journaliste et la date.

b. Créez un titre accrocheur qui donne envie de lire l'article. Quel est le titre qui vous semble le mieux convenir ?

More and More Young Drivers Distracted by Smartphones

Should Texting While Driving Be Illegal?

Phones are getting smarter, not drivers

ARE YOU ADDICTED TO YOUR SMARTPHONE?

c. Quelle phrase allez-vous utiliser pour introduire votre article ?

- *Distracted driving is involved in more than 200,000 vehicle crashes each year, often involving injuries and death.*
- *At 55mph it is like driving the length of a football field completely blind.*
- *When you send a text message while driving you are 23 times more likely to be in a crash.*

d. Recherchez les idées et mobilisez le lexique à l'aide de la carte mentale suivante :

Exposé de la situation : utilisez les informations fournies dans l'affiche. →

behaviour: *comportement*
be addicted to/dependent on
be unaware of risks
widespread phenomenon: *phénomène répandu*
risky/dangerous

Conséquences →

run over sb: *renverser qqn*
take one's eyes off the road
crash into
cause accidents
injuries: *blessures*
damage *(indénombrable)*: *dégâts*

Mesures à prendre

ban/forbid
discourage sb from V-ING
vote tough/strict laws
educate citizens
take action
launch awareness campaigns: *lancer des campagnes de sensibilisation*
fine sb: *faire payer une amende à qqn*

e. Écrivez votre article. Puis concluez de façon optimiste ou pessimiste.

f. Relisez-vous avec attention (→ Relire son devoir, p. 7).

Écrire une lettre informelle ou un e-mail

1. Observez la lettre ci-dessous. Il y manque des informations.

1..........................

2..............

3.........

4..............., I have just found a new job! I applied two months ago and got an interview almost immediately. They said they were extremely interested in my CV and hired me two weeks later.

I really love what I am doing here. I work as a personal assistant, which means I have to organise meetings, maintain my boss's diary, arrange her travel and even travel with her sometimes.

We really have to try and meet up soon.

I'm dying to tell you more about my new life.

Let me know when you are available!

5.........

Lisa

6 ......

A Dear Natalie

B 67 Lillie Road
Birmingham
B19 7TH

C Love

D 22nd September 2016

E xxx

F Sorry for not writing to you earlier

a. Associez chaque bulle à un numéro dans la lettre.

b. Où se trouve la date ? L'adresse ?

c. Que signifie xxx ?

d. Qui est le/la destinataire de cette lettre ? S'agit-il d'un parent, d'un employeur, d'un.e ami.e ? Quels éléments de la lettre vous ont aidé.e à trouver la réponse ?

2. Utilisez la bonne formule.

Sur papier libre, associez chaque salutation de début de lettre à la/les formule(s) de clôture qui lui correspond(ent).

Dear Mrs Smith • My dear Andrew • Dear Aunt

Take care • Best wishes • With love

3. Répondez à cette lettre par un e-mail.

a. Quelle formule d'introduction allez-vous utiliser ?

b. Quelle formule de conclusion allez-vous utiliser ?

c. Attention, certains éléments d'une lettre ne seront pas écrits dans un e-mail. Lesquels ?

Attach | Send ➢

Check mail | New | Reply | Forward | Delete | Print

To: lisa340@gmail.com
From:
Subject:

What great news!: *Quelle bonne nouvelle !*
Congratulations on

I can't wait to + BV
I look forward to V-ING: *j'ai hâte de...*

Écrire une lettre formelle

Here is Wendy's cover letter (= letter of application) for the job of receptionist.

Ms Wendy McKay
63 Main Street
Chicago, IL 60609
Cell phone: (00-1)312-303-1753
Email: wendy.mckay@yahoo.com

March 12, 2016

The Personnel Manager
The Drake Hotel
21 E. Bellevue Place
Chicago, IL 60611

Dear Sir or Madam
With reference to your advertisement on your website, I wish to apply for the position of receptionist in your hotel in July and August. Although I do not have any previous experience in this type of work, I have already worked as a sales assistant and a waitress and I can supply references from my former employers if you would like to see them. I enjoy dealing with customers and I am keen to use my skills in Spanish and French.

I am currently studying accountancy at the City College of Chicago and I will be available from the end of June.
Please find enclosed my resume. Do not hesitate to contact me if you require further details or for an interview.

I look forward to hearing from you.

Yours faithfully

W. McKay

Wendy McKay

Match each colour with the element of the letter it corresponds to:
- sender's address and details
- formal greetings
- signature and name of the sender
- recipient's details
- date

In the letter, find the English equivalents of the following phrases:
- *je serai disponible*
- *mes compétences*
- *fournir des références*
- *expérience antérieure*
- *je souhaite postuler*
- *je fais actuellement des études de comptabilité*
- *si vous souhaitez davantage d'informations*
- *suite à votre annonce*
- *un entretien*

Choose the most appropriate equivalent:
- *J'ai hâte d'avoir de vos nouvelles.*
- *Dans l'attente d'une réponse de votre part…*
- *En espérant vous entendre bientôt.*

Lorsque l'on ne connaît pas l'identité du destinataire, on doit utiliser :
- en début de lettre : *Dear Sir or Madam*
- en formule de clôture : *Yours faithfully*

Lorsque l'identité du destinataire est connue, on doit utiliser :
- en début de lettre : *Dear Mr/Mrs/Ms Jones*
- en formule de clôture : *Yours sincerely*

Attention aux différences entre le Royaume-Uni et les États-Unis :

	UK	USA
Vocabulaire →	*a CV*	*a resumé* /ˈrezumeɪ/
Date →	*12(th) March 2016 • 12/03/2016*	*March 12(th), 2016 • 03/12/2016*
Adresse de l'expéditeur →	En haut à droite ou à gauche	En haut à gauche

Rédiger un dialogue

1. Écoutez le dialogue suivant.

MP3 n° 22 — CD 3 piste 18

My father entered the room. He started to speak but stopped in the middle of his sentence. I turned around. He was staring at me.
"What?" I said.
"I know you've been smoking," my father said. "I could smell it in the car."
"I was just trying it," I said.
"Don't lie to me," he said. "How long have you been smoking?"
"I..., I..."
"Well, that's enough now. You will quit this habit immediately!"

a. Quel est le niveau de langue utilisé ici : formel ou informel (familier) ?

b. Quelles différences avec le français remarquez-vous dans la ponctuation ?

c. Traduisez en français : **my father said • I said**. Que remarquez-vous ?

d. Améliorez ce passage afin de raconter la scène :

– en variant les verbes introducteurs. Choisissez dans la liste suivante : **add** (ajouter) • **admit** • **ask** • **exclaim** • **explain** • **hesitate** • **insist** • **reply = answer** • **suggest** • **wonder** (se demander).

– en enrichissant vos phrases à l'aide d'adverbes.

Dans le dialogue ci-dessus, lesquels pourriez-vous utiliser ? **angrily** • **kindly** (gentiment) • **calmly** • **nervously** • **quietly** • **loudly** (haut et fort) • **shyly** (timidement) • **impatiently**

– en ajoutant des *gap fillers* : **well** • **you know...** • **actually**.

2. Observez ce script.

Dans cet extrait d'une interview de Lance Armstrong par Oprah Winfrey, que remarquez-vous à propos de la ponctuation ? Quelles sont les différences de présentation avec le dialogue de l'exercice 1 ? Comment les justifiez-vous ?

Oprah Winfrey: *"Was it humanly possible to win the Tour de France without doping, seven times?"*
Lance Armstrong: *"Not in my opinion."*
Oprah Winfrey: *"So why now admit it?"*
Lance Armstrong: *"That is the best question. It's the most logical question."*

3. Échangez des arguments.

L'affiche ci-contre a attiré votre attention. Vous avez envie de partir étudier ou travailler à l'étranger. Vous discutez avec un.e ami.e pour le / la convaincre de tenter l'aventure avec vous.

a. Lisez les arguments ci-dessous et classez-les en deux colonnes : pour / contre partir étudier ou travailler à l'étranger.
job mobility is a necessity • **a great opportunity** • **an enriching experience** • **feel homesick** (avoir le mal du pays) • **miss parents and friends** • **an exciting challenge** • **discover the world and learn about new cultures** • **experience abroad is a bonus on your CV** • **easier to stay in your native country** • **get behind with your studies**

b. Imaginez le dialogue avec votre ami.e en utilisant les arguments ci-dessus. N'oubliez pas de faire attention à la ponctuation.

c. Relisez-vous avec attention (→ Relire son devoir, p. 7).

Précis grammatical

1. Adjectifs

En anglais, les adjectifs sont **invariables** (sans ***-s*** du pluriel) :	*These armchairs are* ***comfortable****.* Ces fauteuils sont confortables.
Les adjectifs **épithètes** (= rattachés directement au nom) se placent **avant** le nom :	*There are two* ***comfortable armchairs****.* Il y a deux fauteuils confortables.
En anglais, on emploie les adjectifs comme noms pour désigner **l'ensemble d'une catégorie** : • L'adjectif précédé de ***the*** reste invariable (sans *-s* du pluriel) et le groupe *the + adjectif* a un **sens pluriel**. • Dans les autres cas, l'adjectif est obligatoirement **associé à un nom ou au pronom *one*** :	***The young*** *are for this measure.* Les jeunes sont favorables à cette mesure. Il y avait beaucoup de jeunes. *There were a lot of* ***young people****.* Je préfère la bleue. *I prefer the* ***blue one****.*

- Certains adjectifs sont formés à partir de verbes, auxquels on ajoute soit :
  - la terminaison ***-ing*** — *amuse → amus****ing*** — amusant
  - la **marque du participe passé** — *amuse → amus****ed*** — amusé

La terminaison *-ing* équivaut à la terminaison française « -ant ».
interesting intéressant — *tiring* fatigant
interested intéressé — *tired* fatigué

2. Adverbes : leur place dans la phrase

- Les **adverbes de fréquence**

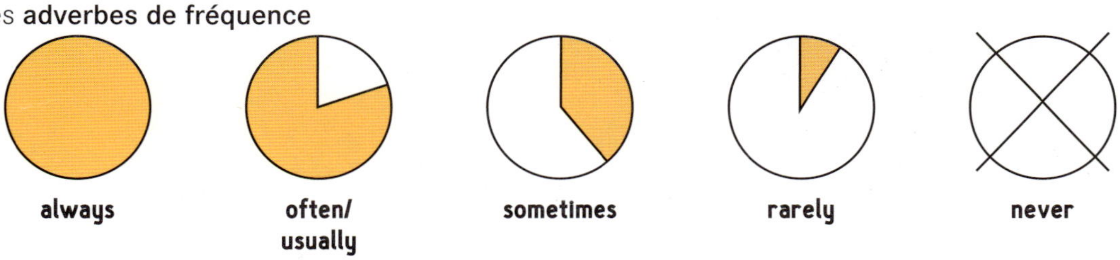

- Les adverbes de fréquence se placent **devant le verbe.**

She sometimes	***drinks*** *coffee.*	Elle boit quelquefois / parfois du café.
She never	***drinks*** *coffee.*	Elle ne boit jamais de café.

- Quand il y a un auxiliaire (*BE*, *CAN*, etc.), ils se placent **après l'auxiliaire.**

He is	***often***	*in front of his computer.*	Il est souvent devant son ordinateur.
I've	***never***	*eaten Jamaican food.*	Je n'ai jamais mangé de nourriture jamaïcaine.

- **L'adverbe ne doit pas séparer le verbe de son complément d'objet.**
  Il connaît bien l'Italie. → *He knows Italy* ***well****.*

3. Article *a/an*

- On utilise ***a*** /ə/ devant un son « consonne » : ***a*** *train*.
- On utilise ***an*** /ən/ devant un son « voyelle » : ***an*** *old man*.
  Lorsqu'un nom commence par le son /j/ (comme dans ***y****ou*), il est précédé de *a* (et non de *an*), même si dans l'écriture la première lettre est une voyelle :
  a *union* /ˈjuːniən/ (un syndicat), ***a*** *European* /jʊərəˈpiːən/ *nation*.
  Attention aussi au ***h*** **initial**, qui est une consonne **prononcée** (***a*** ***h****ard disk*),
  sauf dans *honest*, *honour*, *hour:* ***an*** *honest citizen*, ***an*** *hour*.

> ***On utilise a/an*** pour indiquer le métier de quelqu'un.
> *She's* ***a dentist***. Elle est dentiste.

4. Be

Conjugaison du présent

Affirmation	***I am / I'm***	*he / she / it* ***is / 's***	*we / you / they* ***are / 're***
Négation	***I am not / I'm not***	*he / she / it* ***is not / isn't***	*we / you / they* ***are not / aren't*** /ɑːnt/
Interrogation	***am I?***	***is*** *he / she / it?*	***are*** *we / you / they?*

Conjugaison du prétérit

Affirmation	*I / he / she / it* ***was*** /wɒz/ ou /wəz/	*we / you / they* ***were*** /wɜː/ ou /wə/
Négation	*I / he / she / it* ***was not / wasn't***	*we / you / they* ***were not / weren't*** /wɜːnt/
Interrogation	***was*** *I / he / she / it?*	***were*** *we / you / they?*

« Avoir » en français et *be* en anglais

avoir faim / soif / froid / chaud	*be hungry/thirsty/cold/hot*
avoir peur	*be scared* (plutôt familier)/ *frightened*
avoir de la chance	*be lucky*
avoir 18 ans	*be 18 (years old)*

5. « Beaucoup » et « peu » *(a lot of/many/much, few/little)*

	Nom indénombrable (singulier) : *traffic*	Nom dénombrable au pluriel : *tourists*
Beaucoup de	*There's* ***a lot of/lots of traffic.*** *There isn't* ***much traffic.*** *Is there* ***much traffic****?* Il y a / Il n'y a pas beaucoup de circulation. / Est-ce qu'il y a beaucoup de circulation ?	*There are* ***a lot of / lots of tourists.*** *There aren't* ***many tourists.*** *Are there* ***many tourists****?* Il y a / Il n'y a pas beaucoup de touristes. /Est-ce qu'il y a beaucoup de touristes ?
Peu de	*There's* ***little traffic.*** Il y a peu de circulation.	*There are* ***few tourists.*** Il y a peu de touristes.
Un peu de, quelques	*There's* ***a little traffic.*** Il y a un peu de circulation.	*There are* ***a few tourists.*** Il y a quelques touristes.

6. But et équivalents anglais de « pour »

- ***To/in order to* + base verbale : expression du but :**
  He got off the car ***to ask his way****.*
  Il est sorti de la voiture pour (dans le but de) demander son chemin.

- **« Pour ne pas... »** peut être exprimé par ***in order not to*** :
  I'll make a note of the appointment ***in order not to*** *forget it.*
  Je vais noter le rendez-vous pour ne pas l'oublier.

- Les subordonnées de **but** introduites par ***so*** ou ***so that*** contiennent souvent un **modal**, ***can/could*** (idée de « pouvoir »), ou ***will/would*** :
  I'll do the shopping today ***so we'll have enough food for the weekend****.*
  Je vais faire les courses aujourd'hui pour qu'on ait assez de nourriture pour le week-end.
  I turned up the heating ***so they wouldn't catch cold****.*
  J'ai monté le chauffage pour qu'ils n'attrapent pas froid.

7. « Ce qui », « ce que »

- **Ce qui / ce que** = « la / les chose(s) qui / que » : ***what***
  Je me demande ce qu'il mijote.
  I wonder ***what*** *he is up to.*
  What *he said was very clever.*
  Ce qu'il a dit était très intelligent.

- **Ce qui / ce que** = « chose(s) qui / que » : ***which*** (**résume ce qui précède**)
  Elle a réussi brillamment, ce que j'avais prédit.
  She succeeded brilliantly, ***which*** *I had predicted.*

- **Tout ce qui / tout ce que** : ***all (that)*** ou ***everything (that)***
  J'ai tout ce qu'il me faut / tout ce dont j'ai besoin.
  I've got ***all (that)*** *I need.*
  Il dépense tout ce qu'il gagne.
  He spends ***everything (that)*** *he earns.*

8. « Combien... ? »

How much + nom singulier	*How much money?*	Combien d'argent ?
How many + nom pluriel	*How many years?* *How many times did you meet him?*	Combien d'années ? Tu l'as rencontré combien de fois ?

- **« (Pendant) combien de temps ? » :** ***how long*** + formes verbales diverses (mais pas le *present perfect*).
  Tu y es resté / Tu y resteras combien de temps ?
  How long *did you stay/will you stay there?*

- **« Depuis combien de temps ? » :** ***how long*** + ***present perfect*** ou ***past perfect*** (→ 29 p. 205 et 31 p. 206).
  Tu la connais / connaissais depuis combien de temps ?
  How long *have/had you known her?*

- **« Tous les combien ? » :** ***How often****...?*
  Tu vas chez le coiffeur tous les combien ?
  How often *do you go to the hairdresser's?*

9. Comparatifs et superlatifs

- **Adjectifs courts :** une syllabe, ou deux syllabes avec terminaison *-y* ou *-er*.
  Adjectifs longs : autres adjectifs.

- **Formation**

	Adjectifs courts	Adjectifs longs
Comparatif de supériorité (= plus… que…)	*A rhino is **heavier than** /ðən/ a tiger.* Un rhinocéros est plus lourd qu'un tigre.	*A tiger is **more dangerous than** /ðən/ a rhino.* Un tigre est plus dangereux qu'un rhinocéros.
Comparatif d'égalité (= aussi… que…)	*Tim is **as** /əz/ **enthusiastic as** /əz/ his father.* Tim est aussi enthousiaste que son père.	
Comparatif d'infériorité (= moins… que…)	*A tiger is **not as** /əz/ **heavy as** /əz/ a rhino.* *A tiger is **less heavy than** /ðən/ a rhino.*	

« de plus en plus… »	*Temperatures are **higher and higher**.* Les températures sont de plus en plus élevées.	*The situation is **more and more worrying**.* La situation est de plus en plus inquiétante.
« de moins en moins… »	*He's **less and less optimistic**.* Il est de moins en moins optimiste.	

« plus … plus… » (notez l'emploi de *the* et l'ordre des mots)	***The hotter** it is, **the happier** he feels.* Plus il fait chaud, plus il se sent heureux.	*The more time he spends at work, **the more tired** he is.* Plus il passe de temps au travail, plus il est fatigué.
« moins… moins… »	***The less** he works, **the less** he feels like working.* Moins il travaille, moins il a envie de travailler.	
« plus… moins… »	***The more** exercises you do, **the fewer** mistakes you will make.* Plus vous ferez d'exercices, moins vous ferez de fautes.	

Superlatif de supériorité (= le plus…)	*Is it **the largest city in** the world?* Est-ce que c'est la plus grande ville du monde ?	*Is it **the most polluted city in** the world?* Est-ce que c'est la ville la plus polluée du monde ?

- **Attention : modifications orthographiques** avec les terminaisons **-er/-est** :

happy → happier, happiest — Un ***y*** qui suit une consonne devient ***i***.
big → bigger, biggest — Une consonne **finale** qui suit une voyelle est redoublée.

- Le complément du superlatif est introduit par ***in***, sauf s'il désigne :
  - un groupe d'éléments *(the largest city **of all**)*
  - ou une période de temps *(the coldest year **of the century**)*.

- **Comparatifs et superlatifs de supériorité irréguliers**

Adjectif / Adverbe	Comparatif	Superlatif
good bon ***well*** bien	***better*** meilleur / mieux	***the best*** le / la / les meilleur(e)(s) / mieux
bad mauvais	***worse*** /wɜːs/ pire	***the worst*** /wɜːst/ le / la / les pire(s)
far loin	***farther*** ou ***further*** plus loin	***the farthest*** ou ***the furthest*** le / la / les plus éloigné(e)(s)

10. Condition / hypothèse *(if…)*

Hypothèse **possible** (sur un fait présent ou futur)	*If I **have** the money [now / next month], I'**ll** buy myself a new phone.*	Si j'ai assez d'argent (je ne sais pas si j'ai / j'aurai assez d'argent), je m'achèterai un nouveau téléphone.
Hypothèse **irréelle** portant sur un fait **présent**	*If I **had** the money [now], I'**d** (= **would**) buy myself a new phone.*	Si j'avais assez d'argent (mais je n'ai pas assez d'argent), je m'achèterais un nouveau téléphone.
Hypothèse **irréelle** portant sur un fait **passé**	*If I **had had** the money, I'**d** (= **would**) **have bought** myself a new phone.*	Si j'avais eu assez d'argent (mais je n'en ai pas eu assez), je me serais acheté un nouveau téléphone.

11. Conditionnel (équivalents du conditionnel français)

- En général, l'équivalent du conditionnel français est ***would/'d*** + **BV**.
  Je savais qu'ils **seraient** en retard.
  *I knew they'**d be** late.*
  S'il pleuvait, le match **serait** annulé.
  *If it rained, the match **would be** cancelled.*

> On ne peut pas employer *would* + BV dans les subordonnées de temps.
> À la place, il faut employer le ***prétérit simple*** :
> Il a dit qu'il reviendrait quand il ferait moins froid.
> *He said he'd come back when it **was** less cold.*

- Le conditionnel des verbes modaux du français (« pouvoir », « devoir », « falloir ») se traduit généralement par le **prétérit d'un modal** :

Tu **devrais** leur demander.
*You **should** ask them.*

Je **pourrais** me servir de ton portable ?
***Could** I use your mobile?*

12. Démonstratifs *(this/these* et *that/those)*

This /ðɪs/ (+ nom au **singulier**) et ***these*** /ðiːz/ (+ nom au **pluriel**) s'emploient pour désigner ce qui est **proche** dans l'espace ou le temps, ou ressenti comme proche.	***This music** is fantastic!* Cette musique [= la musique que nous sommes en train d'écouter] est fantastique.
That /ðæt/ (+ nom au **singulier**) et ***those*** /ðəʊz/ (+ nom au **pluriel**) s'emploient pour désigner ce qui est **éloigné** (ou ressenti comme éloigné), a déjà été mentionné, ou fait l'objet d'un rejet.	***That year** there was a big tsunami.* Cette année-là, il y a eu un gros tsunami. ***That music** is much too loud!* Cette musique est beaucoup trop forte !

13. « Depuis »

Depuis	+ indication d'une durée	***for*** • *He <u>has been living</u> in London* ***for twenty years.*** ***(present perfect)*** Il <u>habite</u> Londres depuis **vingt ans**. • *He <u>had been living</u> in London for twenty years.* ***(past perfect)*** Il <u>habitait</u> Londres depuis **vingt ans**.
	+ indication du point de départ / date	***since*** *He <u>has</u> / <u>had been living</u> in London* ***since 2008****.* Il <u>habite</u> / <u>habitait</u> Londres depuis **2008**.

« Depuis que » : ***since***	*I have been suspicious* ***since*** *he tried to cheat.* Je me méfie de lui **depuis qu'**il a essayé de tricher.

- ***Since*** indique un **point de départ d'une période de temps**.
- Emploi du ***present perfect*** dans la **proposition principale**, puisque l'événement dure encore au moment présent.
- Emploi du **prétérit** dans la **proposition introduite par** ***since***, puisqu'on indique un point-repère dans le passé.

■ **« Depuis quand... ? » / « Depuis combien de temps... ? » :** *How long...?* → 8 p. 195

14. « Devoir »

« Je dois... » = « Il faut que je... » :	***Must***, qui est un **modal** (→ 24 p. 203), exprime le point de vue de l'énonciateur (style plutôt formel). *You* ***must*** *give up smoking!* Tu dois arrêter / Il faut que tu arrêtes de fumer ! ***Have to*** exprime une obligation vue de façon neutre (notamment une contrainte extérieure). *He* ***has to*** *take the 7:30 train to be in time for work.* Il doit prendre le train de 7 h 30 pour être à l'heure au travail.

Obligation située dans le **futur**	***will have to*** (« je devrai », « il faudra que je »)	*Next year, he**'ll have to** to take the 7:30 train.* L'an prochain, il devra prendre le train de 7 h 30.
Obligation située dans le **passé**	***had to*** (« j'ai dû », « il a fallu que je »)	*Yesterday he* ***had to*** *to take the 7:30 train.* Hier, il a dû prendre / il a fallu qu'il prenne le train de 7 h 30.

À la forme négative, *must* et *have to* ont deux sens très différents :
You ***mustn't*** *stay here!* Tu ne dois pas rester ici ! (= obligation de ne pas / interdiction de)
You ***don't have to*** *stay here.* Tu n'es pas obligé de rester ici. (= non obligation de)

	should + BV (base verbale)	*should* + *have* + participe passé
« Je devrais... » = « Il faudrait que je... » (conseil, etc.)	*You* ***should take*** *some rest.* Tu devrais prendre un peu de repos.	**« J'aurais dû... »** *He* ***should have told*** *me.* Il aurait dû me le dire.

	must + BV (base verbale)	*must* + *have* + participe passé
« Je dois... » = « Il est probable que je... » (→ 37 p. 209)	*He* ***must be*** *very disappointed.* Il doit être très déçu.	*She* ***must have been*** *frightened.* Elle a dû avoir peur.

15. Discours direct / indirect : rapporter des paroles ou des pensées

Discours direct	Discours indirect
a. *He said, "I'm sorry."*	*He said (that) he **was** sorry.*
b. *He said, "I have found a solution."*	*He said (that) he **had found** a solution.*
c. *He said, "They will like the project."*	*He said (that) they **would like** the project.*
d. *He said, "She may win the match."*	*He said (that) she **might win** the match.*

Caractéristiques du discours indirect

- Pas de guillemets.
- Certains **pronoms** doivent être modifiés (dans les exemples **a.** et **b.**, *I* devient *he*).
- Respecter les règles de **concordance des temps.** Elles s'appliquent dans les **récits au passé**, quand le verbe qui introduit le discours indirect est au **prétérit** *(He **said**/He **thought** that…) :*

Le **présent** du discours direct devient un **prétérit**	*He said, "I'**m** sorry."* → *He said he **was** sorry.* *He said, "I **will** help them."* → *He said he **would** help them.*
Le **prétérit** du discours direct devient généralement un ***past perfect***	*He said, "I **told** you the truth."* → *He said he **had told** me the truth.*
Les **adverbes de lieu et de temps** peuvent être modifiés	*He asked me, "Do you like it **here**."* → *He asked me if I liked it **there**.* *He said, "I'll tell you **tomorrow**."* → *He said he would tell me **the day after/the following day**.*
Autres changements de ce type	• *yesterday* → *the day before* • *last week/month/year* → *the week/month/year before* • *ago* → *before*

Le cas particulier des questions

Les questions rapportées au **style indirect** sont à la **forme affirmative** : pas d'inversion sujet-auxiliaire • pas d'auxiliaire *do/does/did* • pas de point d'interrogation.

She asked me, "What does Tom think of the project?" → *She asked me what **Tom thought** of the project.*

Pour rapporter au style indirect une *Yes/No question*, on utilise ***if*** :

He asked me, "Do you like spaghetti?" → *He asked me **if** I liked spaghetti.*

16. « Faire faire » (*make/have*, etc. + verbe)

Assez souvent, l'équivalent anglais du français « faire + verbe » est un verbe simple ou une expression :
Je vais **faire chauffer** le lait dans cette casserole.
*I'll **heat** the milk in this pan.*
Il nous **a fait attendre** une demi-heure.
*He **kept us waiting** for half an hour.*

Dans les autres cas, « faire » peut avoir pour équivalent *make*, *have* ou *get*, dans des constructions différentes.

make + nom / pronom + base verbale	exprime une idée de **cause ou de forte contrainte** : *He **made the audience cry**.* Il a fait pleurer l'assistance. (Notez l'ordre des mots en anglais.) *They **made him do** the dishes.* Ils lui ont fait faire la vaisselle.
have + nom / pronom + base verbale	exprime une **contrainte plus neutre** : *His mother **had him go** to the hairdresser's.* Sa mère l'a fait aller chez le coiffeur.

17. Futur (situer un événement dans le futur)

■ Pour parler de l'avenir, le français utilise souvent le **présent** : « Le film **sort** la semaine prochaine. » L'anglais fait de même : *"The film **comes out** next week."* Mais attention : en anglais il faut choisir entre le **présent simple** et le **présent en** *BE* **+** *-ING*.

Présent simple	pour un événement qui fait partie d'un **programme** (planning, horaire, calendrier, etc.) : *The film **comes out** next week.*
Présent en *BE* + *-ING*	pour exprimer une **intention** : Ils se marient en mai. *They**'re getting** married in May.*

■ L'équivalent anglais du **futur simple** français est en général le modal ***will*** (+ base verbale) :
Elle **sera** très contente de votre travail. *She**'ll be** very pleased with your work.*

■ L'équivalent anglais de **« aller + infinitif »** est souvent ***be going to*** :
Je pense que ça va leur plaire. *I think they**'re going to** like it.*
Cependant, on emploie ***will*** (et non *be going to*) pour exprimer une **décision prise au moment où l'on parle** :
D'accord, je vais faire la vaisselle. *OK, I**'ll do** the dishes.*

> **Dans certaines propositions subordonnées**, notamment les subordonnées de temps, on ne peut pas utiliser *will* pour exprimer le futur, on utilise le **présent simple** :
> Je vous le dirai quand je le **saurai**. *I'll tell you when I **know**.*
> Il fera ce qui lui **plaira**. *He'll do what he **likes**.*

18. Habitude

■ **« Avoir l'habitude de »**
– Présent simple ou prétérit simple :
*He **takes/took** the bus every morning at eight.*
Il a / avait l'habitude de prendre le bus tous les matins à 8 heures.
– Pour le passé, on peut aussi employer ***would*** (ou ***'d***) + base verbale :
*He**'d take** the bus every morning at eight.*
Il avait l'habitude de prendre le bus tous les matins à 8 heures. (→ 44 p. 212.)

■ **Sens de « être habitué à » : *be used to*** + nom ou pronom / + V-*ING*.
*She**'s used** to the cold/**to being** alone.*
Elle est habituée au froid / à être seule. (→ 44 p. 212)

19. *Had better* et *would rather*

Pour exprimer un **conseil** : ***had better*** (ou ***'d better***) + **base verbale** :		*You**'d better phone** her at once.* Tu ferais bien de lui téléphoner tout de suite. *He**'d better not wake** the baby up!* Il n'a pas intérêt à réveiller le bébé ! (La base verbale peut être précédée de *not*.)
Pour exprimer une préférence : ***would rather*** (ou ***'d rather***)	+ base verbale	***I'd rather (not) stay** here.* Je préfère (ne pas) rester ici. ***Would you rather go** by train?* Vous préféreriez y aller en train ?
	+ nom / pronom + prétérit	***I'd rather you stayed** here.* Je préférerais que vous restiez ici. *He**'d rather you didn't ask** too many questions.* Il préférerait que vous ne posiez pas trop de questions.

20. Have, have got

- ***Have*** **: auxiliaire**
  - utilisé pour former le ***present perfect*** ou le ***past perfect*** :
  She ***hasn't*** *finished./****Has she*** *finished?* (→ 31 p. 206)
  - dans l'expression *have got* :
  *He****'s got*** *a mobile./He* ***hasn't got*** *a mobile./****Has he got*** *a mobile?*

- ***Have*** **: verbe**
  - En dehors de ses emplois comme auxiliaire du *present perfect / past perfect*, *have* peut **toujours** fonctionner comme **verbe,** c'est-à-dire **avec *do/does/did*** pour la négation et l'interrogation (→ 22 p. 202) :
  I ***don't have*** *a mobile./****Do you have*** *a mobile?*
  - *Have* est également employé dans le sens de « prendre » ou dans un sens voisin (manger, boire).

Have *some more tea!*	Prends / Prenez encore un peu de thé !
Have *a nice weekend!*	Bon week-end !
Did *you* ***have*** *a good journey?*	Tu as / Vous avez fait bon voyage ?
have / take *a shower / a bath*	prendre une douche / un bain
have *a chat / a talk with somebody*	bavarder / discuter avec qqn
have / take *a walk*	faire une promenade
have / take *a look*	jeter un coup d'œil

21. « Il y a... / Il y avait... »

- **« Il y a... »** utilisé pour dire que quelque chose **existe** dans tel lieu, dans telle situation, etc. :

Il y a une voiture sur le parking. Il y a deux voitures sur le parking.	***There is*** *a car in the car park* ***There are*** *two cars in the car park.* (Notez **l'accord singulier / pluriel** avec le nom qui suit.)
Il y avait une poste dans le village.	***There was*** *a post office in the village.*
Est-ce qu'il y a un problème ?	***Is there*** *a problem?*
Il doit y avoir un problème.	***There must be*** *a problem.* (Notez la construction « modal + *be* ».)

- **« Il y a... »** suivi d'une **indication de temps** :
  Elle est partie il y a dix minutes. *She* ***left ten minutes ago***.

verbe au **prétérit** (puisque l'événement est situé tout entier dans le passé)	+ nombre de minutes / jours / etc.	+ *ago*

Le cas particulier de « Il y a... que... » / « cela fait... que »
• Pas de problème si « **il y a... que...** » peut être remplacé par « **il y a...** » en changeant l'ordre des mots :
Il y a dix minutes qu'elle est partie. = Elle est partie il y a dix minutes.
She ***left ten minutes ago.***
• Mais attention si ce remplacement est impossible :
Il y a dix minutes que je suis là. ***I've been here for*** *ten minutes.*
(= Je suis là depuis dix minutes.) (→ 13 p. 198)

22. Interrogation

■ Les **constructions interrogatives** utilisent obligatoirement un **auxiliaire** (*BE, HAVE, DO* ou un modal → 24 p. 203), qui est **placé immédiatement avant le sujet.** Le présent et le prétérit simples utilisent ***do/does/did*** à la forme interrogative :

Does Edwin *live in Cardiff?* Est-ce qu'Edwin habite à Cardiff ?

Will they *have finished by five o'clock?* Est-ce qu'ils auront fini avant cinq heures ?

■ Une phrase interrogative peut être introduite par un mot interrogatif ou une expression interrogative :

How *is Susan?*	Comment va Susan ?
What *is Susan* ***like****?*	Comment elle est, Susan ? (mot à mot : « À quoi ressemble Susan ? »)
Who *did they speak to?*	À qui ont-ils parlé ? (Notez la place de la préposition *to*.)
Whose *computer is this?*	À qui est cet ordinateur ?
How far *is the post office from here?*	Elle est loin d'ici, la poste ?
How often *do you have competitions?*	Tous les combien as-tu des compétitions ?

Notez la différence de construction entre ***Who*** *did they help*? (Qui ont-ils aidé ?) et ***Who*** *helped them?* (Qui les a aidés ?) : quand le mot interrogatif est sujet du verbe (cf. ***Peter*** *helped them*), on n'emploie pas *do/does/did*.

23. « Le / la / les » : *the* ou Ø en anglais ?

■ Dans de nombreux cas, « le / la / les » (articles définis) ont pour équivalent ***the*** en anglais.

Je cherche le chemin de la gare. *I'm looking for the way to the station.*

L'article ***the*** se prononce :
- /ðə/ devant un son « consonne » : *the sun, the UK /juːˈkeɪ/, the one /wʌn/* (→ 3 p. 194).
- /ði/ devant un son « voyelle » : *the annual meeting, the honest /ˈɒnɪst/ citizen.*

■ Cependant, l'équivalent de « le / la / les » est **l'article Ø** (= « zéro » / absence d'article) dans les cas suivants :

Mercury *is a metal.* Le mercure est un métal. *That pesticide is dangerous for* ***bees****.* Ce pesticide est dangereux pour les abeilles.	On parle de quelque chose **« en général »**, avec un nom **indénombrable au singulier** *(mercury)*, ou un nom **dénombrable au pluriel** *(bees)*.
Spain, Africa, Minnesota	Devant les **noms de pays, continents** ou **régions**. Exceptions : noms de pays au pluriel *(the USA, the Philippines)*, noms communs (par exemple *kingdom* dans *the UK*), *the Caribbean* (la Caraïbe).
Prince William, President Obama, King George VI (lire George the sixth)	Devant les **noms de titre ou de fonction** suivis d'un nom propre.

24. Modalité et auxiliaires modaux

La modalité (sens de « pouvoir », « devoir », etc.) peut être exprimée soit par des **modaux** (*can*, *will*, etc., voir ci-après) soit par des **expressions de modalité** (*have to*, *be able to*, etc.).

Les cinq modaux principaux :

Présent	***can*** /kæn/, /kən/	***may*** /meɪ/	***must*** /mʌst/, /məs/	***shall*** /ʃæl/, /ʃəl/	***will*** /wɪl/, /wəl/, ***'ll***
Prétérit	***could*** /kʊd/, /kəd/	***might*** /maɪt/		***should*** /ʃʊd/, /ʃəd/	***would*** /wʊd/, ***'d***

La forme négative de *can*, ***cannot***, s'écrit en un seul mot.
Sa forme contractée, ***can't***, se prononce /kɑːnt/ en anglais britannique et /kænt/ en anglais américain.

Formes modales simples et composées : exemples avec le modal MAY

Modal + base verbale	*He **may/might work**.*
Modal + *be* + V-ING	*He **may/might** be **working**.*
Modal + *have* + participe passé	*He **may/might** have **worked**.*
Modal + *have been* + V-ING	*He **may/might** have been **working**.*

Caractéristiques importantes des modaux

- Ce sont des auxiliaires : leur interrogation et leur négation se forment directement (sans *do/does/did*).
- Ils ne prennent pas de *-s* à la troisième personne du singulier.
- Ils ne sont jamais précédés ni suivis de *to*. Ils n'ont pas d'infinitif, ni de forme en -ING, ni de participe passé.
- Quand on a besoin d'un infinitif, d'une forme en -ING ou d'un participe passé, on utilise un **équivalent** (voir ci-après).
- Dans un groupe verbal, il ne peut y avoir qu'un seul modal, qui est nécessairement placé en tête.
  *He **must** be able to do it.* Il doit être capable de le faire.

Équivalents des modaux

Have to **peut remplacer** ***must*** **(pour l'obligation)**	*They'**ll have to** be patient.* Ils devront être patients.
Be able to **peut remplacer** ***can*** **(pour la capacité)**	*She must **be able to** solve the problem.* Elle doit pouvoir (= être capable de) résoudre le problème.
Be allowed to **peut remplacer** ***can*** **(pour la permission / l'autorisation)**	*He **was allowed to** use the company car.* Il a pu (= a été autorisé à) utiliser la voiture de la société.
Be forbidden to **peut remplacer** ***mustn't/can't*** **(pour l'interdiction)**	*She **was forbidden to** take notes.* On lui a interdit de prendre des notes.

25. *Most (of the)* + nom

Most **= « la plupart (de / des) ».** Distinguez bien ***most*** de ***most of the*** :

***Most people** like music.* La plupart des gens aiment la musique.	***Most of the people I know** like music.* La plupart des gens que je connais aiment la musique.
On considère la catégorie *people*, les gens, d'une façon générale : article Ø.	On ne parle pas des gens en général, mais d'une catégorie (= les gens que je connais).

26. Noms indénombrables

■ **Indénombrables singuliers** (***furniture*** = mobilier / meubles • ***news*** = nouvelle(s) • ***progress*** = progrès)...

- L'**accord** du verbe et des pronoms se fait au **singulier** :

*His **progress** is remarkable.*

Ses progrès sont remarquables.

- **Impossibilité de mettre le nom au pluriel** et **d'employer l'article** ***a/an*** :

Quand on veut absolument « dénombrer », il faut utiliser un ***dénombreur*** comme *a piece of* :

This is an interesting piece of news. = C'est une nouvelle intéressante.

■ **Autres indénombrables singuliers à connaître :**

information renseignement(s)	*advice* conseil(s)	*luggage (GB)* *baggage* /ˈbæɡɪdʒ/ *(US)* bagages	*evidence* preuve(s)	*leisure* loisirs	*damage* dégâts

27. « On » (équivalents anglais)

On = nous (en français parlé)	***we***	Tu te rappelles ? On s'est bien amusés. *Do you remember? **We** had a lot of fun.*
On = n'importe qui (vous ou moi, par exemple)	***you***	On ne fait jamais assez attention. ***You** can never be careful enough.* Au Danemark, on voit beaucoup d'éoliennes. *In Denmark **you** see a lot of wind turbines.*
On = une ou plusieurs personnes inconnue(s), ou que je n'éprouve pas le besoin de nommer	**construction passive**	Il y a un mois qu'on a autorisé la vente de ce médicament. *The sale of that medicine **was authorized** a month ago.* Je n'aime pas qu'on me mente. *I don't like **being lied to**.* On dit qu'il est très riche. *He **is said to** be very rich.*

28. Passif (la voie passive)

■ **Formes**

Construction active	Construction passive (*BE* conjugué + participe passé)
*My brother **took** this photo.* Mon frère a pris cette photo	*This photo **was taken** by my brother.* Cette photo a été prise par mon frère.

Si le complément du verbe se construit avec une **préposition**, cette dernière se place **après le participe passé** :

Ses avertissements n'ont jamais été écoutés.

*His warnings **have** never **been listened to**.*

■ **Emplois**

On utilise le passif, en particulier, quand on ne peut pas ou qu'on ne veut pas dire qui accomplit l'action. Dans ce cas, le français utilise généralement **« on »** (→ 27, ci-dessus).

■ **Construction avec les verbes de parole ou d'opinion** (***say***, ***believe***, etc.) :

*He **is said/believed to** have inherited a huge fortune.*

On dit / pense qu'il a hérité d'une fortune immense.

29. *Past perfect* (ou *pluperfect*)

Formes

Auxiliaire ***had*** (forme contractée : ***'d***) pour toutes les personnes + **participe passé.**

*I/You/He ... **had found** the solution.*
J'avais / Tu avais / Il avait ... trouvé la solution.

Sens

- **Valeur de résultat**

*He **had lost** his keys, so he couldn't enter his house.*
Il avait perdu ses clés, donc il ne pouvait pas entrer dans sa maison.

> Différence avec le *present perfect* (→ 31 p. 206) : il s'agit d'un résultat **par rapport à un moment du passé**, et non par rapport au moment présent.

- **Valeur de durée**

*He **had been working** there <u>for twenty years/since 1998.</u>*
Il **travaillait** là depuis vingt ans / depuis 1998.
L'événement dure jusqu'à un moment du passé (alors qu'avec le *present perfect* il dure jusqu'au moment présent). En français, le temps utilisé est ici l'**imparfait**.

- **Valeur imaginaire** (→ 35 p. 208)

*I wish he **had told** me.*
J'aurais aimé qu'il me le dise. / Je regrette qu'il ne me l'ait pas dit.

30. Pluriel des noms dénombrables

Pluriel des noms réguliers

On ajoute la terminaison ***-s*** (*one book* → *two book**s***).
Modifications orthographiques et prononciation → p. 8 ***-s, 's***

Principaux pluriels irréguliers

child /tʃaɪld/ (enfant) → *children* /ˈtʃɪldrən/	*foot* /fʊt/ (pied) → *feet* /fiːt/
man /mæn/ (homme) → *men* /men/	*tooth* /tuːθ/ (dent) → *teeth* /tiːθ/
woman /ˈwʊmən/ (femme) → *women* /ˈwɪmɪn/	*mouse* /maʊs/ (souris) → *mice* /maɪs/

Certains noms qui se terminent par ***-f*** ou ***-fe*** ont un pluriel en ***-ves*** :
half /hɑːf/ → ***halves*** • *wife* → ***wives*** (mais : *roof* → *roofs*).
Parmi les plus courants : *life* • *shelf* (étagère) • *knife* • *leaf* (feuille) • *wolf* (loup).

Avec les **noms collectifs** comme ***people***, ***police*** ou ***personnel***, l'accord se fait au **pluriel.**
*Ten **people were** injured in the accident.*
Dix personnes ont été blessées dans l'accident.
*The **police have** arrested the murderer.*
La police a arrêté le meurtrier.

31. *Present perfect* simple

- **Formes** : auxiliaire HAVE au présent + participe passé.
- **Valeur de résultat** : on s'intéresse au **résultat présent** d'un **événement passé.**
  *I'**ve lost** my keys.* J'ai perdu mes clés.
  Ce qui importe ici, c'est le résultat : « Je n'ai plus mes clés. »

Avec le *present perfect*, on emploie :

already (déjà)	*I've **already** asked him if he'd like to join the club.* Je lui ai déjà demandé s'il voulait adhérer au club.
ever (« *déjà* » dans une question) *never* (jamais)	*Have you **ever** asked him?* Tu lui as déjà demandé ? *I've **never** asked him.* Je ne lui ai jamais demandé.
not... yet (pas encore) *over the past few days* (ces derniers jours)	*I haven't asked him **yet**.* Je ne lui ai pas encore demandé.

- **Valeur de durée :** (→ 13 p. 198) **« Depuis »**
- **Passé récent**

Present perfect + just : exprime un passé récent (action qui vient à peine de s'accomplir)
*I'**ve just seen** her.*
Je viens de la voir.

32. *Present perfect* ou prétérit ?

- Pour le même événement passé, on peut choisir, **en fonction du point de vue qu'on adopte**, soit le *present perfect* soit le prétérit.

Prétérit quand on s'intéresse à l'événement passé, ou à ses circonstances : *"When **did** you **lose** your keys?"* *"[I **lost** them] **last night**."* « Quand est-ce que tu as perdu tes clés ? » « Hier soir. »	***Present perfect*** quand on s'intéresse **au résultat présent** d'un événement passé : *I'**ve lost** my keys. I will be late.* J'ai perdu mes clés. Je vais être en retard.

- Les indications de date, d'heure, etc., sont **incompatibles avec le *presentperfect***, et exigent l'emploi du **prétérit** (→ 35 p. 208) :
  *I asked him **yesterday / on March 2nd / two days ago**.*
  Je lui ai demandé hier / le 2 mars / il y a deux jours.

> Même si le *present perfect* ressemble par sa forme au passé composé français formé avec « avoir », il n'en est pas toujours l'équivalent.

- **Deux emplois de *for* : « depuis » et « pendant »**

Comparez :

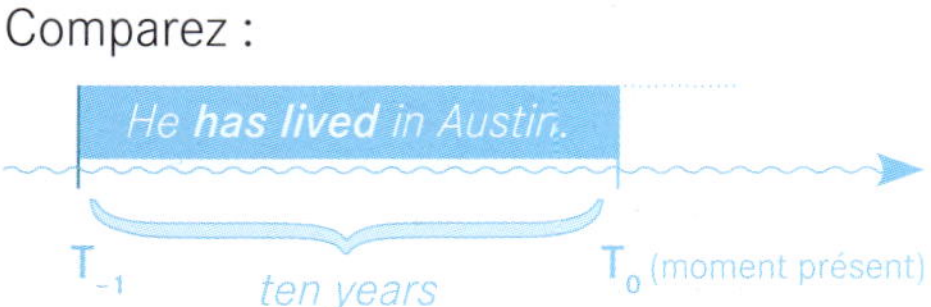

*He **has lived** in Austin **for ten years**.*
Il habite à Austin **depuis** dix ans.
(Il y habite encore.)

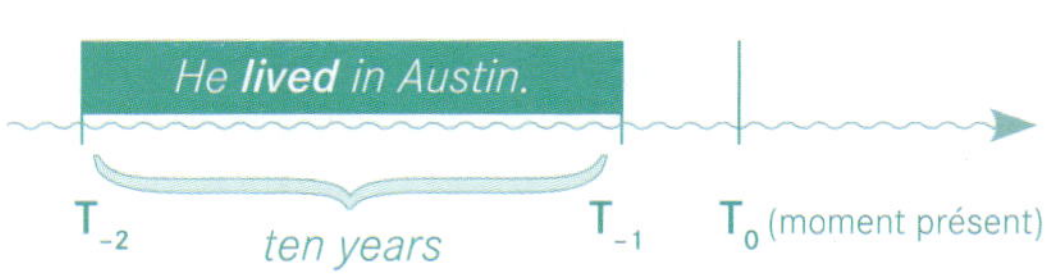

*He **lived** in Austin **for ten years**.*
Il a habité à Austin **pendant** dix ans. (Il n'y habite plus.)
L'emploi du prétérit est normal dans ce cas : l'événement est séparé du présent.

33. *Present perfect* en *BE* + V-*ING*

Valeur de résultat

	Forme	Valeur
Present perfect simple	*Alice **has washed** the dog.* *He doesn't smell any more.* Alice a lavé le chien. Il ne sent plus mauvais.	**Exprime simplement un résultat :** le chien est propre.
Present perfect en *BE* + V-*ING*	*"There's water everywhere!* *What's happened?"* *"Ted **has been washing** the dog."* « Il y a de l'eau partout. Qu'est-ce qui s'est passé ? » « Ted a lavé le chien. »	On a constaté un résultat (« Il y a de l'eau partout »), et la forme verbale en *BE* + V-*ING* exprime un « coup de projecteur » sur l'**action qui a provoqué le résultat** (sur l'action « Ted a lavé le chien »).

Notez qu'en français on a la même forme verbale dans les deux cas (« a lavé le chien »).

Valeur de durée

Avec les verbes exprimant un état tels que ***know, look*** (= paraître) ou ***understand,***	on utilise obligatoirement le *present perfect* **simple** : *He**'s known** her since 2002.* Il la connaît depuis 2002.
Avec les autres verbes,	on utilise généralement le *present perfect* en *BE* + V-*ING* : *He**'s been running** for 45 minutes.* Il court depuis 45 minutes.

34. Présent simple et présent en *BE* + V-*ING*

Forme du présent simple : terminaison *-s* à la 3e personne du singulier.
Modifications orthographiques et prononciation de ***-s*** : → p. 8

Emplois du présent simple
Le présent simple est utilisé pour parler d'un fait, ou d'une série de faits, considérés au moment présent et **vus dans leur totalité**.

Caractéristique du sujet	*Glen **sings** very well.* Glen chante très bien.
Comportement habituel	*Pam **takes** the bus every morning at 8.* Pam prend le bus tous les matins à 8 h.

Emplois du présent en *BE* + V-*ING*
Le présent en *BE* + V-*ING* réalise un « coup de projecteur » **sur un moment de l'événement** (ou sur plusieurs moments). Ce « coup de projecteur » peut prendre plusieurs formes.
– Il se situe au **moment où on parle**, et au milieu de l'action :
*Listen: they**'re trying** to open the door.*
Écoute(z) : ils essaient d'ouvrir la porte.
– Il porte sur un événement **futur** (expression d'une **intention**) :
*Tomorrow I**'m having** lunch with Sonia.*
Demain je déjeune avec Sonia.

> Certains verbes sont difficilement compatibles avec *BE* + V-*ING* : *know* (savoir, connaître) ou *look* (employé dans le sens de « sembler »), etc.
> Ces verbes expriment un sentiment ou un état mental :
> *I know the answer.* Je connais la réponse.
> *I see what you mean.* Je vois ce que vous voulez dire.

35. Prétérit

Terminaison -*ed* du prétérit ou du participe passé, modifications orthographiques

reply → replied	Un ***y*** qui suit une consonne **devient *i***. (Mais *play → played*.)
stop → stopped *prefer → preferred*	Une consonne finale qui suit une voyelle est **redoublée** dans les verbes d'une seule syllabe (*stop*). ou si la **dernière syllabe est accentuée** (*pre**fer***). **Mais *o*ffer → *o*ffered** : la dernière syllabe n'est pas accentuée.

Terminaison -*ed* du prétérit ou du participe passé, prononciation : → p. 8.

Le prétérit de récit

Ce prétérit est utilisé dans le récit d'événements passés, vus comme **nettement séparés du présent** :
President Kennedy ***was assassinated*** *on November 22, 1963.*
Le Président Kennedy a été assassiné le 22 novembre 1963.
L'événement passé est **repéré dans le temps** :
- par un adverbe (*yesterday*, etc.),
- par une date,
- par l'indication d'une période ou d'une heure *(last year)*,
- par une construction formée avec ago *(He left ten minutes ago)*,
- ou par le contexte.

« Pendant » : *for* ou *during* ?

He worked in a fast food restaurant ***<u>for</u> two weeks <u>during</u> the holidays****.*
Il a travaillé dans un fast food pendant quinze jours pendant les vacances.
– ***During*** sert à indiquer **une période**, et répond à la question ***When...?***
– ***For*** sert à indiquer **une durée**, et répond à la question ***How long...?***
(How long did he live in London?)

Le prétérit imaginaire (ou « prétérit modal »)

– Événement « contraire à la réalité »

If I ***had*** *a car I'd drive you there.*
Si j'avais une voiture, je vous y conduirais. (sous-entendu : je n'ai pas de voiture)
Pour BE, il existe une forme pour exprimer ce sens de « non-réalité » : ***were*** utilisé à toutes les personnes.
If I were his brother... (Si j'étais son frère...).
Dans la langue courante, on dit *If I was his brother*...
Cependant, on dit toujours *If I were you*... (Si j'étais toi / vous...)

– Événement présenté comme peu probable

If you ***had*** *an accident the insurance would cover all the expenses.* (sous-entendu : il est peu probable que vous ayez un accident)
Comparez avec *If you* ***have*** *an accident, the insurance* ***would*** *cover all the expenses.*

– Emplois après *wish*, *if only*, etc.

wish *if only...* (si seulement...!)	*I wish* ***I knew*** *the answer.* J'aimerais connaître la réponse. / Je regrette de ne pas connaître la réponse. = Je souhaite connaître la réponse mais je ne la connais pas. *If only* ***I knew*** *the answer!* Si seulement je connaissais la réponse! *I wish they* ***had told*** *me.* J'aurais aimé qu'ils me le disent. / Je regrette qu'ils ne me l'aient pas dit. (Pour exprimer un regret sur un fait **passé**, on emploie ***had*** + **participe passé**.)
it's (high) time	*It's time you* ***got*** *a new phone.* Il est temps que tu te procures un nouveau téléphone.

36. Prétérit simple et prétérit en *BE* + V-*ING*

La différence est la même qu'entre le présent simple est le présent en *BE* + V-*ING*.

Le prétérit simple	Le prétérit en *BE* + V-*ING*
est utilisé dans un récit pour raconter la progression de l'action. *When I broke the news to him, he* ***texted*** *his wife.* Quand je lui ai appris la nouvelle, il a envoyé un SMS à sa femme.	est utilisé pour des événements qui servent de « toile de fond » à l'action. *When I broke the news to him, he* ***was texting*** *his wife.* Quand je lui ai appris la nouvelle, il était en train d'envoyer un SMS à sa femme.

37. Probabilité (degrés) : certain, probable, possible, etc.

Certain	*He* ***will*** *be at home now.* *He* ***will*** *be at home tomorrow.*	Il est certainement chez lui maintenant. Il sera chez lui demain.
Fortement probable	*He* ***must*** *be at home now.*	Il doit être chez lui maintenant.
Logiquement possible	*He* ***could*** *be at home.* *He* ***may*** *be at home.* *He* ***might*** *be at home.*	Il peut / pourrait (très bien) être chez lui. Il se peut qu'il soit chez lui. Il se pourrait qu'il soit chez lui.
Logiquement impossible	*He* ***can't*** *be at home.* *He* ***must*** *not be at home.* (US)	Il ne peut pas / ne doit pas être chez lui. Il ne doit pas être chez lui.

38. Pronoms personnels et possessifs

Pronoms sujets	Pronoms compléments	Déterminants possessifs	Pronoms possessifs	Pronoms réfléchis (→ 39 p. 210)
I	***me*** me, m', moi	***my*** mon/ma/mes	***mine*** le(s) mien(s) / la (les) mienne(s)	***my<u>self</u>*** (accentuation sur *self*)
you	*you*	*your* /jɔː/	*yours* /jɔːz/	*your<u>self</u>*
he	*him*	*his*	*his*	*him<u>self</u>*
she	*her*	*her*	*hers*	*her<u>self</u>*
it	*it*	*its*	*its own*	*it<u>self</u>*
we	*us*	*our* /ˈaʊə/	*ours* /ˈaʊəz/	*our<u>selves</u>*
you	*you*	*your* /jɔː/	*yours* /jɔːz/	*your<u>selves</u>*
they	*them*	*their*	*theirs*	*them<u>selves</u>*

Les **possessifs** (*my*, *your*, etc. / *mine*, *yours*, etc.) s'accordent uniquement avec le « possesseur » :

<u>He</u> called ***his*** *sister/****his*** *brother.* Il a appelé <u>sa</u> sœur / <u>son</u> frère.

<u>She</u> called ***her*** *sister/****her*** *brother.* Elle a appelé <u>sa</u> sœur / <u>son</u> frère.

39. Pronoms réfléchis et réciproques (équivalents des verbes pronominaux français)

- Le français utilise la même forme pour le sens **réfléchi** (« Ils **se sont regardés** [dans la glace] » – action sur soi-même) et pour le sens **réciproque** (« [au moment où ils se sont croisés] Ils **se sont regardés** »).
- En anglais :

Pour le **sens réfléchi**	on utilise un **pronom réfléchi** (*myself, yourself*, etc. → 38 p. 209) *They **looked at themselves** [in the mirror].*
Pour le **sens réciproque**	on utilise l'un des deux **pronoms réciproques *each other/one another*** **(sens identiques)**: *They **looked at each other/one another.***

- Les verbes ***get up, shave, dress, wash, meet*** et ***quarrel*** se construisent sans pronom réfléchi ou réciproque (car le sens réfléchi ou réciproque est évident) :

*He **shaves** every other day.*
Il **se rase** tous les deux jours.

*They **met** in the park.*
Ils **se sont rencontrés** dans le parc.

40. Relatifs : propositions relatives, pronoms relatifs

- Les propositions relatives sont introduites par des **pronoms relatifs**, qui sont :
  - les pronoms relatifs en *wh-* (***who*** /hu:/, ***which***, ***whose*** /hu:z/) ;
  - ***that*** (prononcé /ðət/) ;
  - le relatif « zéro » *(Ø)*, c'est-à-dire un vide :

  The young woman <u>you spoke to</u> is Dr Jones. La jeune femme <u>à qui tu as parlé</u> est le docteur Jones.
- Le choix entre ces pronoms est déterminé par :
  - le type d'**antécédent** (c'est-à-dire de nom que le pronom relatif remplace) ;
  - la **fonction** du pronom relatif (sujet du verbe, complément du verbe, ou complément d'un nom).

Règles à appliquer absolument :
- ***who*** uniquement pour les personnes et ***which*** uniquement pour les choses ;
- Ø n'est **jamais utilisé en fonction sujet.** Il ne peut pas remplacer *who/which/that* dans des phrases comme *The woman <u>**who** answered the phone</u> is my sister.* (La femme qui a répondu au téléphone est ma sœur.) ou comme *The season <u>**which/that** is best to plant a tree</u> is winter.* (La saison qui est la meilleure pour planter un arbre est l'hiver.)

	Antécédent humain	Antécédent non humain
Sujet	*The woman **who** answered the phone…*	*The season **which/that** is best…*
Complément direct	*The woman **Ø** you met…* La femme que tu as rencontrée…	*The film **Ø** you saw…* Le film que tu as vu…
Complément indirect	*The woman **Ø** you spoke **to**…* La femme à qui tu as parlé…	*The book **Ø** you're looking **for**…* Le livre que tu cherches…
Complément de nom	*The woman **whose** flat…* La femme dont l'appartement…	*The film **whose** director…* Le film dont le metteur en scène…

Faites attention lorsque le verbe se construit avec une **préposition** (exemples ci-dessus : prépositions ***to*** et ***for***).
Avec le **relatif Ø**, la préposition est obligatoirement **placée après le verbe** (et éventuellement après son complément direct).

41. *Some*, *any*, *no*, *every* et leurs composés

■ ***Some*** /səm/ **ou *any*** /ˈeni/ **: « une certaine quantité / un certain nombre de… » (= du / de la / des)**

	Nom indénombrable (singulier)	Nom dénombrable au pluriel
Affirmations : *some* /səm/	*He drank* ***some fruit juice****.* Il a bu du / un peu de jus de fruit.	*He ate* ***some pancakes****.* Il a mangé des / quelques crêpes.
Questions pour offrir / demander qqch : *some* /səm/	*Would you like* ***some fruit juice****?* Tu veux du jus de fruit ?	*Would you like* ***some pancakes****?* Tu veux des crêpes ?
Autres interrogations : *any*	*Did he drink* ***any fruit juice****?* Est-ce qu'il a bu du jus de fruit ?	*Did he eat* ***any pancakes****?* Est-ce qu'il a mangé des crêpes ?

■ ***Any*** est souvent utilisé dans des énoncés affirmatifs avec le sens de « n'importe quel(s) / n'importe quelle(s) » :

Take one card from the pack. ***Any*** *card.*
Prends une carte dans le paquet. N'importe quelle carte.

■ ***Not any*** **ou *no*** **: quantité nulle (= « pas de… », « aucun… », etc.)**

	Nom indénombrable (singulier)	Nom dénombrable au pluriel
Construction négative + *any*	*He <u>didn't eat</u>* ***any sugar****.* Il n'a pas mangé de sucre.	*He <u>didn't eat</u>* ***any pancakes****.* Il n'a pas mangé de crêpes.
Construction affirmative + *no*	*He <u>ate</u>* ***no sugar****.* Il n'a pas mangé de sucre.	*He <u>ate</u>* ***no pancakes****.* Il n'a mangé aucune crêpe.

■ ***Every*** **: « chaque, « tous »**

Every *question has its answer.* Chaque question a sa réponse. / Toutes les questions ont leur réponse.
(Notez qu'avec *every* les accords se font au **singulier**.)

■ **Composés de *some, any, no* et *every***

Le choix entre les composés de *some* et ceux de *any* se fait de la même façon qu'entre *some* et *any* (voir ci-dessus).

Personnes	Choses	Temps	Lieux
somebody /ˈsʌmbədi/ ***someone*** quelqu'un	***something*** /ˈsʌmθɪŋ/ quelque chose	***sometimes*** quelquefois	***somewhere*** ***someplace*** (US) quelque part
anybody /ˈenibɒdi/ ***anyone*** quelqu'un / n'importe qui	***anything*** /ˈeniθɪŋ/ quelque chose	***anytime*** n'importe quand	***anywhere*** quelque part, n'importe où
nobody /ˈnəʊbədi/ ***no one*** personne	***nothing*** /ˈnʌθɪŋ/ rien		***nowhere*** nulle part
everybody /ˈevribɒdi/ ***everyone*** (+ singulier) tout le monde	***everything*** /ˈevriθɪŋ/ (+ singulier) tout		***everywhere*** ***everyplace*** (US) partout

42. *Tags* et reprises par auxiliaire

Réponse abrégée *(tag answer)*	*"Can you be here at four?"* *"Of course **I can**."* *"Do you think he liked the film?"* *"I'm sure he did/he didn't."*	« Tu peux être ici à quatre heures ? » « Bien sûr que oui. » « Tu penses qu'il a aimé le film ? » « Je suis sûr(e) que oui / que non. »
Reprise interrogative *(question tag)*	*Ted left yesterday, **didn't** he?* * *Clara can't speak Russian, **can** she?*	Ted est parti hier, hein ? / non ? / pas vrai ?/ n'est-ce pas ? Clara ne sait pas parler Russe, hein ?
Reprise avec un sujet différent	*I think he's competent. **Don't you?*** *"Who said that?" **"Nora did!"***	Je pense qu'il est compétent. Pas toi ? « Qui a dit ça ? » « C'est Nora ! »
SO / NEITHER NOR + auxiliaire + sujet	*Sue plays the guitar, and **so does Ian**.* *"I can't swim." **"Neither can I."** / **"Nor can I."***	Sue joue de la guitare, et Ian aussi. « Je ne sais pas nager. » « Moi non plus. »
SO + sujet + auxiliaire (confirmation étonnée)	*"She looks pleased!" **"So she does!"***	« Elle a l'air contente ! » « Mais oui ! / En effet ! »

* En règle générale, la reprise interrogative est **négative** après un groupe verbal **positif**, et **positive** après un groupe verbal **négatif**.

43. *They're, their, theirs, there's*

Les prononciations de ces mots sont voisines ou identiques. Apprenez à les distinguer et à reconnaître la prononciation de chacun d'entre eux.

***They're** /ðeə/ pleased.* Ils / Elles sont content(e)s.

***Their** /ðeə/ house isn't far from here.* Leur maison n'est pas loin d'ici.

*That car isn't **theirs** /ðeəz/.* Cette voiture n'est pas à eux.

***There's** /ðeəz/ a lot of noise.* Il y a beaucoup de bruit.

44. *Used to* et *be used to*

Dans ces deux expressions, *used* se prononce /juːst/ (notez le son « s »).

*He **used to** live in Cardiff.* Il habitait / a habité Cardiff autrefois. *There **used to** be a pub here.* Autrefois, il y avait un pub ici.	L'expression invariable ***used to*** **+ base verbale** sert simplement à indiquer qu'un événement ou une série d'événements ont eu lieu **dans le passé**. (Elle n'exprime pas, en elle-même, une habitude.)
be used to **+ V-ING**	*He **is used to getting up** early.* → 18 p. 200

45. Verbes suivis d'un infinitif et verbes suivis d'un gérondif (V-ING)

Verbes + infinitif sans *to*

Let (laisser), ***help*** (aider), ainsi que ***have*** et ***make*** (sens de « faire faire » → 16 p. 199).

*Let Brian **do** as he likes.*

Laisse(z) Brian faire comme il veut.

*Help me (to) **tidy up** the bedroom.*

Aide(z)-moi à ranger la chambre.

> Attention à l'**ordre des mots** en anglais. En français, « laisser » ou « faire » peuvent être suivis immédiatement de l'infinitif : « Ils ont laissé participer / Ils ont fait participer tout le monde. »
> En anglais, il faut respecter l'ordre ***let*** **+ nom / pronom + BV** :
> *They let everybody participate./They made everybody participate.*

Verbes de perception : *see*, *watch*, *hear*, *feel*, etc.

*I saw several people **go in**.*

J'ai vu entrer plusieurs personnes. (Notez l'ordre des mots en anglais.)

Après ces verbes, on peut également avoir V-ING, utilisé lorsque l'action est vue en cours de déroulement : *I saw him trying to open the door.* Je l'ai vu [en train d']essayer d'ouvrir la porte.

Verbes + infinitif avec *to* : verbes exprimant une volonté et / ou une cause (on est tourné vers ce qui va ou ce qui peut se passer).

*She intends **to go** by bus.*

Elle a l'intention d'y aller en bus.

*She managed **to pass** her exam.*

Elle a réussi à passer son examen.

> En français, des **verbes de volonté** comme « vouloir » ou « préférer » sont souvent suivis d'une proposition en « que... ». Leurs équivalents anglais (***want***, ***would like***, ***prefer***) sont normalement suivis d'une **proposition infinitive**, et non d'une proposition en *that* (~~*I want that...*~~) :
> J'aimerais qu'il réponde à mes questions.
> ***I'd like** him to answer my questions.*
> *I **want** (Ben) to help you.*
> Je veux que Ben vous aide / vous aider.

Verbes + gérondif (V-ING) :

– Verbes ou constructions exprimant une opinion, une appréciation, un sentiment :
*She enjoys liv**ing** in that house.* Elle apprécie d'habiter dans cette maison.
*She can't stand wait**ing** for hours.* Elle ne supporte pas d'attendre pendant des heures.

– Verbes ***go on***, ***keep (on)***, ***stop***... :
*He went on/kept/stopped walk**ing**.* Il a continué à / arrêté de marcher.

– ***It's worth***
*This film is worth see**ing**.* Ce film vaut la peine d'être vu.

– ***It's no use***
*It's no use cheat**ing**.* Cela ne sert à rien de tricher.

– ***Look forward to***
*I look forward to see**ing** you.* J'ai hâte de te / vous voir.

MP 3 n° 23 — CD 3 PISTE 19

	Base verbale	Prétérit	Participe passé	Traduction
B	be	was / were	been	*être*
	bear /eə/	bore /ɔː/	borne /ɔː/	*porter*
	beat /iː/	beat /iː/	beaten /iː/	*battre*
	become /ɪ/ /ʌ/	became /ɪ/ /eɪ/	become /ɪ/ /ʌ/	*devenir*
	begin /ɪ/ /ɪ/	began /ɪ/ /æ/	begun /ɪ/ /ʌ/	*commencer*
	bend /e/	bent /e/	bent /e/	*courber*
	bet /e/	bet /e/	bet /e/	*parier*
	bite /aɪ/	bit /ɪ/	bitten /iː/	*mordre*
	bleed /iː/	bled /e/	bled /e/	*saigner*
	blow /əʊ/	blew /uː/	blown /əʊ/	*souffler*
	break /eɪ/	broke /əʊ/	broken /əʊ/	*casser*
	breed /iː/	bred /e/	bred /e/	*élever*
	bring /ɪ/	brought /ɔː/	brought /ɔː/	*apporter*
	build /ɪ/	built /ɪ/	built /ɪ/	*bâtir*
	burn /ɜː/	burnt /ɜː/, burned /ɜː/	burnt /ɜː/, burned /ɜː/	*brûler*
	burst /ɜː/	burst /ɜː/	burst /ɜː/	*éclater*
	buy /aɪ/	bought /ɔː/	bought /ɔː/	*acheter*
C	cast /ɑː/	cast /ɑː/	cast /ɑː/	*lancer*
	catch /æ/	caught /ɔː/	caught /ɔː/	*attraper*
	choose /uː/	chose /əʊ/	chosen /əʊ/	*choisir*
	come /ʌ/	came /eɪ/	come /ʌ/	*venir*
	cost /ɒ/	cost /ɒ/	cost /ɒ/	*coûter*
	cut /ʌ/	cut /ʌ/	cut /ʌ/	*couper*
D	deal /iː/	dealt /e/	dealt /e/	*distribuer*
	do /uː/	did /ɪ/	done /ʌ/	*faire*
	draw /ɔː/	drew /uː/	drawn /ɔː/	*tirer*
	dream /iː/	dreamt /e/, dreamed /e/	dreamt /e/, dreamed /e/	*rêver*
	drink /ɪ/	drank /æ/	drunk /ʌ/	*boire*
	drive /aɪ/	drove /əʊ/	driven /ɪ/	*conduire*
E	eat /iː/	ate /e/	eaten /iː/	*manger*
F	fall /ɔː/	fell /e/	fallen /ɔː/ /ə/	*tomber*
	feed /iː/	fed /e/	fed /e/	*nourrir*
	feel /iː/	felt /e/	felt /e/	*(res)sentir*
	fight /aɪ/	fought /ɔː/	fought /ɔː/	*combattre*
	find /aɪ/	found /aʊ/	found /aʊ/	*trouver*
	fly /aɪ/	flew /uː/	flown /əʊ/	*voler (dans les airs)*
	forbid /ə/ /ɪ/	forbad(e) /ə/ /eɪ/	forbidden /ə/ /ɪ/ /ə/	*interdire*
	forget /ə/ /e/	forgot /ə/ /ɒ/	forgotten /ə/ /ɒ/ /ə/	*oublier*
	forgive /ə/ /ɪ/	forgave /ə/ /eɪ/	forgiven /ə/ /ɪ/ /ə/	*pardonner*
	freeze /iː/	froze /əʊ/	frozen /əʊ/	*geler*
G	get /e/	got /ɒ/	got /ɒ/, gotten /ɒ/ (US)	*obtenir*
	give /ɪ/	gave /eɪ/	given /ɪ/	*donner*
	go /əʊ/	went /e/	gone /ɒ/	*aller*
	grow /əʊ/	grew /uː/	grown /əʊ/	*pousser (= croître)*
H	have /æ/	had /æ/	had /æ/	*avoir*
	hang /æ/	hung /ʌ/	hung /ʌ/	*pendre, suspendre*
	hear /ɪə/	heard /ɜː/	heard /ɜː/	*entendre*
	hide /aɪ/	hid /ɪ/	hidden /ɪ/	*cacher*
	hit /ɪ/	hit /ɪ/	hit /ɪ/	*frapper*
	hold /əʊ/	held /e/	held /e/	*tenir*
	hurt /ɜː/	hurt /ɜː/	hurt /ɜː/	*blesser*
K	keep /iː/	kept /e/	kept /e/	*garder*
	know /əʊ/	knew /uː/	known /əʊ/	*connaître*
L	lay /eɪ/	laid /eɪ/	laid /eɪ/	*poser à plat*
	lead /iː/	led /e/	led /e/	*mener*
	leap /iː/	leapt /e/	leapt /e/	*sauter*
	learn /ɜː/	learnt, learned /ɜː/	learnt, learned /ɜː/	*apprendre*

	Base verbale	Prétérit	Participe passé	Traduction
	leave /iː/	left /e/	left /e/	*quitter*
	lend /e/	lent /e/	lent /e/	*prêter*
	let /e/	let /e/	let /e/	*laisser*
	lie /aɪ/	lay /eɪ/	lain /eɪ/	*être couché*
	light /aɪ/	lit /ɪ/	lit /ɪ/	*éclairer*
	lose /uː/	lost /ɒ/	lost /ɒ/	*perdre*
M	make /eɪ/	made /eɪ/	made /eɪ/	*faire*
	mean /iː/	meant /e/	meant /e/	*signifier*
	meet /iː/	met /e/	met /e/	*rencontrer*
P	pay /eɪ/	paid /eɪ/	paid /eɪ/	*payer*
	put /ʊ/	put /ʊ/	put /ʊ/	*mettre*
R	read /iː/	read /e/	read /e/	*lire*
	ride /aɪ/	rode /əʊ/	ridden /ɪ/	*aller à cheval*
	ring /ɪ/	rang /æ/	rung /ʌ/	*sonner*
	rise /aɪ/	rose /əʊ/	risen /ɪ/	*s'élever*
	run /ʌ/	ran /æ/	run /ʌ/	*courir*
S	say /eɪ/	said /e/	said /e/	*dire*
	see /iː/	saw /ɔː/	seen /iː/	*voir*
	sell /e/	sold /əʊ/	sold /əʊ/	*vendre*
	send /e/	sent /e/	sent /e/	*envoyer*
	set /e/	set /e/	set /e/	*placer*
	shake /eɪ/	shook /ʊ/	shaken /eɪ/	*secouer*
	shoot /uː/	shot /ɒ/	shot /ɒ/	*faire feu, tirer*
	show /əʊ/	showed /əʊ/	shown /əʊ/	*montrer*
	shut /ʌ/	shut /ʌ/	shut /ʌ/	*fermer*
	sing /ɪ/	sang /æ/	sung /ʌ/	*chanter*
	sink /ɪ/	sank /æ/	sunk /ʌ/	*couler, sombrer*
	sit /ɪ/	sat /æ/	sat /æ/	*être assis*
	sleep /iː/	slept /e/	slept /e/	*dormir*
	smell /e/	smelt /e/	smelt /e/	*sentir*
	speak /iː/	spoke /əʊ/	spoken /əʊ/ /ə/	*parler*
	spell /e/	spelt /e/	spelt /e/	*épeler*
	spend /e/	spent /e/	spent /e/	*dépenser*
	spill /ɪ/	spilt /ɪ/	spilt /ɪ/	*répandre (par mégarde)*
	split /ɪ/	split /ɪ/	split /ɪ/	*fendre*
	spoil /ɔɪ/	spoilt /ɔɪ/	spoilt /ɔɪ/	*gâter*
	spread /e/	spread /e/	spread /e/	*répandre, étaler*
	spring /ɪ/	sprang /æ/	sprung /ʌ/	*bondir*
	stand /æ/	stood /ʊ/	stood /ʊ/	*être debout*
	steal /iː/	stole /əʊ/	stolen /əʊ/ /ə/	*voler (qqch)*
	stick /ɪ/	stuck /ʌ/	stuck /ʌ/	*coller*
	strike /aɪ/	struck /ʌ/	struck /ʌ/	*frapper*
	swear /eə/	swore /ɔː/	sworn /ɔː/	*jurer*
	sweep /iː/	swept /e/	swept /e/	*balayer*
	swim /ɪ/	swam /æ/	swum /ʌ/	*nager*
	swing /ɪ/	swung /ʌ/	swung /ʌ/	*(se) balancer*
T	take /eɪ/	took /ʊ/	taken /eɪ/ /ə/	*prendre*
	teach /iː/	taught /ɔː/	taught /ɔː/	*enseigner*
	tear /eə/	tore /ɔː/	torn /ɔː/	*déchirer*
	tell /e/	told /əʊ/	told /əʊ/	*dire*
	think /ɪ/	thought /ɔː/	thought /ɔː/	*penser*
	throw /əʊ/	threw /uː/	thrown /əʊ/	*lancer*
U	understand /æ/	understood /ʊ/	understood /ʊ/	*comprendre*
W	wake /eɪ/	woke /əʊ/	woken /əʊ/	*réveiller*
	wear /eə/	wore /ɔː/	worn /ɔː/	*porter (un vêtement)*
	win /ɪ/	won /ʌ/	won /ʌ/	*gagner*
	write /aɪ/	wrote /əʊ/	written /ɪ/	*écrire*

Corrigés des pages Apprendre à apprendre

(téléchargeables sur le site www.editions-hatier.fr/langues-eleves)

Unit 1 Yes, We Care!

1. a. demonstrator: *manifestant* • banner: *banderole* • protest march: *manifestation* • work placement/internship: *stage* • memories: *souvenirs* • scholarship: *bourse d'études*
determined: *déterminé* • involved in/with: *impliqué dans* • self-confident: *sûr de soi* • convincing: *convaincant*
empower: *donner les moyens de* • support a cause: *soutenir une cause* • achieve one's goals: *atteindre ses objectifs* • improve: *améliorer*

b. In a democracy, people **go to the polls** to elect their representatives. To be eligible to vote you must first **register** in order to be on a list. On the day of the election, you go to the **polling station,** you enter a **voting booth** so that your choice can remain secret and then you **cast** your **ballot** into a **ballot box**.

c. although • teenager • voting booth • candidate • parliament • empower • scholarship

2. a. My best experience has been my gap year, although I missed my friends.

b. Although she is very young, she is really involved in politics.

c. She is very self-confident in spite of her young age.

d. Zoella is very influential although she is very young.

Unit 2 Black Voices of Protest

1. *racines*: roots • *force*: strength • *(un) moyen de*: (a) means of • *paroles d'une chanson*: lyrics • *outil*: tool • *quartier*: neighbo(u)rhood •
insupportable: unbearable • *profondément ancré*: deep-rooted • *inquiet*: concerned • *engagé*: committed • *démuni*: deprived
surmonter des préjugés: overcome prejudices • *sensibiliser*: raise awareness • *faire tomber des barrières*: break down barriers • *exiger*: demand • *atteindre*: reach • *sortir un album*: release an album • *donner un spectacle*: give a performance • *lutter*: struggle

2. This rap singer used to live in a deprived area in L.A.
For him, songs are a means of denouncing social injustice.
He wants to make the audience aware of the recent riots.
Is a singer influential enough to make the government react?

3. a. He gave this concert to help deprived people after the hurricane/storm.

b. Tracy Chapman wrote this album to denounce/expose the racial divide.

c. Music is a powerful tool to make people react.

d. The video clip I've seen denounces deep-rooted prejudices.

Unit 3 Guns Under Fire

► **1.** a. f**i**rearm: *arme à feu* • sl**au**ghter: *massacre* • s**a**fety: *sécurité* • (eye)w**i**tness : *témoin*
d**e**sperate: *désespéré* • h**e**lpless/p**o**werless: *impuissant* • ast**o**nishing: *surprenant* • eff**e**ctive: *efficace* •
w**ou**nded: *blessé (par balle)*
aim at sb: *viser qqn* • thr**ea**ten sb with sth: *menacer qqn avec qqch* • shoot sb down: *abattre qqn* • make sb r**e**alize: *faire prendre conscience à qqn* • supp**o**rt: *soutenir*

b. illegal, impossible, unusual, unsafe, ineffective, unnecessary

c. T**e**xas • Color**a**do • Louisi**a**na • Massach**u**setts • Virg**i**nia • Fl**o**rida • Calif**o**rnia

► **2.** a. At Bear Creek High School the students are protected by the police.

b. Firearms/Weapons/Guns are forbidden in the high school.

c. In 2010 a teacher was threatened by intruders.

d. An anti-gun (awareness) campaign was launched by some parents.

e. Students/Pupils must open their bags at the entrance gate.

Unit 4 Screen Tourism

► **1.** a. h**o**lidaymaker: *vacancier* • boost: *élan, impulsion* • tr**a**veller: *voyageur* • film set: *plateau de tournage* • trip: *voyage* • b**e**nefit: *avantage* • m**e**dia hype: *battage médiatique*
enthusi**a**stic: *enthousiaste*
b**e**nefit from: *tirer profit de* • app**ea**l to: *plaire à* • make sb feel like +V-ING: *donner envie à qqn de* • boost the ec**o**nomy: *stimuler l'économie* • attr**a**ct: *attirer* • fulf**i**l a dream: *réaliser un rêve*

b. Some fans are so **enthusiastic** that they dream of seeing all the places where their favourite film or **series** was shot. Film **locations** have become very popular **holiday destinations** and many cities or countries are now trying to **cash in on** this new **trend**. They know that the **economic** impact can be phenomenal.

c. b**e**nefit • ec**o**nomy • econ**o**mic • enthus**ia**stic • h**o**lidaymaker • p**u**rchase • film-ind**u**ced • phen**o**menon

► **2.** a. In order to attract tourists, guided tours are organised in the cities or countries where films or series have been shot.

b. New Zealand is one of the first countries to really benefit from film(-induced) tourism.

c. Fans go to hotels, eat in restaurants, buy postcards of the place where they are staying. In fact, they boost the economy of the country or the region (that) they visit.

Unit 5 Building a Global World

► **1.** a. handy = **convenient** • fight = **struggle** • problem = **issue** • useless = **pointless** • eliminate = **eradicate** • overseas = **abroad**

b. More and more people are addicted **to** technological devices. Sometimes, we are so absorbed **in** our phones that we don't interact **with** others around us. Some people blame technology **for** our lack **of** communication.
Bill and Melinda Gates are involved **in** the fight **against** inequalities. Mark Zuckerberg wants to provide everyone **with** an Internet access. He is committed **to** the fight against inequalities.

c. - globalisation
- a means to
- share
- prevent somebody from doing something
- the digital divide
- enable somebody to
- His/Her goal/aim is to bridge the gap between the haves and the have-nots.

d.

Première syllabe	Deuxième syllabe
border • **ob**stacle	con**nect** • trans**form** • di**vide** • ex**change** • com**mu**nicate

► **2.** a. We don't have much time to act. As global citizens, we have many/a lot of responsibilities.

b. Bill Gates's last speech/The last speech by Bill Gates may inspire future generations to get involved in the protection of the environment.

c. New technologies offer a lot of advantages, but it is easy to become addicted to/hooked on them.

Unit 6 The New Face of America

► **1.** a. pro**jec**tion: *prévision* • youth: *jeunesse* • shift: *changement* • suc**cess**: *succès* • **in**come: *revenu*
cur**rent**: *actuel* • af**for**dable: *abordable (= pas trop cher)* • incr**ea**sing: *croissant* • **e**thnic: *ethnique*
make up: *composer, constituer* • rate: *classer* • resh**a**pe: *refaçonner* • achi**e**ve one's goals: *atteindre ses buts* • set up a b**u**siness: *monter une affaire, une entreprise*

b. mos[a]ic • div[e]rsity • decr[ea]se (verb) • ret[i]rement • b[u]siness • comp[e]titiveness

c.

/ɪ/ (fish)	/iː/ (key)	/aɪ/ (five)
hit • shift	achieve • decrease • dream • succeed	rise • decline

► **2.** a. When she graduates, she will look for a job.

b. As soon as they have become American citizens, they will be able to make their dreams come true.

c. As long as there is diversity in the population, there will be dynamism.

d. Once I have set up my business in Silicon Valley, I will think I have succeeded.

e. They won't give up until they have achieved their goal(s).

Unit 7 Work in Progress

► 1. a.

The future of the workplace
remote worker • multi-task • telework • telecommute • convenient • digital • on the move

Robots
tireless • improve • mechanised/automated • concerned/worried • threaten

New jobs
efficient • exploit • mechanical Turk • slave • complete tasks

b. 1. worried 2. automated 3. beneficial 4. employers 5. tireless

c. automation • application • competition • position

d.

/æ/ (cat)	/eɪ/ (cake)	/ə/ (banana)
laptop • distracting • staff	placement • make • wage • labour • vacancy	manual • apply

► 2. a. If my company uses robots, I will quit (my job).

b. If his workplace was far from his home, he would ask his boss to telecommute/telework/work remotely.

c. The more CVs/resumés and cover letters people send, the more opportunities they will have to get a job interview.

d. The happier employees are at work, the more efficient they are: it's a win-win situation!

Unit 8 More Than Meets the Eye

► 1. a. tank-top: *débardeur* • hooded sweatshirt: *sweat-shirt à capuche* • suit: *costume* • swimsuit: *maillot de bain* • skill: *capacité/compétence*
narrow-minded: *étroit d'esprit* • suspicious: *louche* • open-minded: *large d'esprit* • daring: *audacieux* • self-assured: *sûr de soi*
deceive: *tromper* • judge by: *juger sur/d'après* • be prejudiced against: *avoir des préjugés envers/contre* • be discriminated against: *être victime de discrimination*

b. prejudice • cliché • stereotype • tolerance • discrimination • open-mindedness

c. Banksy, a street artist, disapproves of **stereotypes or clichés** because he thinks people are all different and you can easily be **misled or deceived or fooled** by appearances. You can be **misled or deceived or fooled** by the way somebody looks. A young man with dreadlocks and baggy pants looks **suspicious** to people who only **judge by** appearances! The way he is dressed is not **traditional** enough, and yet he is a brilliant student. A young girl with a ponytail may look nice or shy, and yet she is **daring** enough to hit a boy with a spiked club.

► 2. a. If only people who are different/different people were better accepted!

b. He wishes his boss didn't criticize the way he dresses.

c. Young people wish older people did not judge them by their style.

Unit 9 Wind of Change for Women?

1. a. Many women now **succeed** in reaching a **powerful or top** position in a company. They are **determined** to climb the social **ladder**. However, most women must still fight for **equal** pay, because their **salary or income** is lower than a man's. Many campaigns denounce this **unfair or unjust** situation and encourage men and women to get **involved** in the fight against gender **inequality or discrimination**.

b. **1.** She wants to make people aware of the glass ceiling that exists in companies.
2. Women don't always believe in their abilities, and suffer from prejudices. They are sometimes discriminated against at work.
3. She fights for a better salary/better wages, (in order) to be on an equal footing with men.

c. succeed • career • esteem

d.

/ɪ/ (fish)	/aɪ/ (five)
ambitious • prejudice • embody • determined	ideal • strike • apply

2. a. Women have had the right to vote since 1928 in the United Kingdom.

b. Over the last few years, more and more men have joined the cause of gender equality.

c. Before the 90s/nineties, few women were CEOs.

d. For a long time, Hollywood actresses have been fighting* for equal pay between men and women.

** Ici, on utilise BE + ING pour montrer que la lutte est toujours en cours.*

Unit 10 Dreamers

1. a. standard of living: *niveau de vie* • fence: *barrière* • living conditions: *conditions de vie* • wages: *salaire* • attempt: *tentative/essai*
daring: *audacieux* • disappointed with: *déçu de* • undocumented: *sans papiers*
integrate into: *s'intégrer dans* • climb the social ladder: *grimper dans l'échelle sociale* • tell the truth: *dire la vérité* • succeed: *réussir* • achieve one's goals: *atteindre ses buts* • improve: *améliorer*

b. hesitant ≠ confident • optimistic ≠ pessimistic • poverty ≠ wealth • manage to ≠ fail to • skilled ≠ unskilled

c. Immigrants from South America want to **cross** the US **border**. They know it is a **risky** journey. **Smugglers** and **thieves** can steal from them. They are very courageous because they know they can **die of thirst** in the hot desert. They know they can be **deported** if they are caught. But they want to **escape** poverty.

2. a. Why did Alejandro risk his life? To have a better life and fulfil his dream.

b. Immigrants cross the border at night not to be caught.

c. How many miles did they travel to reach the border?

d. How many times did she try to cross the desert?

Unit 11 Sports Heroes

► **1.** a. sportsperson (sportsman/sportswoman): *un sportif/une sportive* • track and field events: *compétitions d'athlétisme* • (do) athletics: *(faire) de l'athlétisme* • title holder: *détenteur d'un titre*
committed: *engagé* • impressive: *impressionnant* • involved in: *impliqué dans*
score a goal: *marquer un but* • worship: *adorer/vénérer* • beat/defeat an opponent: *battre un adversaire* • overcome obstacles: *surmonter les obstacles* • play by the rules: *respecter les règles* • cheat: *tricher* • tell a lie: *dire un mensonge*

b. hero ≠ villain • able-bodied ≠ disabled • admire ≠ despise/look down on • respect ≠ disrespect • honest ≠ dishonest

c. Many people **admired** Lance Armstrong for his outstanding **results**. People respected him until they discovered he took **performance-enhancing drugs**.
His behaviour was **shameful**. He **deceived** doctors and organizers because he lied, he also **avoided** detection. He **pretended** he had never taken any drugs. To **achieve his goals or break records** he was ready to **jeopardize** his career.

► **2.** a. Who is the best basketball player that/Ø you know?

b. What this athlete did is stunning. He has an artificial leg which/that enables him to run very fast.

c. This blind athlete is more courageous than able-bodied athletes.

d. Are the athletes that/Ø we admire all trustworthy?

Unit 12 Ambassadors of Conscience

► **1.** a. opponent to: *adversaire de* • damage: *dégâts* • oil platform/rig: *plateforme de forage* • spokesperson: *porte-parole* • lack of: *manque de*
fearless: *qui n'a pas peur, sans crainte* • huge: *énorme* • discouraged: *découragé*
violate basic rights: *violer des droits de base* • urge people to: *inciter les gens à* • fight for one's rights: *se battre pour ses droits* • destroy: *détruire* • assert one's rights: *affirmer ses droits* • target/aim at: *viser*

b. offended: outraged • strong-willed: determined • bold: daring • reckless: fearless • stand up against: resist • defy: challenge • expose: denounce

c. Edward Snowden had the courage to **disclose** secrets. He **released** NSA documents on the United States government's surveillance programme. He **accused** the US government **of** spying on people all over the world. He **broke** the **law** by keeping journalists **informed** about the US global surveillance because he wanted to **limit** the excesses of the NSA. He was considered a public enemy because his revelations **threatened** the security of the country.

► **2.** a. The journalist asked who Chelsea Manning was. He/She asked what she exposed/had exposed.

b. The expert answered Manning was serving 35 years in prison for revealing secrets about the US army.

c. He added that Manning had chosen to risk her life to tell the truth. Her revelations had opened up a public debate on war and diplomacy.

Crédits textes

19 YouTube star Zoella becomes digital ambassador for mental health, by Stuart Dredge. Copyright Guardian News & Media Ltd 2015 **20** copyright 2015 Lauren Forcella credited to StraightTalkAdvice.org **22** © Letty Hardy, D.R. **23** © Lattitude Global Volunteering **28 Text A** © Global Citizen Academy **28 Text B** General Election 2015: E4 to shut down on polling day to encourage young people to vote.Daisy Wyatt, The Independent. April 2015 **31** Hip-Hop Lives, Lawrence Parker © Because.tv © Kobalt **32** Across the Lines (Tracy Chapman) © 1988 EMI April Music Inc / Purple Rabbit Music. Avec l'a mable autorisation d'EMI Music Publishing France. Droits protégés. **33** Race relations arguably worse in 'Age of Obama', By Anita Kumar - McClatchy Washington Bureau, © 2016 The McClatchy Company **34** D'Angelo and Bobby Seale on the Past and Future of Political Protest, by Dan Hyman, June 2015 © 2016 The New York Times Company **35** Baltimore, Prince © Because.tv **38** The world 's coming to an end, by Prince EA © PrinceEa.com **42 Text A** A Change is Gonna Come, written by Sam Cooke. Published by © 1964 AbKCO Music, Inc. Used by permission. All rights reserved. Avec l'aimable autorisation d'EMI Publishing France. Droits Protégés. **42 Text C** The Freedom Riders by Bernice Johnson Reagon, Eyes on the Prize © Blackside, Inc. D.R. **46** Excerpt fromThe Life Before her Eyes by Laura Kasischke. Copyright © 2002 by Laura Kasischke. Reprinted by permission of Houghton Mifflin Harcourt Publishing Company. All rights reserved **49** No Guns Allowed (Angela Hunte / Aubrey Graham / Calbin Broadus / Zachary Condon / Andrew Bain / Ariel Rechtshaid / Thomas Wesley Pentz / Wayne Henry / Andrew Herschey) © 2013 EMI Foray Music / Masani El Shabazz Music / EMI Blackwood Music Inc / Live Write Llc / My Own Chit Music / EMI Music Publishing Ltd / Songs Of Ingrooves / Galactic Soul Music / Lion Of God Publishing Co / Songs Of SMP / I Like Turtle Music / Jahdan Blakkamoore Music / Party Machine Music **50** Guns Blazing on the Silver Screen, by Leslie Marshall November 2013, 2016 © U.S. News & World Report LP. **54 Text A** What does gun violence really cost?, a special investigation by Mark Follman, Julia Lurie, Jaeah Lee, and James West. Based on research by Ted Miller © 2016 Mother Jones and the Foundation for National Progress. All Rights Reserved. **54 Text B** © Complex/Andrew LaSane 60 'Game of Thrones' puts Northern Ireland on the map, by ASSOCIATED PRESS, 22 June 2014, D.R. **62** Tourism Ireland launches Skellig Michael video to entice Star Wars fans, Frances Mulraney, January 06, 2016 © IrishCentral.com **63** Introducing Great Britain's $1M Tourism Ambassador: James Bond, by Mark Johanson, October 2012 © 2016 IBT Media Inc. All Rights Reserved. **68 Text A** How does movie tourism change a city's environment?, by Stephen Kelly 27 June 2014 © virgin.com, D.R **68 Text B** © Sue Beeton, 28 July 2008 **75** As budgets dwindle, high schools and youth sports teams turn to crowdfunding, By Jason Wolf, Special for USA TODAY, July 28, 2015, D.R. **80 Text A** Eat, Pray, Love, de Elizabeth Gilbert, 2006 © Elizabeth Gilbert, Used by permission of The Wylie Agency (UK) Limited **80 Text B** To Unite the Earth, Connect It, by Bono and Mark Zuckerberg, September 2015 © 2016 The New York Times Company **83** Cincy in 2060: 1 in 7 of us will be biracial, by Mark Curnutte, Photos and video by Cara Owsley © 2016 www.cincinnati.com. All rights reserved. **84** Latinos play a growing role in America's future, by Monica C. Lozano, May, 2015, Courtesy CNN **86** "A woman with the heart of a tiger": My mother risked everything to flee from the Khmer Rouge with her children, by SREYRAM KUY and SREYREATH KUY, June 2015, Copyright © 2016 The Associated Press, D.R. **87** The worldwide web, India should make more of a valuable asset abroad, May 2015 © The Economist Newspaper Limited, London 2016 **88** Black immigration is remaking U.S. black population, report says, by Fredrick Kunkle, April 2015 © 1996-2016 The Washington Post **92 Text A** © myimmigrationstory.com **92 Text B** © First appeared in TribTalk, a publication of The Texas Tribune **97** The future of your workplace, by RISHI BHATNAGAR, July 22, 2015, © 2016, The Hindu, D.R. **98** Secret to successful telecommuting? Moderation, research shows, By Patricia Kozicka, September 28, 2015 © Shaw Media Inc., 2016. All rights reserved. D.R **100** 4 Businesses that are Cutting Costs With Robot Workers, by Sam Becker, March 27, 2015 © The Cheat Sheet **106 Text A** "This Robot Is Cute, Artificially Intelligent and Employed", by Adam Satariano, Dina Bass, Jack Clark, May 2015 © 2016 Bloomberg L.P. All Rights Reserved **106 Text B** © 2016 Scenario Magazine, D.R. **109** 21-Year-Old Poses as Fake Celebrity, Gets His 15 Minutes of Fame By Eliza Murphy - 8/23/12, © ABC News **111** © Voice of America **112-113** Givonte Latimore Created on: February 09, 2008, D.R. **118** WE SHOULD ALL BE FEMINISTS by Chimamanda Ngozi Adichie, copyright © 2014 by Chimamanda Ngozi Adichie. Used by permission of Alfred A. Knopf, an imprint of the Knopf Doubleday Publishing Group, a division of Penguin Random House LLC. All rights reserved. Copyright © Chimamanda Ngozi Adichie 2014, used by permission of The Wylie Agency (UK) Limited **119** I lost a job because of my tattoos, September 2014. From BBC News at bbc.co.uk/news. With courtesy of BBC Motion Gallery **122** Made in Dagenham, script de James Ivory (2010). D.R. **124** What girls say about equality for girls, © Royal Academy of Engineering **130 Text A** Guilt – the one thing women shouldn't have in trying to have it all, by India Knight, July 2014 © Times Newspapers Ltd 2015 D.R. **130 Text B** Erin Kaye, Closer to Home, Poolbeg Press Ltd 2006; D.R. **136** Enrique's Journey by Sonia Nazario, 2007. Used by permission of Sonia Nazario **138** My life as an undocumented immigrant, by Jose Antonio Vargas, June 2011 © 2016 The New York Times Company **144 Text A** Texas,by James A. Michener, copyright © 1985 by James Michener. Used by permission of Random House, an imprint and division of Penguin Random House LLC; All rights reserved. **144 Text B** Deported to Mexico: a lost generation, by Nina Lakhani. Copyright Guardian News & Media Ltd 2015 **148** What It's Like To Be Me: Aimee Mullins, By Corrie Pikul, April 1, 2015, www.self.com **150** Cover image and Extract from "Welcome Home" from Silent Gesture: The Autobiography of Tommie Smith by Tommie Smith with David Steele. Used by permission of Temple University Press. © 2007 by Temple University. All Rights Reserved. **156 Text A** "The Hero In You" by Ellis Paul, Ellis Paul Publishing (SESAC), www.EllisPaul.com **156 Text B** Imperfect Heroes, Thomas Ehrlich and Ernestine Fu, July 2015 © 2016 Forbes.com All Rights Reserved 159 from Kalpona Akter's foreword to INVISIBLE HANDS: VOICES FROM THE GLOBAL ECONOMY (ed. Corinne Goria) published by Voice of Witness **160** Edward Snowden: the whistleblower behind the NSA surveillance revelations. Copyright Guardian News & Media Ltd 2015 **162** Offshore fracking fight washes up on the pristine shores of Arnhem Land by Zoe Holman. Copyright Guardian News & Media Ltd 2015 **168 Text A** Cobra by Deon Meyer. Copyright © 2014 Deon Meyer. Reproduced by permission of Hodder and stoughton Limited. **168 Text B** Dear Future Generations: Sorry, by Prince EA © PrinceEa.com **184** The Terrible Privacy of Maxwell Sim by Jonathan Coe, (Penguin Books, 2010) Copyright © Jonathan Coe, 2010 **186** Should employers pay for women to freeze their eggs?, October 2014. From BBC News at bbc.co.uk/news. With courtesy of BBC Motion Gallery

Table des illustrations

Rabat avant ph © Alamy / Photo 12 **8** : Illustrations Shutterstock et Clipart **10h** : Joe Brusky/Light Brigading **10m** : yienkeat/Shutterstock.com **10b** : George Frey/Getty Images/AFP **11h** : Charles McQuillan/Getty images **11m** : © Matt Herring/debut art **11b** : © Jon Berkeley for the Economist/debut art **12h** : Danomyte/Shutterstock.com **12m** : © Fakestencils/Deviant Art **12b** : Kevin Winter/Getty Images/AFP **13h** : John Moore/Getty Images/AFP **13m** : Dan Kitwood/Getty Images **13b** : kirstypargeter/CanStockPhoto **16-17** : Collection Christophel © Licnsgate/D.R. **18** : Joe Brusky/Light Brigading **19h** : Richard Goldschmidt/LNP/Visual Press **19b** : Reproduced with the approval of Google UK/Alphabet Inc. **21h** : © British Youth Council **21m** : UK Youth Parliament elections 2015: Luke Sabourn, Euan Nankervis, Sarah Trott, Crystal Lily Mills © UK Youth Parliament, D.R. **22** : Ishara S.Kodikara/AFP **23** : The Catholic Institute for International Relations **24** : *One Stitch Closer: Veronika Scott empowers other women* © Gap, Inc. / Be what's possible, D.R. **26** : © Joel Pett, Dec 13, 2010/Cartoonist Group **27h** : Giacomo PIROZZI/PANOS-REA **27b** : Laflor/Getty images **29** : © Bite the Ballot, London **30hg** : Hulton-Deutsch Collection/Corbis/Getty images **30hd** : Kevin Mazur/Getty images **30bg** : Simon Laessoee/Corbis/Getty images **30bd** : Agence Fastimage **31h** : Peter Newark American Pictures/Bridgeman images **31b** : Glenn Pinkerton/AP Photo/SIPA **32** : *Girl with a Balloon*, by Banksy, London, 2005. Courtesy of Pest Control Office **33** : *Ferguson Christmas*, 3 dec 2014 © David Fitzsimmons/Cagle Cartoons, inc **34** : MCT/Getty images **35h** : Carolyn Van Houten/San Antonio Express-News via AP/Sipa **35b** : Joe Brusky/Light Brigading **36** : SONY (26,67%) I CAN (Roy Hammond / Nasir Jones / Salaam Rem) © EMI APRIL MUSIC INC. / SALLAM REMI MUSIC INC. Avec l'aimable autorisation de EMI Music Publishing France **38** : Courtesy Poetry Slam/FBISD, designer of the logo, Fred Benitez **40** : William Gottlieb/Redferns/Getty images **41** : yienkeat/Shutterstock.com **43** : Warner Bros / The Kobal Collection/Aurimages **44** : George Frey/Getty Images/AFP **45** : hotdogsandguns.com 2012/D.R. **46** : © Gamma Acosta **47** : Africa Studio/

Shutterstock.com **48** : Lynne Sladky/AP Photo/SIPA **49** : © Jack Gambro/JackGambroDesign.com **50** : Collection Christophel © StudioCanal/ Silver Pictures **51** : Graphique inspiré de Brady Campaign to Prevent Gun Violence **52** : *Gun Machine*, Dec 14, 2012 Bill Day/Cagle Cartoons, inc **53** : *Too easy to buy a gun*, Jan 12, 2011 Olle Johansson/Cagle Cartoons, inc **54** : © 2016 Mother Jones and the Foundation for National Progress. All Rights Reserved. **56-57** : Collection Christophel © Lionsgate D.R. **58** : © Game of Thrones Tours Ltd **59hg** : Brandon Farris. Remerciements à airlinereporter.com **59hd** : New Zealand Post/AFP **59b** : Alexandre Gendron /www.ag-photo.fr **60** : Photo GaryMcParland, graphisme John Lambert © Game of Thrones Tours Ltd **61** : Charles McQuillan/Getty images **62** : DeAgostini/Getty Images **63** : © Jackdaws/debut art **64** : Antoine Lorgnier/Onlyworld.net **66** : Sherlock Série TV 2010, Benedict Cumberbatch et Martin Freeman, Collection Christophel/Hartswood Films/D.R. **69g** : Alessandro Lai/Shutterstock.com **69d** : Love actually 2003 réal. : Richard Curtis, Collection Christophel/D.R. **70** : © Statista. com, avec l'aimable autorisation de comScore **71** : © Matt Herring/debut art **72** : AFP **74** : *The millennials seeking out careers in social media*, Samira Hussain, July 2014. From BBC News at bbc.co.uk/news. With courtesy of BBC Motion Gallery **75** : USA Today Sports / Reuters **76** : *Wendy, Brian, Hunter, and Harper*, 2014, Eric Pickersgill **77** : Alex Mac/ Fotolia **78** : *Mobile Couple*, by Banksy, Bristol, 2014. Courtesy of Pest Control Office **79** : © Global Goals Campaign/Virgin.com **81** : D.R. **83h** : Judith F. Baca © 2001 *Shoulder II Shoulder Project: Are we both Americans? White /Latina* Photo courtesy of SPARC sparcinla.org **83b** : City of Cincinnati, Ohio **84** : © Jon Berkeley for the Economist/debut art **85** : D.R. 86 : Remerciements à SreyRam Kuy **87** : George Gutenberg/Moodboard/Photononstop **89** : Monticello/Shutterstock.com **90** : *Dancing Frida & Lady Liberty* © Felipe Galindo **91h** : Jim McMahon /Scholastic.com **91m** : JasonMillstein/iLLume/Novus Select **91b** : Joshua Hodge Photography/Getty Images **93**: *Wendy Cervantes Celebrates Immigrant Heritage Month* © Welcome.us, D.R. **94-95** : Collection Christophel © Twentieth Century Fox Film Corporation/D.R. **96hg** : Arleta Chojnacka/CITimages **96hd** : Georgia Kuhn/plainpicture **96b** : Uwe Umstätter/ plainpicture **98** : Turba/plainpicture **99g** : akg-images **99d** : Granger NYC/Rue des Archives/Bridgeman images **100** : DearFuture © Abi Jones **101g** : laraslk/Shutterstock.com **101m** : Macrovector/Shutterstock.com **101d** : america365/Shutterstock.com **102** : Wright's Media Copyrighted 2016. Conde Nast Publications **103** : Konstantin Inozemtsev/Getty images **104** : Danomyte/Shutterstock.com **105h** : © The Economist Newspaper Limited, London (January 18th, 2014). **105b** : David Mareuil / Anadolu Agency/AFP **107** : *Factory Man*, Adam Levey **108** : *Fake Love* © Fakestencils/Deviant Art 109 : © Brett Cohen 110 : Commemoration of the 10th anniversary of the Durban Declaration, UN.org/D.R. **111** : © Voice of America **112** : Edgar Gonzales image from the series Judging America © Joel Parés **114** : © Go Sprout Festival, Remerciements à Abdool Corlette **115h** : Shutterstock.com **115b** : © Licra 2010. Remerciements à Publicis. **116** : © 2016 Luxottica Group S.p.A. **117** : Courtesy of STARS/Ohio University **118** : Joint Council for the Welfare of Immigrants **120g** : Sean Gallup/Getty Images/AFP **120m** : Minas Panagiotakis/ Icon SMI/Corbis/Getty images **120d** : Tannen Maury/epa/Corbis/Getty images **121hd** : From the pages of TIME. © 2013 Time Inc. All rights reserved. Translated from TIME and published with permission of Time Inc. Reproduction in any manner in any language in whole or in part without written permission is prohibited. TIME and the TIME logo are registered trademarks of Time Inc. Used under license **121bg** : Bryan Mitchell/© 2014 Bloomberg Finance LP/Getty Images **121bm** : Mark Wilson/Getty Images/AFP 1**21bd** : PepsiCo Inc./AP Photo/Sipa **122** : *We want sex equality,* 2011, Real Nigel Cole ; Collection Christophel ARP Selection/D.R. **123** : Kevin Winter/Getty Images/AFP **124** : Défilé automne-hiver 2016, NY Wenn/Visual Press **125** : Creative by Dennis Ahlgrim, President and Creative Director of Ahlgrim Design Group, photography by Richard Brathwaite © NY City Government **126** : *How to raise a hand in 47 seconds* © Kommunal, D.R. **127** : © 2015 Let Toys Be Toys, UK **128** : Collection Christophel ® Ruby films/D.R. **129** : © 2015 Benetton Group. Remerciements à Paola Innocente **132-133** : Collection Christophel © 2013 Home Box Office/D.R. **134hg** : John Moore/Getty Images/AFP **134hd** : John Moore/Getty Images/AFP **134bg** : John Moore/Getty Images/AFP 134bd : David McNew/Getty Images/AFP **135** : John Moore/Getty Images/AFP **136h** : Rebecca Blackwell/AP Photo/Sipa **136b** : Alex Webb/Magnum Photos **137** : Jorge Luis Plata/Reuters **138** : David McNew/Getty Images/AFP **139** : Reed Saxon/AP Photo/Sipa **140** : *The illegal immigrants "afraid" of US visa amnesty*, by Aleem Maqbool, January 2015. From BBC News at bbc.co.uk/news. With courtesy of BBC Motion Gallery **141** : *Land of the Free*, April 17, 2008 © Clay Bennett/Cartconist Group **142** : © Kevin Kallaugher « Kal », kaltoons.com **143h** : John Moore/Getty Images/AFP **143b** : *4th of July* © Felipe Galindo **145** : *Mexican Wall Relations*, Oct 28, 2006 © Dario Castillejos/Cagle Cartoons, Inc. **146** : Dan Kitwood/Getty Images **148g** : Phil Cole/Getty Images **148d** : Yann Gamblin/PARISMATCH/Scoop **149** : Eric Gay/AP Photo/Sipa **150** : Cover image From "Welcome Home" from Silent Gesture: The Autobiography of Tommie Smith by Tommie Smith with David Steele. Used by permission of Temple University Press. © 2007 by Temple University. All Rights Reserved. **151** : *The Gunman*, 2015 Real Pierre Morel. Collection Christophel © StudioCanal / Silver Pictures/D.R. **152** : *Doping Lance*, Oct 13, 2012 © David Sack/Cagle Cartoons, Inc. **153** : *What makes Olympians sprint* © Dave Granlund www.davegranlund.com **154** : Imago/Panoramic 155 : *Long Live Sport*, by Charlie Johnston. Photo courtesy of Bob Buchanan, www.themuralsofwinnipeg.com **157** : *Hi... we're your sports heroes* © Paul Fell/CartoonStock Cartoons 1**58** : Campagne *Little Fighters* © 2015 Amnesty International **160** : Sashkin/Shutterstock.com **161h** : *Liberty*, June 10, 2013 © David Fitzsimmons/Cagle Cartoons, Inc. **161b** : *Government Is Watching*, June 10, 2013 © Nate Beeler/Cagle Cartoons, Inc. **162** : *Fracking Blowout,* Oct 31, 2014 © Nate Beeler/Cagle Cartoons, Inc. **163h** : Shutterstock.com 1**63b** : © Alice Eather 2015 **164** : *Become David and fight against Goliath,* campagne de Greenpeace Suisse, 2012. Graphisme Anatolij Pickmann © Greenpeace. Remerciements à Hina Struever **165** : *Privacy Apathy,* June 12, 2013 © Rick McKee/Cagle Cartoons, Inc. **166** : *Whistle Blower*, June 17, 2013 © Jeff Koterba/Cagle Cartoons, Inc. **167h** : kirstypargeter/CanStockPhoto **167b** : iqoncept/CanStockPhoto **170-1** : ph © Finnbarr Webster / Alamy / Photo 12 & Alamy / Photo 12 **170-2** : ph © Ullstein Bild / Akg-Images **170-3** : Cedric Weber / Shutterstock **170-4** : Walker Art Gallery, Liverpool/Google Cultural Project/ Commons Wikimedia **170-5** : National Maritime Museum, Greenwich/Leemage **170-6** : Heritage Images/Leemage **170-7** : Peter Connolly/ akg-images **171-1** : © Photo by dryo http://en.wikipedia.org/wiki/ **171-2** : ph © Garethwiscombe/http://upload.wikipedia.org **171-3** et **4** : ph © Devid Iliff. Licence : CC-BY-SA 3.0 http://en.wikipedia.org **171-5** : ph © http://en.wikipedia.org/wiki/ **171-6** : ph © Michelle Walz Eriksson http://upload.wikipedia.org 1**71-7** : ph © http://en.wikipedia.org **171-8** : ph © Christine Matthews http://en.wikipedia.org **171-9** : ph © Ham http://upload.wikipedia.org **171-10** : ph © Cedric Weber / Shutterstock **171-11** : ph © Cultura / hemis.fr **171-12** : ph © Devid Iliff. Licence : CC-BY-SA 3.0 http://en.wikipedia.org **171-13** : ph © Shutterstock **171-14** : ph © Devid Iliff. Licence : CC-BY-SA 3.0 http://en.wikipedia.org **171-15** : Heritage Images/Leemage **171-16** : Photoshop/MAXPPP **171-17** : BCA/Rue des Archives **171-18** : David Farrell/Lebrecht/Rue des Archives **171-19** : Ing. Andrej Kaprinay / Shutterstock **172-1** : ph © http://en.wikipedia.org/ **172-2** : ph © Pen Waggener http://www.flickr.com **172-3** : ph © Pict rider / Fotolia **172-4** et **5** : ph © jacobulus http://fr.wikipedia.org/ **172-6** : ph © Dominique James http://www.flickr.com **172-7** : Ohran Cam/Shutterstock **172-8** : PVDE/Rue des Archives **172-9, 10** et **11** : The Granger Collection NYC/Rue des Archives **172-12** : Ullstein Bild/Photo12.com **173-1** : ph © Tony the Mist http://en.wikipedia.org/ **173-2** : ph © Dean Franklin http://en.wikipedia.org/ **173-3** : ph © http://en.wikipedia.org/ **173-4** : Francis Miller/Time & Life Pictures/Getty Images **173-5** : NASA/Neil Armstrong **173-6** : Brendan Hoffman/The New York Times-REDUX-REA **174** : Collection Christophel © Lucas Film / Walt Disney /D.R. **176hg** : Collection Christophel © 2012 Home Box Office / DR **176hd** : Collection Christophel © 2015 Home Box Office / DR **176mg** : Collection Christophel © 2012 Home Box Office / DR **176md** : Collection Christophel © 2013 Home Box Office / DR 176bg : Collection Christophel © 2013 Home Box Office / DR **176bd** : Collection Christophel © 2013 Home Box Office / DR **180** : Andy Baker/Ikon Images / Photononstop **182** : Jason LaVeris/FilmMagic/Getty images **183** : Pool Bouvet/De Keerle/Gamma-Rapho via Getty Images **185** : © Fragicomics/Toonpool **187** : © Pennsylvania Newsmedia Association **190** : 4ever.eu/D.R. **Rabat arrière** « The English-speaking world » : ph © Alamy / Photo 12 « The United States of America » : ph © Alamy / Photo 12

D.R. : Malgré nos efforts, il nous a été impossible de joindre certains photographes ou leurs ayants droits, ainsi que les éditeurs ou leurs ayants droit pour certains documents, afin de solliciter l'autorisation de reproduction, mais nous avons naturellement réservé en notre comptabilité des droits usuels.

Achevé d'imprimer en Italie par STIGE - Dépôt légal n° 99294-0/02 - juin 2017